Hawaii Islands Environment

Travel and Tourism

Author
David Mills.

SONITTEC PUBLISHING. All rights reserved. No part of this publication may be reproduced, distributed, or transmitted in any form or by any means, including photocopying, recording, or other electronic or mechanical methods, without the prior written permission of the publisher, except in the case of brief quotations embodied in critical reviews and certain other noncommercial uses permitted by copyright law. For permission requests, write to the publisher, addressed "Attention: Permissions Coordinator," at the address below.

Copyright © 2019 Sonittec Publishing
All Rights Reserved

First Printed: 2019.

Publisher:
SONITTEC LTD
College House, 2nd Floor
17 King Edwards Road,
Ruislip
London
HA4 7AE.

Table of Content

SUMMARY 1
ABOUT HAWAII 3
    LAND 4
        Relief 4
        Drainage 6
        Soils 6
        Climate 6
        Plant and animal life 8
HAWAII PEOPLE 11
    POPULATION COMPOSITION 11
    SETTLEMENT PATTERNS 14
HAWAII ECONOMY 17
    AGRICULTURE, FORESTRY, AND FISHING 18
    RESOURCES AND POWER 19
    MANUFACTURING 19
    SERVICES, LABOUR, AND TAXATION 20
    TRANSPORTATION 21
GOVERNMENT AND SOCIETY 24
    CONSTITUTIONAL FRAMEWORK 24
    HEALTH AND WELFARE 27
    EDUCATION 27
HAWAII CULTURAL LIFE 28
    THE ARTS 29
    CULTURAL INSTITUTIONS 29
    SPORTS AND RECREATION 30
    MEDIA AND PUBLISHING 32
HAWAII HISTORY 33
    EARLY HISTORY 33
    THE ARRIVAL OF EUROPEANS 33
    ESTABLISHMENT OF U.S. DOMINANCE 34
    HAWAII AFTER STATEHOOD 37
    KAUAI 38
        Kauai Regions 39
            North Shore 39
                Kilauea Point Lighthouse 40
                Napali Coast 41
                Hanalei Town 42
                Waioli Huuia Church 44
            East Side (Royal Coconut Coast), Kauai 45
                Opaekaa Falls 45
                Wailua River 46
                Fern Grotto 47
                Kapaa Town 48
            Lihue 49
                Kauai Museum 50
                Alekoko Fishpond 50

  Wailua Falls 51
  Kilohana Estate 52
  Grove Farm Homestead Museum 53
 South Shore 54
  Poipu Beach Park 55
  Koloa Heritage Trail, Kauai 57
  Spouting Horn 59
  Allerton Garden 60
 West Side 61
  Waimea Town 63
  Kokee State Park 64
  Hanapepe Town 65
Things to Do on Kauai 66
 Kauai Beaches 66
  North Shore Beaches 66
  East Side Beaches 68
  South Shore Beaches 70
  West Side Beaches 71
 Kauai Land Activities 73
  Outdoor Activities 74
   Biking on Kauai 74
   Hiking on Kauai 75
   Kauai Golf 76
   Kauai Gardens & Parks 76
   Horseback Riding on Kauai 77
 Kauai Water Activities 78
  Kayaking on Kauai 78
  Snorkeling and Scuba on Kauai 79
  Kauai Surfing 80
  Stand-Up Paddleboarding on Kauai 81
 Kauai Accommodations 84
  Waimea Plantation Cottages 86
  River Estate 87
  Courtyard Kauai at Coconut Beach 88
  Hanalei Colony Resort 89
  Hanalei Inn 90
  Kauai Vacation Home Rental 91
  Kauai Banyan Inn 92
  Kauai Shores Hotel 93
  Grand Hyatt Kauai Resort & Spa 94
  Aqua Kauai Beach Resort 95
 Transportation 96
  Alaska Airlines 98
  Hawaii Car Rentals 98
  Aloha Rents Hawaii Car Rental 99

- Kauai Luxury Transportation 100
- Polynesian Adventure Tours 101
- Roberts Hawaii 103
- Discount Hawaii Car Rental 104
- Hawaiian Airlines 105
- Enterprise Rent-A-Car - Kauai 105
- Weddings on Kauai 106
  - Honeymoons 107
  - Wedding Venues and Services 109

OAHU 114

Oahu Regions 118
Honolulu 118
Arts & Culture in Honolulu 118
- Bishop Museum 118
- Honolulu Museum of Art and Shangri La 119
- Iolani Palace 121

Oahu Restaurants 123
Landmarks & Attractions 125
- Waikiki 125
- Leahi (Diamond Head) 127
- Downtown Honolulu 129
- Kapahulu, Oahu 129
- National Memorial Cemetery of the Pacific Oahu 130

Shopping in Honolulu 131
More Places to See in Honolulu 132
- Duke Kahanamoku 132
- Aloha Tower 134
- Kawaiahao Church, Oahu 135

Central Oahu 136
- Pearl Harbor 137

North Shore, Oahu 144
- Haleiwa 144

Leeward Coast, Oahu 145
- Kaena Point 146

Windward Coast 147
- Makapuu Point Lighthouse 148
- Nuuanu Pali Lookout, Oahu 149
- Byodo-in Temple 151

Things to Do on Oahu 152
Oahu Surfing 152
Scuba & Snorkeling 155
Oahu Accommodations 155
- Aston at the Waikiki Banyan 157
- Paradise Bay Resort 158
- OHANA Waikiki Malia by Outrigger 159

    Shoreline Hotel Waikiki 159
    OHANA Waikiki East by Outrigger 160
    Hilton Hawaiian Village Waikiki Beach Resort.. 161
    The Royal Hawaiian, a Luxury Collection Resort 162
Oahu Activities... 164
    Oahu Water Activities 164
        Fishing on Oahu 165
        Snorkeling & Scuba on Oahu 165
        Oahu Surfing.. 166
        Whale Watching on Oahu 169
    Beaches of Oahu... 169
    Oahu Land Activities 174
    Local Culture... 174
        Farms Tours on Oahu 174
        Oahu Historic Places 176
        Hula on Oahu... 181
        Museums of Oahu.. 184
    Get Outdoors.. 189
        Hiking on Oahu 189
        Horseback Riding on Oahu 190
        Oahu Golf 191
        Oahu Parks & Gardens 196
    Relax and Unwind.. 198
        Still & Moving Center 198
        Waikiki Massage and Foot Spa LLC... 200
        Spa Pure Corp.. 200
        The Spa at the Modern Honolulu... 204
        Na Ho'ola Spa 205
        Spa Suites at the Kahala Hotel & Resort 205
        Moana Lani Spa 206
    Arts & Culture... 207
        Art on the Zoo Fence.. 208
        Honolulu Museum of Art... 209
        Hawaiian Mission Houses Historic Site and Archives 210
        Mahinalani Gift Shop at the Polynesian Cultural Center 211
        Malama Loko Ea Foundation 212
        Hawaii Okinawa Center... 213
        Polynesian Cultural Center 214
        Hawaii Temple Visitors' Center.. 216
        Bishop Museum... 217
        Hawaii State Art Museum... 218
    Oahu Air Activities 219
        Paradise Helicopters 220
        Novictor Helicopters 222
        Magnum Helicopters... 223

Honolulu Soaring	223
Blue Hawaiian Helicopters	224
Hawaii Activities Discount	226
MOLOKAI	**226**
Regions of Molokai	227
Central Molokai	227
Molokai Ancient Hawaiian Fishponds	228
Kalaupapa National Historical Park	230
Kapuaiwa Coconut Grove	232
Kaunakakai, Molokai	233
West End	234
Maunaloa, Molokai	235
Papohaku Beach	235
East End, Molokai	236
Things to Do on Molokai	237
Molokai Beaches	237
Molokai Water Activities	239
Snorkeling and Scuba of Molokai	239
Fishing on Molokai	240
Boating on Molokai	241
Molokai Land Activities	241
Hiking on Molokai	243
Halawa Valley	243
Molokai Farms & Gardens	244
Molokai Golf	245
Molokai Historic Places	246
Kalaupapa National Historical Park	248
Molokai Ancient Hawaiian Fishponds	250
Kaunakakai, Molokai	251
Halawa Valley	252
Kapuaiwa Coconut Grove	254
Molokai Restaurants	255
Molokai Accommodations	255
Ka Hale Ola / Ka Hale Kealoha	255
Molokairentals.net	257
Dunbar Beachfront Cottages	257
1-888-282-3459 Molokai Rentals	258
A116 - Wavecrest	259
Beautiful Condo at Paniolo Hale Unit T2	259
Hotel Molokai	260
Molokai Wedding	261
Molokai Honeymoons	261
Relaxation and Romance	262
LANAI	**264**
Regions of Lanai	267
Central Lanai	267

- Lanai City 268
- Munro Trail 269
- Things to Do on Lanai 270
  - Lanai Restaurants 270
    - Nobu Lana'i 271
    - Sports Bar & Grill 271
    - ONE FORTY, American Steak and Hawaiian Seafood 272
    - Lanai City Grille 273
    - VIEWS at Manele Golf Course 273
    - Malibu Farm 274
  - Lanai Accommodations 275
    - Four Seasons Resort Lanai 276
    - Hotel Lanai 276
  - Attractions on Lanai 277
    - Lanai Beaches 279
      - Polihua Beach 280
    - Lanai Land Activities 281
      - Hiking on Lanai 281
      - Lanai Golf 283
      - Lanai Gardens, Plantations & Parks 284
      - Horseback Riding on Lanai 286
    - Lanai Water Activities 287
      - Boating on Lanai 287
      - Snorkeling and Scuba on Lanai 289
    - Lanai Wedding 292
      - Lanai Honeymoons 292
      - Relaxation and Romance 293

MAUI 295
- Regions of Maui 298
  - Central Maui 298
    - Wailuku 299
    - Iao Valley State Park Maui 300
  - East Maui 301
    - Hana Maui 302
    - Pools of Oheo 303
  - South Maui 305
    - Kihei 305
    - Makena Beach State Park (Big Beach) 307
    - Molokini 307
    - Wailea 308
  - West Maui 310
    - Honolua Bay Maui 311
    - Lahaina, Maui 312
    - Kapalua Maui 314
    - Kaanapali Beach 315

- Upcountry Maui 316
  - Paia, Maui 317
  - Haleakala National Park Maui 318
  - Kula 319
  - Makawao, Maui 320
- Things to Do on Maui 322
  - Maui Restaurants & Dining 322
    - Japengo Maui 322
    - Ama Bar & Grill 323
    - Kimo's 324
    - Royal Ocean Terrace Restaurant 324
    - Kai Cafe 324
    - Lahaina Grill 325
    - Gannon's Restaurant 326
    - Kahili Restaurant 327
    - Royal Scoop 328
  - Maui Hotels & Accommodations 328
    - Mana Kai Maui (CRH) 329
    - Paia Surf Vacation Home 330
    - WaileaEkahiVillage.com, Pauli Family Condos 330
    - Maui Kai 331
    - Aston at The Whaler on Kaanapali Beach 332
    - Sunsets in Paradise 333
    - Hotel Wailea Maui 333
    - Destination Residences Hawaii, Inc. 335
    - Polo Beach Club, A Destination Residence 336
  - Maui Activities 337
    - Land Activities 338
      - Biking on Maui 338
      - Family Activities on Maui 340
      - Golfing on Maui 341
      - Hiking on Maui 342
      - Nightlife on Maui 345
      - Ziplines on Maui 348
      - Attractions on Maui 351
    - Water Activities 352
      - Boating & Sailing on Maui 352
      - Dolphin Encounters on Maui 354
      - Fishing on Maui 356
      - Scuba Diving on Maui 358
      - Snorkeling on Maui 361
      - Water Sports on Maui 363
      - Whale Watching on Maui 365
      - Maui Beaches 368

Summary

The world is a book and those who do not travel read only one page.
It is indeed very unfortunate that some people feel traveling is a sheer waste of time, energy and money. Some also find traveling an extremely boring activity. Nevertheless, a good majority of people across the world prefer traveling, rather than staying inside the confined spaces of their homes. They love to explore new places, meet new people, and see things that they would not find in their homelands. It is this very popular attitude that has made tourism, one of the most profitable, commercial sectors in the world.

People travel for various reasons. Some travel for work, others for fun, and some for finding mental peace. Though every person may have his/her own reason to go on a journey, it is essential to note that traveling, in itself, has some inherent advantages. For one, for some days getting away from everyday routine is a pleasant change. It not only refreshes one's body, but also mind and soul. Traveling to a distant place and doing exciting things that are not thought of otherwise, can rejuvenate a person, who then returns home, ready to take on new and more difficult challenges in life and work. It makes a person forget his worries, problems, frustrations, and fears, albeit for some time. It gives him a chance to think wisely and constructively. Traveling also helps to heal; it can mend a broken heart.

For many people, traveling is a way to attain knowledge, and perhaps, a quest to find answers to their questions. For this, many people prefer to go to faraway and isolated places. For believers, it is a search for God and to gain higher knowledge; for others, it is a search for inner peace. They might or might not find what they are looking for, but such an experience certainly enriches their lives

About Hawaii

Hawaii, constituent state of the United States of America. Hawaii (Hawaiian: Hawai'i) became the 50th U.S. state on August 21, 1959. Hawaii is a group of volcanic islands in the central Pacific Ocean. The islands lie 2,397 miles (3,857 km) from San Francisco, California, to the east and 5,293 miles (8,516 km) from Manila, in the Philippines, to the west. The capital is Honolulu, located on the island of Oahu.

Hawaii was characterized by Mark Twain as "the loveliest fleet of islands that lies anchored in any ocean." The name is thought to derive from Hawaiki, the former name of Raiatea, the ancestral home of Polynesians.

Hawaii is economically vigorous, with diversified agriculture and manufacturing. Hawaiian activities of national and international importance include research and development in oceanography, geophysics, astronomy, satellite communications, and biomedicine. Often called the Crossroads of the Pacific, the state is strategically important to the global defense system of the United States and serves as a transportation hub of the Pacific basin. Finally, Hawaii is a cultural centre and a major tourist mecca. Area 10,970 square miles (28,412 square km). Population (2010) 1,360,301; (2017 est.) 1,427,538.

Land

Relief

The land area of the state of Hawaii consists of the tops of a chain of emerged volcanic mountains that form 8 major islands and 124 islets, stretching in a 1,500-mile (2,400-km) crescent from Kure Island in the west to the island of Hawaii in the east. The eight major islands at the eastern end of the chain are, from west to east, Niihau, Kauai, Oahu, Molokai, Lanai, Kahoolawe, Maui, and Hawaii. Each volcanic mountain formed during the transit of the Pacific Plate across a hotspot (a region of Earth's upper mantle that upwells to melt through the crust) located beneath the central Pacific Ocean, and erupting magma added mass to the crust above.

The origin of Hawaii's islands, islets, and seamounts can be traced to at least 70 million years ago, near the end of the Cretaceous Period (145 million to 66 million years ago). Volcanic activity has become dormant, with the exception of the emergent volcanoes of Mauna Loa, Kilauea, and the Lōʻihi Seamount. Mauna Loa and Kilauea are located on the easternmost and largest island, Hawaii (often referred to as the

"Big Island"), where spectacular eruptions and lava flows take place from time to time. The Lōʻihi Seamount, a growing volcano that could break the surface of the ocean tens of thousands of years from the present, is located 18.6 miles (30 km) southeast of the island of Hawaii. The highest Hawaiian mountains are Mauna Kea and Mauna Loa, both on the island of Hawaii, reaching 13,796 feet (4,205 metres) and 13,678 feet (4,169 metres) above sea level, respectively.

There has been little erosion in the geologically young areas, where the terrain is domelike or scattered with hardened lava, and the volcanic craters are clearly defined. In the older areas the mountains have been shaped and eroded by sea, rain, and wind. Their aspects thus include sharp and craggy silhouettes; abrupt, vertically grooved cliffs pocked with caves; deep valleys; collapsed craters (calderas); and coastal plains. The powerful Pacific surf, churning and crashing against the fringing coral shelves and the lava shorelines, has carried minute shells onto the shore and reduced coral and large shells to sand, creating the state's famous expanses of beach.

Heavy rainfall in mountainous areas produces an extremely voluminous runoff, which is responsible for the erosion that forms the numerous grooves, ridges, and V-shaped valleys characteristic of the older volcanic islands such as Kauai and Oahu. The action of rain combined with waves has had a particularly dramatic effect on the more exposed windward sections of the islands.

Drainage

Because the topography of Hawaii is generally abruptly descending or sloping, there are few surfaces that collect water. Excess rainfall seeps through porous mountain areas to gather in subterranean chambers and layers retained by less-permeable lava and ash beds, or it is prevented by underlying salt water from seeping to the sea. The resultant artesian water supply is tapped for use in irrigation and also for human consumption. Many streams in Hawaii are intermittent, depending on the volume of rainfall. The island of Kauai has numerous perennial streams, the largest of which is the Wailua River.

Soils

As a result of the weathering of basaltic lava and volcanic ash, Hawaii is rich in arable soils. Given local conditions, with variations in rainfall and organic matter, the islands contain a wide variety of soils. Of these the most significant are the andisols and mollisols that are the product of lava flows that occurred more than 3,000 years ago on the islands of Maui and Hawaii and that are agriculturally productive when irrigated. Also suitable for agriculture are the oxisols of Oahu and Kauai, both of which are red from iron oxidation.

Climate

Hawaii lies just below the Tropic of Cancer, and its mild tropical climate is considered by many people to be the world's ideal. Although the weather is often humid by U.S. mainland standards, temperatures are conditioned by the northeast trade winds, which prevail most of the year and make living on the islands delightfully comfortable. As moisture-laden air is carried over the islands, most frequently by the trade winds, it is apt to condense, form cap clouds, and dissipate against the shores and mountains of the windward coasts, which are therefore more lush in foliage than the leeward coasts.

Most Hawaiians recognize only two seasons: summer and winter. Summer (*kau*) lasts from May through October, with high temperatures and reliable trade winds. The rainy season, winter (*hoʻoilo*), lasts from November to April, with cooler temperatures and frequent rainstorms.

The average temperature in Honolulu is in the low 70s F (about 22 °C) in the coolest month and in the high 70s F (about 26 °C) in the warmest, though extreme temperatures in the high 50s F (about 14 °C) and low 90s F (about 33 °C) have been recorded there. The average water temperatures off Waikiki Beach in Honolulu range from the mid-70s F (about 24 °C) in late February to the high 70s F (about 26 °C) in late September. The temperature falls about 3.5 °F (2 °C) with every 1,000 feet (300 metres) of elevation, so mountainous regions are considerably cooler, especially during the winter months, when there can be frost; a temperature of 1.4 °F (−17 °C) has been recorded on the summit of Mauna Kea, and winter snows frequently blanket the crests of Mauna Kea and Mauna Loa.

Rainfall variations throughout the state are dramatic. Mount Waialeale, on the island of Kauai, is often called the wettest spot on Earth, with an annual average rainfall of about 450 inches (11,430 mm). The driest area of the state is at Kawaihae, on the island of Hawaii, where the average annual rainfall is only about 9 inches (220 mm). The average yearly rainfall in Honolulu is 23 inches (590 mm), and in Hilo, one of the state's wettest cities, it is about 130 inches (3,300 mm).

Plant and animal life

The plants and animals that have migrated to Hawaii evolved in a relatively benignenvironment, creating species that live nowhere else on the planet. The seeds of endemicplant species were carried to Hawaii by birds, winds, or currents and tides, bringing about extensive forestation, shrubbery, and grasslands where soil and precipitation were favourable. However, as greater and greater numbers of species were introduced by humans, either purposely or accidentally, the native species, both plant and animal, came under increasing pressure. About one-third of the more than 1,000 animal species that the U.S. government has declared threatened or endangered are located in

Hawaii. More than 1,000,000 acres (400,00 hectares) of land in the state have been set aside in an attempt to protect native ecosystems.

Polynesians and Europeans introduced mongooses, rats, frogs, toads, and, in the more remote regions of some of the islands, deer, sheep, pigs, and goats. Endemic birds, which may have evolved from a small number of original immigrants and which have been isolated from others of their kind, have taken on certain characteristics of their own. These include the nene (Hawaiian goose), the Hawaiian stilt, and a variety of small forest birds known as honeycreepers. Some species of birds have become extremely rare, but, as the result of an increased environmental awareness, steps have been taken to preclude their extinction. Seabirds nest in profusion on the western islands of the archipelago and to a far lesser extent among the major eastern islands. There has been considerable importation of birdlife. Mynas, sparrows, cardinals, and doves live in the trees in both urban and rural areas. Every autumn the small golden plover make an awe-inspiring, nonstop 3,000-mile (4,800-km) flight from Alaska to Hawaii, where they spend the winter, together with ducks from Alaska, Canada, and the northwestern United States.

The insect population contains about 10,000 native species, of which about nine-tenths are unique to the islands. The ocean sustains a diversity of marine ecosystems, from tide pools to the deep ocean floor, with about one-fourth of all the species being unique to Hawaii.

The waters surrounding the islands are home to a wide variety of marine mammals, including about a dozen species of whales.

Hawaii People
Population composition

Most anthropologists believe that the original settlement of Hawaii was by Polynesians who migrated northwest from the Marquesas Islands between the 4th and 7th centuries CE, to be followed by a second wave of immigrants that sailed from Tahiti during the 9th or 10th century. The capabilities demonstrated by the revival of the use of the voyaging canoe and traditional navigation methods in Hawaii beginning in the 1970s indicate that the islands may not have been as isolated after their initial colonization as was once thought; indeed, there may have been considerable purposeful voyaging between Hawaii and far-flung Polynesian destinations. Still, Hawaii's isolation was great enough that Hawaiian culture developed its own distinctive characteristics, even though there are still rather close resemblances in language and culture between the Hawaiians and their Polynesian relatives.

The original Hawaiians were highly skilled in fishing and farming. By the late 18th century their society had evolved into a complex one with a rigid system of laws set down by chiefs and priests. They worshipped and feared a group of gods not unlike the ancient Greek deities of Mount Olympus in character and power.

The arrival of foreigners to Hawaii began after British Capt. James Cook came upon the islands in 1778. During the ensuing four decades, European and American explorers, adventurers, trappers, and whalers stopped for fresh supplies at the Hawaiian Islands contact that would have a profound effect on the islanders. Not the least of these effects was the introduction of diseases from both the East and the West against which the islanders, theretofore virtually disease-free, had no natural immunities. Venereal disease, cholera, measles, and tuberculosis all contributed to the decimation of the native peoples, whose population fell from approximately 300,000 to fewer than 40,000 by the 1890s, little more than a century later.

The collapse of the population, coupled with the impact of outside cultures, most likely caused crisis in Hawaiian society and sparked social and political change. Most notably, Hawaiians, led by members of the royal family, overthrew the complex *kapu* (taboo) system of laws and punishments in 1819. Loss of faith in the old gods, intense curiosity about the ways of people of the United States and Europe, and avid interest in learning to read and write brought about a swift adoption of Christianity on the part of many Hawaiians. The first group of Christian missionaries arrived from the United States in 1820, and by the mid-19th century Hawaii was largely a Christian kingdom, with a small but significant European and American population.

Since that time the ethnic and religious makeup of Hawaii has undergone dramatic change. As the number of Native Hawaiians declined, other ethnic groups arrived, mainly to work on the plantations. Contract labourers came first from China, then from Japan, the Azores, Puerto Rico, the Philippines, and Korea. They were joined by immigrants from the U.S. mainland, Europe, and elsewhere in the Pacific. Over the course of two centuries, people from all over the world had settled in Hawaii, creating a multiethnic society. Each group brought its own customs, languages, and religions into the Hawaiian way of life, broadening it far beyond its Polynesian cultural origins. The descendants of these later settlers now far outnumber the descendants of the original Hawaiians. There is also a continuous influx and outflow of military personnel and their dependents as a result of Hawaii's importance as a base for all branches of the U.S. armed forces.

The two official languages of Hawaii are English and Hawaiian. In the early 1990s the Hawaiian language was all but extinct, spoken by only a handful of Native Hawaiians. However, a program that established Hawaiian-language immersion schools created a new generation of Hawaiian speakers, and instruction in Hawaiian is now offered from kindergarten through the graduate school level. The language also lives on in place-names and street names and in songs. Most Hawaiian residents can also speak what has come to be called Hawaiian Creole English. Commonly referred to as pidgin, Hawaiian Creole English is a dialect of English created by children in the multilingual environment of Hawaiian plantation camps. Hawaiian Creole English has been used increasingly in Hawaiian fiction, poetry, and drama.

With a continued influx of Asian immigrants as well as tourists from Asia, notably from Japan, Hawaii has remained multilingual. Japanese, Chinese, Korean, and several major Filipino languages are widely spoken, and it is not uncommon to see signage in these languages. The largest religious groups are Roman Catholics and Protestants. There are, however, small but important groups of Buddhists and of adherents of other Asian religions.

Settlement patterns

Until the end of World War II, Hawaii's population was scattered in rural settlements, ranging from tiny fishing villages far off the main roads, scant clusters of small houses in isolated valleys, and solitary farm or ranch houses to large coastal and upland villages and plantation and ranch towns.

During the 1950s and '60s there was a building boom in Hawaii of such magnitude that the configuration of entire towns was altered. Single-family dwellings, individual businesses and shops, small markets, and three- or four-story hotels were overrun by high-rise hotels and apartment buildings, shopping centres, and supermarkets. The most graphic example of this was in the city of Honolulu, where construction of 30- and 40-story buildings gave the city once sprawling and low a thrusting, multileveled skyline. The Waikiki area on Oahu became so densely built up that (despite its world-famous beach) it transformed into an urban resort. Resort development on the other islands, notably Maui, Kauai, and Hawaii, was better planned, with less density and more open space along the shorelines. On Oahu, much agricultural land was developed for housing, rural towns became suburbs, and a second city, Kapolei, was founded in 1990 on the leeward plains, once home to vast sugarcane fields.

Most of the state's residents live on Oahu, and nearly three-fourths of them reside in Honolulu proper and its metropolitan area. Because there are vast areas of Oahu still devoted to agriculture and forest reserves, the majority of the population actually resides in high-density clusters. Honolulu is the only legally incorporated town or city in the state.

Many of the older houses in agricultural villages on the islands are largely raised frame structures, often with corrugated-iron roofs. More modern homes are found in some smaller towns. Plants of native origin skirt the foundations of homes, and the yards are informally planted with fruit and flower trees. In all but the smallest villages, there are a school, markets, a post office, a fire station, and at least one church.

Since the late 1990s the population of the state has increased substantially, largely due to immigration from the Philippines, China, Korea, Vietnam, and Japan. By the early 21st century, Asians were the dominant ethnic group, accounting for about two-fifths of the total population.

Hawaii Economy

Hawaii ranks relatively low among U.S. states in terms of personal income, farm products sold, value of manufacturing shipments, retail sales, and bank deposits. Largely because of its insularity and dependence on imports, Hawaii has a high cost of living. Transportation costs are included in the prices of nearly all consumer goods. As Hawaii's population rose, housing became increasingly difficult to acquire, and it is disproportionately expensive when compared with housing costs in many mainland states. Building materials, most of which are imported, are expensive. Historically, residential land has been limited and highly priced, since much of the property, notably on Oahu, is owned by corporations and trusts (though legislation has largely remedied this situation for owners of single-family homes if not for condominium owners). One solution to the shortages and expense associated with urban housing has been the development of mixed-housing communities consisting of single-family homes, high-rise dwellings, townhouses, and apartment complexes.

Agriculture, forestry, and fishing

Agriculture is a major component of the local economy. Since the first Polynesian settlement on the islands, a tremendous variety of food and ornamental plant life from many parts of the world has been introduced. Food plants grown commercially or in backyards for home consumption include sugarcane, pineapple, papaya, banana, mango, guava, litchi, coconut, avocado, breadfruit, lime, passion fruit, taro, and tamarind, though sugarcane and pineapple production have decreased as the world market for them has been changed by lower labour costs in other pineapple- and sugarcane-producing places such as the Philippines. Nearly all varieties of common garden vegetables are raised on the islands, and flowers abound year-round. Since the early 2000s there has been a slow but steady growth of diversified crops, including coffee, macadamia nuts, ginger root, and seed crops.

Most of Hawaii's islands have ranches, with the majority concentrated on the Big Island, where the ranching tradition dates from the 1830s. Mexican vaqueros (cowboys) taught Hawaiians how to manage their herds, beginning a tradition of *paniolos*, or Hawaiian cowboys, who derived their name from these vaqueros and predated the cowboys of the American West. The *paniolos* still run their ranches in much the same way today. Livestock raising, together with some lumbering and commercial fishing, are other important sources of income. Nearly half of the commercial fish catch is tuna, especially yellowfin.

Resources and power

Hawaii has no important mineral deposits; its only natural resources are its climate, water supply, soil, vegetation, and surrounding ocean, as well as the rock, gravel, sand, and earth quarried for use in construction and landscaping. Electric power is supplied by a small number of power companies operating oil-powered steam and diesel generators. Several military installations and some private institutions generate their own power. A small amount of hydroelectric power is generated on several of the islands, and in the mid-1980s a geothermal plant began producing electricity on Hawaii, which supplies about one-fifth of the total electricity to the island. On Maui, the Kaheawa wind farm was opened in 2006. Hawaii still relies on imported oil for most of its energy, but the state has set out to increase its use of renewable energy sources.

Manufacturing

Hawaii has several hundred companies engaged in diversified manufacturing. Heavy-manufacturing plants, using raw materials for the most part imported from the U.S. mainland, include oil refineries that produce a variety of petroleum products and chemical **compounds**, a concrete-pipe plant, and an aluminum-extrusion plant. Heavy manufacturing is confined mainly to the island of Oahu. Most lumber is imported from the mainland. A number of garment manufacturers, largely situated in Honolulu, produce printed fabrics and apparel marketed locally, nationally, and abroad.

A wide variety of Hawaii-grown foodstuffs, sold locally and exported to the mainland, are processed in the state. These include Asian and Hawaiian food specialties as well as tropical fruit juices, jams and jellies, candies, coffee, macadamia nuts, and various alcoholic beverages. Exports include sugar, garments, flowers, and canned fish. Major imports are fuel, vehicles, food, and clothing.

Services, labour, and taxation

Tourism is Hawaii's largest industry. Expansion has been particularly rapid since World War II, and the growth has resulted in part from continued improvements in transportation and the stimulus provided by the state government and local businesses. The majority of visitors come from the U.S. mainland, Canada, Australia, and Asia, particularly Japan. Cruise ships make regular stops in Honolulu, and interisland luxury cruises are available. About half of the hotel units are on Oahu, chiefly in Waikiki and the adjacent Ala Moana area. Visitors have access to a wide range of recreational and cultural facilities, including golf courses, tennis courts, parks, surfing sites, beaches, restaurants, theatres, musical attractions, and sporting events. Tourism has helped Hawaii to become the centre of the international market of the Pacific basin. Capital investment by U.S. mainland and foreign companies has increased tremendously.

About one in four Hawaiian workers belong to a union, making the state among the most unionized in the country. Major Hawaiian manufacturing industries are unionized, as are many of the service and construction industries. The International Longshore and Warehouse Union (ILWU), the state's largest private-sector union, has an important and turbulent history. In 1949 its members held a six-month dock strike against the five shipping companies that controlled most of Hawaii's economic activity (mainly the sugar and pineapple plantations). All shipping to and from the islands was stopped. The union's successful action helped strengthen the Hawaiian Democratic Party, allowing it to more ably challenge the Republicans, who had been in power since the annexation of Hawaii in 1900. With the decline of sugar and pineapple production since the early 2000s, however, the ILWU's influence in Hawaii has faded, and it has been superseded in membership by the Hawaii Government Employees Association, which has had considerable political clout.

State taxes are collected under a centralized tax system. The chief sources of the state's revenue are a general excise tax, individual income taxes, and federal grants-in-aid.

Transportation

Ocean surface transportation is Hawaii's lifeline, and Honolulu Harbor, with its extensive docks, warehouses, and storage sheds, is the centre of Hawaiian shipping. A large percentage of the cargo ships ply between Hawaii and California ports, a few between Hawaii and the East Coast of the United States via the Panama Canal, and others between Hawaii and western Pacific island ports. Tug-pulled barges and small freighters transport goods from Honolulu to the outer islands, returning with agricultural crops and livestock.

The majority of voyagers to and from Hawaii travel by air, as do most interisland passengers. The major civilian airports capable of serving large-jet traffic are Honolulu International Airport, on Oahu; Hilo International Airport at Hilo and Kona International Airport at Keahole in Kailua-Kona, both on Hawaii; and the Kahului Airport, on Maui. There are several smaller airports and a number of small private airfields on the islands. Military authorities maintain a number of airports throughout the state.

Hawaiian roads range from narrow country paths to multilane freeways, which are most common on Oahu. Most of the roads follow lowland contours, circling the islands along or near the shorelines and crossing islands only between mountain ranges. There are many spectacular mountain roads providing dramatic vistas. On Oahu two tunnels bring traffic from the heads of two valleys behind Honolulu through the Koolau Range and out into the windward, or northeastern, side of the island.

Government and Society
Constitutional framework

Hawaii is governed by a constitution that was originally adopted in 1950; it was amendedin 1959, at the time of admission to statehood, and further amended at the constitutionalconvention of 1968. The governor and lieutenant governor are elected on a joint ticket for four-year terms. They are not permitted to serve more than two consecutive terms. The only other elected members in the 17 departments of the executive branch are the members of the Board of Education. Hawaii's bicameral legislature consists of the Senate, with 25 elected representatives from 25 senatorial districts, serving four-year terms, and the House of Representatives, consisting of 51 members elected from single-member districts for two-year terms. Honolulu is the regional headquarters of the federal government.

Hawaii's local governmental structure is unique among the U.S. states in that it is limited to two levels of government: the state and the four counties, each with a mayor and a council. There are no municipal governments. State and county governments are also major employers.

The state judicial system consists of the Supreme Court, an intermediate appellate court, circuit courts, and district courts, as well as a family court, a land court, and a tax appeal court. Judges in the higher courts are appointed by the governor, subject to approval by the Senate.

Primary elections are held in September, and general elections take place in November. During the first half of the 20th century, the Republican Party dominated Hawaiianpolitics. In the 1956 elections the Democrats, gaining strength from labour unions and from returning Japanese American World War II veterans, surged to power. The Democrats won the governorship in 1962 and held it until 2002, and they have been dominant in state legislative elections and in federal elections. Hawaiian Democratic Sen. Daniel Akaka (since 1990) was the first U.S. senator of Hawaiian descent. He was the sponsor, along with long-serving (1963) Democratic Sen. Daniel Inouye, of the Native Hawaiian Government Reorganization Act, also known as the Akaka Bill, which would establish a Native Hawaiian governing body to negotiate with the state and federal governments on issues relating to land, assets, and natural resources. Although the bill has not been passed by the U.S. Senate, the Office of Hawaiian Affairs has begun an initiative to register all Native Hawaiians for participation in a new Native Hawaiian government.

Hawaii holds a strategic position in the defense system of the United States. Pearl Harbor, a vast shipyard for the repair and overhaul of U.S. fleet units, is the home port for many U.S. naval ships. It serves as a training base for submarine and antisubmarine warfare forces. The headquarters of the U.S. Pacific Command are at Camp H.M. Smith in Halawa Heights on Oahu. Other major military installations include the army posts of Schofield Barracks, Fort Shafter, and Fort De Russy; the Hickam and Wheeler air force bases; and the Marine Corps Base Hawaii at Kaneohe Bay. In addition to these, there are military installations, camps, and airfields of varying sizes throughout the state. More than 100,000 U.S. military personnel and their dependents are stationed in or have their home port in Hawaii, and their presence has an important influence on the local economy and social life.

More than half of the land in the state is owned by private individuals or corporations, although the state itself, holding more than one-third of the land, is the largest single landowner. The northwestern islands are part of the Hawaiian Islands National Wildlife Refuge. Midway Island, near the western end of the archipelago, was for many years a U.S. naval preserve. It has since come under the management of the U.S. Fish and Wildlife Service, which allows limited ecotourism.

Health and welfare

The U.S. Department of Health maintains hospitals, health centres, clinics, care centres, and nursing services. The Hawaiian Home Lands Commission controls the transfer of land use to qualified persons of Hawaiian ancestry for homesteading.

Education

Hawaii's school system provides educational facilities from nursery school through the graduate school level. Institutions of higher learning include the University of Hawaii, with campuses at Hilo, Manoa, and West Oʻahu; several smaller private colleges; and a state-established system of two-year community colleges. The Brigham Young Universitycampus at Laie is an undergraduate institution that has one of the most multicultural student bodies of any university in the United States. Private business, technical, and specialized schools provide additional educational facilities and opportunities.

The Center for Cultural and Technical Interchange Between East and West, commonly referred to as the East-West Centre, is a project of the federal government housed at the Manoa campus of the University of Hawaii. It provides specialized and advanced academic programs and technological training to students from the United States and from countries in Asia and the Pacific.

Hawaii Cultural Life

Hawaii's cultural milieu is the result of overlay after overlay of varied cultural groups. The original culture remains evident in the islands, but the Native Hawaiian aesthetic has become diminished and diluted over the years through death and intermarriage. Today, Hawaiian culture reflects a mixture of Eastern and Western influences. The traditions of many ethnic groups have become mainstream in contemporary Hawaii, including the celebration of the Chinese New Year in late January or early February and the annual Japanese Bon festival in July or August.

Native Hawaiian culture underwent a renaissance beginning in the 1970s, most notably with the resurgence of the hula, the voyaging canoe, the art of tattooing, and its music and language. Most Hawaiian inhabitants know at least some Hawaiian words and observe cultural practices including the giving of the lei, a garland of flowers. The "Aloha Spirit," however commercialized it has become, is reflective of the way many diversegroups live together on the small islands.

The arts

Interest in the arts is high, and many distinguished artists, photographers, and performers have been residents of Hawaii. Appreciation of classical, modern, and experimental art forms is manifest in attendance figures at galleries, film festivals, concerts, legitimate theatre performances, and museums. Honolulu has converted its Chinatown neighbourhood into a cultural district, which draws crowds on the first Friday of each month to its art galleries and performance spaces. Numerous hula exhibitions and competitions are held; foremost among them is the weeklong Merrie Monarch Festival in Hilo.

Hawaiian music is also a vital cultural force. It draws from many musical sources, including *ki ho'ala* (Hawaiian slack-key guitar), brought to the islands by vaqueros from Mexico. (In 2005 the National Academy of Recording Arts and Sciences added a Hawaiian music category to its Grammy Awards, and many of the winners in the category have been slack-key musicians.) Don Ho (1930 2007) was one of the best-known Hawaiian musicians. Israel Kamakawiwo'ole was a popular Hawaiian singer whose support of Hawaiian sovereignty made him a cultural hero in Hawaii.

Cultural institutions

An assortment of cultural and scientific institutions in Hawaii provides a wide variety of opportunity for the appreciation and understanding of the fine arts, history, traditions, and sciences. The Bernice P. Bishop Museum, founded in 1889 in Honolulu, is a research centre and museum dedicated to the study, preservation, and display of the history, sciences, and cultures of the Pacific and its peoples. The Honolulu Academy of Arts (1927), often called the most beautiful museum in the world, houses a splendid collection of Western art, including works by late 19th- and early 20th-century masters Claude Monet, Vincent van Gogh, Henri Matisse, Paul Gauguin, and Pablo Picasso. Its collection of Asian art is one of the finest in the Western world. The active art, music, and drama departments in Hawaiian schools and colleges and at the University of Hawaii contribute to the expanding cultural life of Hawaii, while the state has several theatre organizations, professional and amateur. The Honolulu Symphony Orchestra (1900) and the Hawaii Opera Theatre (1960) perform in Honolulu and on the other major islands. Their home is the Neal Blaisdell Center, a municipal theatre concert-hall arena complex where touring theatrical companies and ballet troupes and musical artists of international renown also perform. Honolulu's Chamber Music Society gives a concert series each year.

Sports and recreation

In terms of sports, Hawaii is probably most associated with surfing, which has roots in ancient Polynesia but emerged as a modern sport in Hawaii in the early 20th century. No one looms larger in the early history of the sport than Hawaiian Duke Paoa Kahanamoku, who was also an Olympic champion swimmer once considered the greatest freestyle swimmer in the world. The islands have long been a surfers' mecca, especially at the Banzai Pipeline, Waimea Bay, and Sunset Beach on Oahu's North Shore. In November and December, the North Shore is the site of major surfing competitions known collectively as the Vans Triple Crown of Surfing (though one of the women's events is held at Maui's Honolua Bay).

Baseball's history in Hawaii dates from the 1850s, when Alexander Cartwright, one of the men responsible for the invention of the game, brought it with him when he relocated to the islands. In the 1920s a semiprofessional league was founded in Hawaii featuring teams representing the islands' many ethnic groups. The Honolulu-based Hawaiian Islanders (1961 88) were for a time one of the most prominent franchises in the minor leagues, and since 1993 the Hawaiian Baseball League, which plays in the winter, has been a proving ground for professional players from the United States, Japan, Korea, and elsewhere in Asia.

Hawaiians also take great interest in gridiron football, especially in the fortunes of the University of Hawaii's team, and the islands play host to the National Football League's all-star game, the Pro Bowl, as well as college football's Hula Bowl all-star game and Hawaii Bowl.

The Honolulu marathon, first run in 1973, is one of the world's largest. International windsurfing competitions often take place on Oahu. Cycling and swimming are also popular recreations. Skiing is common at Mauna Loa and Mauna Kea during winter months.

Hawaii has two national parks Hawaii Volcanoes (designated a UNESCO World Heritage site in 1987), on the island of Hawaii, and Haleakala, on Maui as well as the much-visited USS *Arizona* Memorial in Pearl Harbor. There are also many state and county parks, including the Waimea Canyon State Park on Kauai. All beaches in the state are open to the public.

Media and publishing

Hawaii's major daily newspapers are the *Honolulu Star-Advertiser*, *Hawaii Tribune-Herald*(Hilo), and *Maui News*. *Hawaii Herald* (founded in 1912 as *Hawaii Hochi*) serves the Japanese American community in Hawaii. The state has several radio and television stations, including some television stations that broadcast in Japanese and Korean.

Hawaii History
Early history

The first inhabitants of Hawaii may have reached the islands as early as 300 CE from the Marquesas Islands. Contact with and settlement by Tahitians began in the 9th century CE. Powerful classes of chiefs and priests arrived and established themselves but became embroiled in conflicts that were similar to the feudal struggles in Europe, with complicated land rights at the centre of the disputes. The early Hawaiians lacked a written language. Their culture was entirely oral and rich in myth, legend, and practical knowledge, especially of animals and plant life. The material life of the islands was hampered by the lack of metal, pottery, or beasts of burden, but there was great skill in the use of wood, shell, stone, and bone, and the huge double and outrigger canoes were technical marvels. Navigational methods were well developed, and there was an elaborate calendar. Athletic contests encouraged warrior skills.

The arrival of Europeans

Capt. James Cook, the British explorer and navigator, is generally credited with having made the first European discovery of Hawaii; he landed at Waimea, Kauai Island, on Jan. 20, 1778. Upon his return the following year, he was killed during an affray with a number of Hawaiians at Kealakekua Bay.

The initial appearance of Cook was followed by a period of intermittent contact with the West. During this period King Kamehameha I used European military technology and weapons to emerge as an outstanding Hawaiian leader, seizing and consolidating control over most of the island group. For 85 years thereafter monarchs ruled over the Hawaiian kingdom. In the early 19th century the American whaling fleet began wintering in Hawaii, and the islands were visited with mounting frequency by explorers, traders, and adventurers. Capt. George Vancouver introduced livestock to the islands in 1792. In 1820 the first of 15 companies of New England missionaries arrived. By the middle of the century there were frame houses, horse-drawn vehicles, schools, churches, taverns, and mercantile establishments. A written language had been introduced, and European and American skills and religious beliefs Protestant and Roman Catholic had been imported. Hawaiian culture was irrevocably changed.

Establishment of U.S. dominance

After the arrival of missionaries, a small but powerful "white" minority began to exert greater and greater power over the Hawaiian monarchy. This minority urged upon King Kamehameha III a written constitution in 1840 and, more importantly, the Great Mahele, or division of lands, in 1848, which guaranteed private ownership of property. Kamehameha III sustained insults to his sovereignty from both the French and the British. U.S. interests grew paramount, however, in the succeeding years, culminating in the signing of the Reciprocity Treaty of 1875, essentially a free-trade agreement between the United States and Hawaii in which the former guaranteed a duty-free market for Hawaiian sugar and the latter gave the United States special economic privileges that were denied to other countries. (When the treaty was renewed in 1887, the United States received exclusive rights to enter and establish a naval base at Pearl Harbor.)

King Kalakaua, who would be the last king of Hawaii, had lobbied for the Reciprocity Treaty. He lost the support of the planter class because of his attempts to revive Hawaiian culture and because of his profligate spending. In 1887 a company of "white" troops, the Honolulu Rifles, helped force upon him the Bayonet Constitution, which severely limited his powers and which allowed suffrage for the wealthy residents (who were generally American or European). When his successor, Queen Liliuokalani, seemed as if she would abrogate that constitution, the Committee of Safety, a group of American and European businessmen, some of whom were citizens of the kingdom, seized power in 1893, with the help of a company of U.S. Marines from the U.S.S. *Boston*, at anchor in the harbour. The U.S. government, under Pres. Grover Cleveland, refused to annex the territory, however, noting that the overthrow of the monarchy was an "act of war" accomplished against popular will using U.S. armed force. A short-lived republic (an oligarchy of American and European businessmen) ensued, until the administration of Pres. William McKinley annexed the islands as U.S. territory in 1900.

As a U.S. territory, Hawaii until 1940 was distinguished by a rapid growth in population, the development of a plantation economy based on the production of sugar and pineapples for consumption on the U.S. mainland, and the growth of transport and military links. Movements for statehood, based in part on Hawaii's obligation to pay U.S. taxes without having corresponding legislative representation, began to emerge. The Japanese attack on Pearl Harbor, on Dec. 7, 1941, brought not only Hawaii but the United States as a whole into World War II, and the islands were beset by an upsurge of military activity and a sometimes controversial curtailment of civil liberties. The post-1945 period was marked by further economic consolidation and a long constitutional path to statehood, a status finally achieved in 1959.

Hawaii after statehood

Since statehood both the population and the economy boomed in Hawaii, with ever-increasing numbers of visitors. Outside investment, notably from the U.S. mainland and Japan, along with rising real estate values, made the islands seem especially bountiful. However, wages have not kept up with the cost of living, and many Hawaiians work multiple jobs to survive. Also, much of the land that had been occupied by Native Hawaiians was cleared for new developments and state parks. Beginning in the 1980s, a sovereignty movement emerged on the islands in which Native Hawaiians demanded legal restoration of sovereignty or reparations for the U.S. takeover of their kingdom. Some groups have pressed for Hawaii to become its own nation, while others have advocated for federal recognition of Native Hawaiians equivalent to that of Native Americans. In 1993 U.S. Pres. Bill Clinton apologized for America's role in the overthrow of the Hawaiian monarchy.

After decades of growth, the islands underwent a protracted recession in the early 1990s. By the end of that decade, however, the economy had recovered, and much development took place on Maui and the Kona side of Hawaii Island. Tourism remained the dominant industry in the early 21st century. Visitors are lured not only by the warm climate and exotic beauty of the islands but also by a growing number of world-class resorts, built on such a grand scale that they are destinations in themselves. Moreover, the Mauna Kea Observatory has helped Hawaii become a major world centre of astronomy.

Despite the draw of Hawaii for tourists, foreigners, and researchers, Native Hawaiians continue to demand land rights, more autonomy in their internal affairs, and the right to self-governance. The establishment of a Native Hawaiian governing entity continues to be debated between Native Hawaiians and those who oppose ancestry-based sovereignty.

Kauai

Kauai is Hawaii's fourth largest island and is sometimes called the "Garden Island," which is an entirely accurate description. The oldest and northernmost island in the Hawaiian chain is draped in emerald valleys, sharp mountain spires and jagged cliffs aged by time and the elements. Centuries of growth have formed tropical rainforests, forking rivers and cascading waterfalls! Some parts of Kauai are only accessible by sea or air, revealing views beyond your imagination. More than just dramatic beauty, the island is home to a variety of outdoor activities. You can kayak the WAILUA RIVER, snorkel on POIPU BEACH, hike the trails of KOKEE STATE PARK, or go ziplining above Kauai's lush valleys. But, it is the island's laid-back atmosphere and rich culture found in its small towns that make it truly timeless. Make your escape to Kauai and discover the undeniable allure of the island.

Kauai Regions

North Shore

Kauai's dramatic North Shore is an enchanting setting full of rugged mountains, lush taro fields, heavenly beaches and spectacular sea cliffs. You'll be amazed at how much beauty can be found in just one area of Kauai.

Begin your journey on the island's northernmost point. Historic Daniel K. Inouye Kilauea Point Lighthouse is a wildlife sanctuary and a scenic spot during whale watching season. Visit lovely Hanalei Town, home to stretches of green taro fields alongside colorful shops, galleries and restaurants. You'll also find some of Kauai's best beaches here including Lumahai Beach, the setting for the film "South Pacific," and Kee Beach, ideal for sunbathing. You can also learn about native plants and see scenic ocean views at Na Aina Kai Botanical Gardens or at the 17-acre Limahuli Gardens, part of the National Tropical Botanical Garden.

But the most stunning feature of Kauai's North Shore is the magnificent Napali Coast. This 17-mile stretch of coastline is lined with cliffs up to 3,000-foot tall, accented with lush green valleys, cascading waterfalls and sea caves. Inaccessible by car, you can hike or take an air or boat tour to view this breathtaking natural wonder.

The North Shore is also home to the upscale resort area of Princeville where you can indulge in world-class hospitality and play at some of Kauai's premier golf courses. You can also find other accommodations here ranging from historic bed and breakfasts to rental homes allowing everyone the opportunity to experience the beauty of Kauai's North Shore.

Kilauea Point Lighthouse
Daniel K. Inouye Kilauea Point Lighthouse

What: Beautiful views from Kauai's northernmost tip
Where: A 45-minute drive north of Lihue

Perched at the northernmost tip of Kauai, the 52-foot Daniel K. Inouye Kilauea Point Lighthouse was built in 1913 as a beacon for traveling ships. Although its light was turned off in the 1970s and has been replaced by an automatic beacon, it still serves as one of the island's most frequented attractions.

The view off the rugged northern coastline and the deep-blue Pacific makes this the perfect vantage point for photos. This is also the location of the Kilauea Point National Wildlife Refuge, a sanctuary for seabirds. Signage throughout the refuge identifies the area's bird species, including frigates, shearwaters, boobies and Laysan albatrosses nesting on the property. You'll see them soar the skies above the refuge, many landing on a small nearby island covered in birds. During December through May, you may even catch a glimpse of humpback whales. This scenic peninsula, 200-feet above sea level, is a must-see on your visit to the North Shore.

Tours are offered Wednesdays and Saturdays at 10:30 and 11:30 a.m. and at 12:30, 1:30 and 2:30 p.m. pending availability of staff or volunteers. Tour involves walking up steep, narrow steps. Restrictions: Children must be at least 44 inches tall. No infants. Backpacks, tripods and other large items are not allowed in the Kilauea Lighthouse.

Napali Coast
What: Iconic, mountainous shoreline on Kauai's North Shore
Where: About 90 minutes north of Lihue

Spanning 17 miles along Kauai's North Shore, the Napali Coast is a sacred place defined by extraordinary natural beauty. These emerald-hued cliffs with razor-sharp ridges tower above the Pacific Ocean, revealing beautiful beaches and waterfalls that plummet to the lush valley floor. The rugged terrain appears much as it did centuries ago when Hawaiian settlements flourished in these deep, narrow valleys, existing only on the food they could grow and the fish they could catch.

There are many ways to explore the Napali Coast, but the safest access and best views are found by sea or by air. Boat tours depart from Port Allen on the West Side, and during the summer months, guided kayaking trips bring you up-close to soaring cathedral cliffs. When conditions are right, raft tours are available to guide you to hidden sea caves and remote beaches.

Aerial tours, most lifting off from Lihue Airport, are perhaps the best way to grasp the magnitude of the Napali Coast. You'll also get a front-row seat to scenic areas that are largely inaccessible by land or water, like majestic Manawaiopuna Falls, a backdrop in the film "Jurassic Park." Whichever tour you choose, the natural splendor of the Napali Coast will leave a deep impression on your soul.

Hanalei Town
What: Charming small town on Kauai's north shore
Where: In northern Kauai, a few minutes west of Princeville

West of Princeville, on Kauai's North shore, is peaceful Hanalei Town. Graced with timeless beauty, this lovely small town is home to everything from historic places to contemporary art galleries. Hanalei Town is an unforgettable stop on your visit to Kauai.

Visit the Waioli Mission House and step back into Kauai's history.

Browse Hanalei's art galleries for made-in-Kauai art and carvings made from rare, native Hawaiian woods. Locals and visitors come to Hanalei for ukulele concerts held at the Hanalei Community Center, a regular Kauai event.

At the foot of Hanalei's misty green mountains, you'll also discover fields of taro ("kalo" in Hawaiian). These heart-shaped plants grow intensely green in flooded patches and are used to make poi, a Hawaiian staple starch that you can taste at any Kauai luau. You can get a good view of this emerald quilt of land from the Hanalei Valley Lookout. Note that these taro farms are on private property, so only step foot on them during an authorized farm tour.

The historic Hanalei Pier was built in 1892 and has long been a favorite gathering place for local residents, who go there to fish, swim and play music on Hanalei Bay. In 1957, the pier became world famous when Oscar Hammerstein II and 20th Century Fox featured the pier in the classic film, "South Pacific." After a busy day of soaking up Hanalei Town's history and charm, kick back, relax and watch a luminous sunset over Hanalei Bay.

Note: To get to Hanalei, visitors need to pass over a one-lane bridge. Drivers must use local etiquette: all the vehicles on one side cross, followed by all the vehicles on the other side.

Waioli Huuia Church

Waioli Huuia Church and Mission House
What: Hanalei landmark built in 1837

Where: In Hanalei, minutes from Princeville

Step back in time at the 1837 home of early Christian missionaries Abner and Lucy Wilcox. This Hanalei Town landmark, restored in 1921 and listed on the National Register of Historic Places, reflects the southern roots of its architect, the Reverend William Alexander of Kentucky.

Inside, synchronize your watch with the wall clock, which was installed in 1866 and still keeps perfect time. View the significant features like the lava rock chimney and the fine koa furniture. Lucy Wilcox gave birth to eight sons in the master bedroom, a significant feat on its own.

In front of the house is the old Waioli Huuia Church, which was founded in 1834. Its green shingles and stained glass windows are a picturesque symbol of Hanalei.

Tours are offered Tuesdays, Thursdays and Saturdays from 9 a.m. to 3 p.m. on a first come, first served basis.

East Side (Royal Coconut Coast), Kauai

Kauai's East Side is sometimes referred to as the Royal Coconut Coast for the groves of coconut palms that grow in its resort areas. The most populated district on the island, about 16,000 of the island's 71,000 residents reside in the Wailua/Kapaa area. Amongst the clusters of coconut trees you'll find historic places, amazing beaches and memorable attractions.

In Wailua, you'll find a variety of sightseeing opportunities and outdoor activities. Kayak the Wailua River in Wailua River State Park, take a boat ride to the Fern Grotto, or take photos at Opaekaa Falls. Don't forget to try and spot the Sleeping Giant in the Nounou Mountain or take a hike up this scenic ridge. Sacred places like Poliahu Heiau can also be found on the East Side. And be sure to visit Kapaa Town to discover fine Hawaiian craft pieces, aloha-print shirts, jewelry and art.

But the golden beaches of the Coconut Coast may be the area's biggest draw. Unwind at Lydgate Beach Park in Wailua, where you'll find two lava rock enclosed ocean pools that are perfect places for families and first-time snorkelers. Fun in the sun awaits you on the Coconut Coast.

Opaekaa Falls

What: One of Kauai's most accessible major waterfalls

Where: In Wailua, two miles up Route 580

Cascading down into a hidden pool, this 151-foot-tall, 40-foot-wide waterfall is easily one of the island's most accessible major waterfalls. Located on the East Side about two miles up Kuamoo Road (Route 580) from Hwy. 56, signs clearly point to the roadside lookout on the right. This convenient stop offers visitors a great view from a scenic lookout and access to picnic tables and restrooms. "Opaekaa" means "rolling shrimp," which were once abundant in the stream. Walk uphill from the Opaekaa lookout and across the road for another great view of the Wailua River valley and interior plains beyond.

Wailua River

What: Kauai's largest navigable river

Where: About 15 minutes north of Lihue, on Kauai's East Side

The tranquil Wailua River weaves by gorgeous waterfalls and lush, jungle landscapes along the island's East Side. Kauai has the only navigable rivers in Hawaii, and the Wailua River is the largest.

The 20-mile long river, that once wove through the settings of seven different *heiau* (temples), flows from the 5,148-foot Mount Waialeale in the center of the island. The Wailua River feeds two popular and accessible waterfalls: Opaekaa Falls and Wailua Falls. The scenic river itself can be explored by kayak, SUP or outrigger canoe, and a boat tour is also available. Open-air boats also offer guided tours of the Fern Grotto, a natural lava rock cave sheltered by draping ferns. This romantic area is a popular wedding venue. Also look for the Nounou Mountains (Sleeping Giant), a formation on a mountain ridge between Wailua and Kapaa that looks like a human figure lying on its back.

You can also see the river by car. Take Kuamoo Road (Hwy. 580), which goes inland along the north side of the river from Kuhio Highway (Hwy. 56). You'll want to take in the special and sacred landmarks along the way, including heiau (temples), historical sites, Opaekaa Falls and the Keahua Arboretum.

Fern Grotto

What: Natural, fern-filled grotto on the Wailua River
Where: Up the Wailua River on the East Side

On Kauai's East Side, the Fern Grotto is one of Kauai's signature attractions. Accessible only by a short boat trip up the Wailua River, the grotto is a natural lava-rock grotto, lush with hanging ferns and tropical foliage, cooled by the mists of a waterfall. There was a time when the Grotto was off-limits to all but Hawaiian royalty. But for more than 50 years, riverboats have provided tours of the site.

In this serene setting, the grotto acts like a natural amphitheatre. Taking advantage of the incredible natural acoustics, visitors are often treated to musicians playing beautiful Hawaiian music. It's no wonder why this unique Kauai setting is such a popular destination for wedding ceremonies.

Kapaa Town
What: Unique local shopping on Kauai
Where: North of Wailua on the East Side

North of Wailua on the East Side is Kapaa Town, a great area for shopping on Kauai. Kinipopo Shopping Village offers a variety of fun shops and eateries. It has a water sports shop that carries everything you need to purchase or rent for a water adventure. You can also arrange for water skiing or kayak rental in Kapaa. Aloha shirts, vintage maps, fine art and jewelry can be found as you browse this shopping village.

Other stops include the Wailua Shopping Plaza, which houses several restaurants and an eclectic antique shop, and the Coconut Marketplace, with dozens of shops in which you'll find Hawaiian mementos, fine artwork, antiques, jewelry and craft items. Find the perfect, made in Hawaii keepsake on your trip to Kapaa. And if you're there on the first Saturday of the month, Old Kapaa Town features live music, local crafts and food.

Lihue

Lihue is the government and commercial center of the island, as well as a cultural and historical area. This may be the most traveled town on Kauai since it is home to Kauai's main airport (the Lihue Airport) and Nawiliwili Harbor, the island's major commercial shipping center and cruise ship port.

Lihue has a variety of natural wonders to explore. Kalapaki Beach is the home of the Kauai Marriott Resort and Beach Club and the Hokuala Golf Resort. Bodysurfing, SUP, surfing and swimming make Kalapaki a popular destination. Ninini Beach is home to an automated lighthouse, in operation since 1897. And just north of Lihue, don't forget to stop at the Wailua Falls lookout for an amazing waterfall view.

The Lihue area also has numerous historical spots including Alekoko Fishpond, a roughly 1,000-year-old aquaculture reservoir; Kilohana, a historic plantation estate home to one of the island's most iconic luau; and both the historic Kauai Museum and Grove Farm Homestead Museum. Lihue is your gateway to adventure on Kauai.

Kauai Museum

Name: Kauai Museum

What: Museum showcasing local artists and Hawaiian history

Where: On Rice Street in Lihue

When: Monday-Saturday 9 a.m.-4 p.m.

How Much: General admission $15, Kamaaina $10, seniors $12, students age 8-17 $10, children under 7 & active military free

More Info: (808) 245-6931

Located in a lava rock structure in Lihue, the Kauai Museum features amazing collections from the artisans of Kauai and Niihau (a small eastern island part of Kauai county). Visitors can learn about the geological formation of the Hawaiian Islands, early Native Hawaiian life, Captain Cook's arrival on Kauai's shores in Waimea and the Hawaiian Monarchy. Plus, visitors can view galleries showcasing the work of multi-cultural artists, sculptors and craftsmen. Guided tours are available (upon request).

Alekoko Fishpond

What: Legendary ancient Hawaiian fishpond

Where: In Nawiliwili, minutes from Lihue

Built nearly 1,000 years ago, the Alekoko Fishpond, minutes from Lihue, has been on the National Register of Historic Places since 1973.

Ingenious ponds were built to catch fish, and this is one of the finest examples of ancient Hawaiian aquaculture.

The legend that surrounds the fishpond is based on the mythical Menehune, Hawaii's mischievous little people who performed legendary engineering feats. The Menehune lived in the forest and hid from humans. According to Hawaiian legends, the Menehune built this entire fishpond in one night. They managed this amazing task by lining up from the village of Makaweli for 25 miles, passing stones hand-to-hand to build the pond. Though Menehune legends abound, some say the word may have derived from the Tahitian word manahune meaning commoner, or small in social standing, not in physical size.

The Alekoko Fishpond is located near the Huleia National Wildlife Refuge, about a half-mile inland from Nawiliwili Harbor and can be viewed from an overlook on Hulemalu Road. The wall separating the pond from Huleia Stream is 900 feet long, five feet high and meticulously assembled with lava rock.

Note: Kayak tours are an enjoyable way to explore the fishpond. You can kayak past the pond entrance, but the refuge is closed to the public.

Wailua Falls

What: Dramatic waterfalls that are easily accessible

Where: North of Lihue, at the south end of the Wailua River

Wailua Falls, just north of Lihue, is a step off the beaten path. Located at the south end of the Wailua River, it cascades into two streams, dropping 80 feet below. Some even say the distance is more accurately described as 200 feet. Perhaps this is because the size and appearance of the falls is determined by the amount of rainfall farther up the mountains.

Like other spectacular spots on Kauai used as film locations, Wailua Falls is most recognized in the opening credits of the long-running television show "Fantasy Island." Easily accessible, Wailua Falls can be seen from the roadside, so you can leave your hiking boots behind. To get there, head north from Lihue and follow Maalo Road in Hanamaulu. Travel uphill for about 3 miles. If you visit in the mornings, you may be treated to a rainbow as the sunlight meets the mist of the falls, which makes for an amazing photo opportunity.

Kilohana Estate

What: Historic plantation estate

Where: Lihue on Kaumualii Highway

Past Lihue and headed toward the Kauai Community College campus is

Kilohana, a restored plantation estate that provides a glimpse of life in the 1930s. The site of a 16,000 square-foot Tudor mansion that was home to one of the island's most prominent families, Kilohana is now a picturesque venue for tours, gatherings and a theatrical luau.

Manicured green lawns surround the estate, which now features Gaylord's restaurant and a number of unique shops like the Koloa Rum Company. Once the center of a 27,000-acre sugar plantation and the hub of Kauai business, cultural and social life, the 35-acre estate now features tropical gardens and an old plantation village. Classic Kauai Plantation Railway gives you a tour of Kilohana's working farm, and the festive Luau Kalamaku is held regularly. Banquet facilities also make this a perfect venue for weddings, receptions and special events.

Grove Farm Homestead Museum
What: A historic sugar plantation museum
Where: In Lihue on Nawiliwili Road
More Info: (808) 245-3202

A visit to the Grove Farm Homestead in Lihue provides visitors with a fascinating look into the island's past. Hawaii's booming sugar plantation industry in the late 1800s had its origins on Kauai. Grove Farm, one of the earliest sugar plantations and the former home of George N. Wilcox and his descendants, was founded in 1864. Today, this 100-acre, historic site showcases life during Kauai's plantation era more than a century ago. By appointment, a tour takes visitors throughout the property, which includes the gracious old Wilcox home and the cottage of the plantation housekeeper situated amidst tropical gardens, orchards and rolling lawns. Make a reservation and learn more about how sugar plantations influenced the history of the islands.

Note: Tours are available Monday, Wednesday, and Thursday at 10 a.m. and 1 p.m. Advanced reservations are required for the two-hour tour.

South Shore

Drive through a tunnel of trees to arrive on the warm and beautiful south shore of Kauai. The biggest attractions here are the perfect beaches around the Poipu area and Spouting Horn, a blowhole that releases a spout of water up to 20 feet into the air. Poipu stretches around Makahuena Point and is a spectacle to any onlooker. At night, you can stroll through charming boutiques and dine on Pacific Rim cuisine at ocean-side restaurants. Other towns you'll find on the south side include Old Koloa Town, Kalaheo, Lawai, and Omao. Filled with resorts, golf, shopping, beaches and sights, there's never a dull moment on the South Shore of Kauai that is unless you just want to take a break and nap on the beach.

Poipu Beach Park

Where: South Shore

Activities: Surfing, fishing, snorkeling, bodyboarding

Amenities: Parking, lifeguard (seven days a week), restrooms, showers, picnic tables

Popular with visitors and locals alike, this crescent-shaped beach offers crystal-clear waters and occasional Hawaiian monk seal appearances. (If you do spot a monk seal, please be mindful by staying at least 100 feet away and no flash photography as they are currently on the endangered species list.) With lifeguards, picnic facilities, showers and a natural wading pool for young swimmers, it's also a great destination for a family beach day. There's a bodyboarding site directly in front of the park for older children and novice adults, a surfing site for experienced surfers and a good reef for snorkeling. From December through April, you can sometimes spot humpback whales in the distance.

Old Koloa Town

What: Charming town rooted in its plantation past

Where: About 20 minutes west from Lihue

Historic and picturesque, the Koloa district spans from Old Koloa Town to Kauai's beautiful South Shore in Poipu. Koloa opened its first sugar mill in 1835 and set the precedent for commercial sugar production across the islands. The sugar era opened the door to a wave of immigrants that make up Hawaii's multicultural population today.

The gateway to the Koloa/Poipu area is called the Tree Tunnel, a stretch of Maluhia Road lined with eucalyptus trees first planted a century ago. The Tree Tunnel still thrives and welcomes visitors today.

Old Koloa Town has retained much of its charm with shops now occupying the plantation buildings along Koloa Road. Stroll by old-fashioned storefronts and discover special local gifts. Stop by the Koloa History Center any day of the week from 9 a.m. to 9 p.m. to learn about the town's sweet heritage. Then cool down with an island-style Lappert's ice cream cone under the shade of the large monkey pod trees. Lappert's Ice Cream Store is a Kauai original and is still made fresh daily in nearby Hanapepe. Hawaii-inspired favorites include Heavenly Hana, Big Island Inspiration and Kauai Pie.

You can also explore the Koloa Heritage Trail, which covers 14 cultural, historical and geological sites from Old Koloa Town to Poipu. But to really experience all that this area has to offer, go to the Koloa Plantation Days Celebration (July), an annual summer event that celebrates Kauai's rich plantation past. Further south you'll discover the resorts around beautiful Poipu Beach, a modern change from charming Old Koloa Town.

Koloa Heritage Trail, Kauai

What: 10-mile tour of important sites in Koloa and Poipu

Where: South Shore of Kauai through Koloa and Poipu

Ka Ala Hele Waiwai Hooilina o Koloa, or the Koloa Heritage Trail, is a 14-stop, self-guided 10-mile tour of the Koloa and Poipu area's most important cultural, historical and geological sites, with descriptive plaques that explain each spot's significance.

Koloa is a historic South Shore area, home to Hawaii's first commercial sugar plantation. In the mid 1800's, sugar replaced the whaling industry to become the principal industry of Hawaii. As a result of the sugar boom, approximately 350,000 immigrants from around the world came to Hawaii to work in the sugar plantations. Although tourism supplanted sugar as Hawaii's major industry (Kauai's last sugar mill closed in 2008), the legacy of the era lives on in the unique ethnic diversity of Hawaii's people today.

Beyond the shower tree in the center of Old Koloa Town you'll discover the Sugar Monument, just one of the stops on the Koloa Heritage Trail. This circular concrete sculpture suggesting a millstone holds a bronze sculpture depicting the eight principal ethnic groups that brought the sugar industry to life (Hawaiian, Caucasian, Puerto Rican, Chinese, Korean, Japanese, Portuguese and Filipino). The sculpture opens up to face the remnants of the Koloa sugar mill's stone chimney, built in 1841.

Koloa Heritage Trail Locations

Encompassing the south shore of Kauai, look for these special spots on your next visit:

1. Spouting Horn Park - Famous south shore blowhole.
2. Prince Kuhio Birthplace & Park - Prince Kuhio, known as the "People's Prince," was born here in 1871.
3. Hanakaape Bay & Koloa Landing - Formerly the third largest whaling port in Hawaii.
4. Pau A Laka (Moir Gardens) - Botanical garden founded in the 1930s.
5. Kihahouna Heiau - Site of an ancient Hawaiian temple.
6. Poipu Beach Park - Popular beach home to endangered monk seals.
7. Keoneloa Bay - Home to some of Kauai's oldest occupied sites (200-600 A.D.).
8. Makaweha & Paa Dunes - A fossil bed that has become a popular spot for bird watching
9. Puuwanawana Volcanic Cone - A younger volcanic cone in a formation dating back more than 5 million years.
10. Hapa Road - Hawaiians have lived in this area since 1200 A.D.
11. Koloa Jodo Mission - Buddhist temple built in 1910.

12. <u>Sugar Monument</u> - Commemorates the site of Hawaii's first sugar mill.

13. <u>Yamamoto Store & Koloa Hotel</u> - Former plantation-era mainstay from the 1920s. Note that these two businesses are now the present day Crazy Shirts and the South Shore Pharmacy respectively.

14. <u>Koloa Missionary Church</u> - The first Congregational church in Kauai.

Spouting Horn

What: Scenic blowhole of Hawaiian legend
Where: On Kauai's South Shore near Poipu

On Kauai's South Shore you'll find the spectacular Spouting Horn blowhole, one of the most photographed spots on Kauai. The Poipu surf channels into a natural lava tube here and releases a huge spout of water that can reach as high as 50 feet into the air. You'll also hear a hiss and a roar that is the basis of a Hawaiian legend.

One legend says that this coastline was once guarded by a giant moo (lizard) named Kaikapu. Everyone was afraid of the moo because it would eat anyone who tried to fish or swim in the area. One day, a young boy named Liko entered the ocean to outwit the lizard. Kaikapu attacked him, but Liko thrust a sharp stick into her mouth, swam under the lava shelf, and escaped through a small hole to the surface. The moo followed Liko and got stuck in the lava tube. To this day, you can hear the lizard's roar and see her breath spraying from the blowhole.

Access to Spouting Horn Park is convenient with ample parking and the view from the lookout is luminous at sunset. The Poipu coastline is also a great vantage point to look for humpback whales during whale watching season from December to May.

Allerton Garden

What: Botanical garden and landscape architecture masterpiece
Where: On Kauai's South Shore

Part of the network of National Tropical Botanical Garden, Allerton Garden is a must-see on the south shore of Kauai. Also known as Lawai Kai, the garden is a paradise, transformed through time by the hands of a Hawaiian Queen, by a sugar plantation magnate, and most significantly by an artist and an architect, Robert Allerton and John Gregg Allerton, who in 1938 began designing and developing the mistifying garden "rooms" and water features. You might also recognize the garden's enormous Moreton Fig Trees from their role in "Jurassic Park," as well as other areas of the garden that have served as a backdrop for numerous blockbuster films.

Today the garden continues to serve as a refuge for those who appreciate beauty in nature carefully cultivated and balanced with human artistry and ingenuity, along with the beautiful story of the garden's devoted caretakers.

West Side

About an hour's drive from Lihue and other major towns on the Coconut Coast, Kauai's West Side feels like it's a world away. Here, spectacular natural wonders and historic sites meet funky small towns, rewarding visitors with a glimpse of Kauai mainly seen by locals.

The most famous attraction on the West Side is breathtaking Waimea Canyon, also called the "Grand Canyon of the Pacific." Hiking trails and scenic overlooks offer sweeping views of rugged crags and plunging valleys dipping more than 3,600 feet into the earth. There's nothing else in Hawaii quite like it.

Neighboring Kokee State Park offers 45 miles of trails and endless opportunities to see native plants and wildlife. At the north edge of the park, Kalalau Lookout and Puu O Kila Lookout provide panoramic views of the vibrant, green cliffs of one of the valleys of the Napali Coast two of the best (and safest) ways to see Kalalau Valley from land.

The two small towns of Waimea and Hanapepe are also worth a visit on the West Side. In 1778, Captain James Cook first landed in the

Hawaiian Islands here at Waimea Bay. Today, a statue of Cook stands in Waimea Town commemorating this historic event. About seven miles south of Waimea, Hanapepe is the island's art capital, with eclectic galleries, shops and eateries lining the streets of "Kauai's biggest little town" a perfect place to shop for made-in-Hawaii gifts and souvenirs.

Waimea Canyon

What: On the southwest side of Kauai in Waimea
Where: Scenic canyon nicknamed "The Grand Canyon of the Pacific"
When: Open daily during daylight hours
How much: free admission
More Info: Parking lot, restrooms, lookout

Waimea Canyon, on Kauai's West Side, is described as "The Grand Canyon of the Pacific." Although not as big or as old as its Arizona cousin, you won't encounter anything like this geological wonder in Hawaii. Stretching 14 miles long, 1 mile wide and more than 3,600 feet deep, the Waimea Canyon Lookout provides panoramic views of crested buttes, rugged crags and deep valley gorges. The grand inland vistas go on for miles.

The main road, Waimea Canyon Drive, leads you to a lower lookout point and the main Waimea Canyon Overlook, offering views of

Kauai's dramatic interior. The road continues into the mountains and ends at Kokee State Park. There are numerous trails to traverse for beginners and seasoned hikers alike.

Waimea Town
What: Historic seaport town
Where: In southwest Kauai, west of Hanapepe

On your way to Waimea Canyon, make a stop in Waimea Town on the West Side. This historic seaport town is a stone's throw from where British discoverer Captain James Cook first landed in Hawaii in 1778. A statue of Captain Cook can be found in the center of town, a replica of the original statue found in Whitby, England. Rich in paniolo history (Hawaiian cowboys), this charming town is home to a variety of small shops and businesses as well as a growing number of tech companies.

While you're in Waimea Town, stop by the West Kauai Technology & Visitor Center, a great place to learn more about Kauai's past. The center features exhibits, programs and weekly activities that reflect the diversity of Kauai's agricultural community. Call for more information (registration is required for some events and programs). Along with Hanapepe, Waimea Town is an off-the-beaten-path discovery that's a great place to stop as you explore Kauai's West Side.

Kokee State Park

What: State park with hiking trails and the Kalalau Lookout

Where: North beyond Waimea Canyon

When: Open daily during daylight hours

How much: tent camping fees start at $12 per campsite

More Info: Hiking trails, restrooms, camping, picnic areas.

North of Waimea Canyon on Kauai's West Side is Kokee State Park. Spread over 4,345 acres on a plateau 3,200 to 4,200 feet above sea level, Kokee State Park is covered in forest, wild flowers and hiking trails making it an excellent spot to see native plants and colorful endemic Hawaiian forest birds like the apapane, iwi and moa. The park also offers roughly 45 miles of the state's finest hiking trails. Some trails lead to views of Waimea Canyon, others wind through wet forests with sweeping views of valleys opening up to the North Shore.

The Kokee Natural History Museum is a must-stop shop for information about the park and the trails. Exhibits will give you an overview of the park and Waimea Canyon. Staff will also provide you with helpful assistance, advice and information on trail and weather conditions.

Beyond the museum and the Lodge at Kokee (12 rustic rental cabins for campers) are two amazing lookouts. Both the Kalalau Lookout and the Puu O Kila Lookout offer commanding views of the Kalalau Valley stretching out to the sea. This view offers a glimpse at the towering cliffs of the Napali Coast. Note that the temperature drops as you climb up to the 3,200 to 4,200 foot elevations of the park. Temperatures range from 45 degrees in January to 68 degrees in July with annual rainfall of about 70 inches, so remember to dress warmly.

Note: *If you are scuba diving during your visit to Kauai, you should wait at least 24 hours before visiting this location due to the higher elevation of Waimea Canyon and Kokee State Park.*

Hanapepe Town
What: Small town, art capital of Kauai
Where: Southwest Kauai, between Koloa and Waimea

Located on the south shore west of Koloa, Hanapepe Town once flourished as one of Kauai's largest communities. From World War I to the early 1950s, West Side Hanapepe was also one of Kauai's busiest towns, alive with G.I.s and sailors who were stationed there for training.

Today, "Kauai's biggest little town" hasn't changed much over the last century at first look. Its historic buildings are so authentic that the town was used as a location for films like "The Thornbirds" and "Flight of the Intruder," and even served as the model for the Disney film "Lilo and Stitch." But now those plantation-style buildings are home to charming shops, local eateries and more art galleries than any other spot on Kauai.

Hanapepe Town hosts a farmer's market on Thursdays starting at 3 p.m. And it celebrates its artists every Friday from 5-9 p.m., as painters, sculptors and craftsmen open the doors of their galleries and studios to celebrate the arts. Visit the galleries, take a walk on the "Hanapepe Swinging Bridge" which is always an adventure to cross then shop and dine in one of Kauai's most famous small towns.

Things to Do on Kauai

Kauai Beaches

Beaches

While Kauai is famous for its dramatic cliffs, canyons and rainforests, it's also home to some of Hawaii's most picturesque beaches. The island is surrounded by 50 miles of shimmering white-sand coast where you can enjoy jaw-droppingly beautiful unspoiled views. Find activities for both daring and more relaxed travelers, from surfing Hanalei Bay's waves in the North Shore to spotting whales and sea turtles at Poipu Beach Park in the south.

North Shore Beaches

<u>Haena Beach Park</u> has the picturesque backdrop of Mount Makana (Bali Hai) and is perfect for a day or relaxing or some great sunset shots.

Where: North Shore, Kauai
Activities: Swimming, surfing, snorkeling, sunbathing
Amenities: Parking, restrooms, camping, lifeguard

With Mount Makana (Bali Hai) looming above and lush tropical jungles just beyond the sand, Haeana Beach is a picturesque backdrop for relaxing on the beach or taking sunset photos. During winter and spring, water conditions can become hazardous due to pounding shorebreaks and powerful rip currents. In summer, the water is much calmer, making it a great place for snorkeling. While visiting, be sure to check out the Maniniholo dry cave just across the street.

<u>Anini Beach Park</u> features miles of white sandy beach protected by a huge coral reef. The quiet lagoon and tranquil waters are perfect for beginning snorkelers and windsurfers. Facilities are available, but there are no lifeguards.

<u>Kee Beach</u> is located at the end of Highway 560. The reefs here make for great shoreline snorkeling on calm days, or you might be able to grab some glimpses of the Napali Coast while you sunbathe. Kee

Beach is also where you'll find the trailhead for the Napali Coast's Kalalau Trail. Lifeguards are on duty.

East Side Beaches

<u>Lydgate Beach Park</u> is shielded from the open ocean by a lava rock wall, so the snorkeling lagoon at Lydgate is a popular place for keiki (children) to play. Restrooms, picnic grounds and lifeguards are available at this family-friendly East Side beach.

Where: East Side (Coconut Coast), Kauai

Activities: Swimming, windsurfing, bodyboarding, surfing

Amenities: Parking, lifeguard, restrooms, showers

Located on the shoreline near the mouth of the Wailua River, Lydgate Beach is one of the most popular beach parks on Kauai and attracts many swimmers, picnickers, campers, fishermen, surfers, divers and beachcombers. Windsurfers also visit the area when south, or kona, winds offer favorable sailing conditions for this side of the island. Protected from the open ocean by a lava-rock wall, Lydgate Beach Park uniquely hosts a variety of tropical fish in protected calm waters, ideal for keiki (children) and beginner snorkelers. With its many facilities, including a picnic area and restrooms, this spot is ideal for a family beach day.

Lydgate Pond.

Where: East Side (Coconut Coast)

Activities: Swimming

Amenities: Parking, lifeguard, playground

Located in Lydgate State Park, this large salt-water pool is one of Kauai's safest year-round swimming sites. Constructed by placing huge boulders in a semicircle facing the beach, the pond is divided into one large, deep pool and one small, shallow pool. The boulders provide protection from strong currents and seasonally high surf. It's a great beach for keiki (children), with a nearby wooden play structure at Kamalani Playground that will occupy them for hours.

Kealia Beach Park is a half-mile stretch of golden coast that hugs the curve of Highway 56. Its long sand-bar bottom provides a nice surf break. Swim or boogie board near the north end, where a breakwater creates a protected area. Facilities and lifeguards are available.

Where: East Side (Coconut Coast), Kauai

Activities: Swimming, bodyboarding, surfing

Amenities: Parking, lifeguard, restrooms, showers, picnic tables

This half-mile stretch of white sand beach hugs the curve of Highway

56. Popular with surfers, its sand-bar bottom provides a good surf break. Enjoy strolling on the sand or whale watching in winter. Calmer water in summer months make it a nice spot for swimming or bodyboarding near the north end, where breakwater creates a protected area.

Kalapaki Beach fronts the Marriott Kauai Beach Club. Pack a picnic, grab a shave ice and watch Kauai surfers ride the waves. The beach is partially protected from the open ocean, creating calm and safe conditions for kids.

Welcome to Marriott's Kauai Beach Club - a tropical paradise located on beautiful Kalapaki Beach. From here, you can explore lush valleys and timeless canyons, majestic waterfalls and rainforests that merge into the blue and green sea. Play a few rounds of golf or lounge by the spectacular 26,000-square-foot swimming pool, rimmed by colonnades and waterfalls. After a day of sun and exploration, return to your comfortable guestroom or villa where you will enjoy living and dining space, plus thoughtful conveniences to enhance your stay.

South Shore Beaches

Poipu Beach Park is one of Kauai's most popular beaches, with its crystal-clear waters and occasional Hawaiian monk seal appearances. Poipu also has a natural wading pool for young swimmers. Lifeguards, picnic facilities, showers and pavilions make this South Shore beach a great day trip for families.

Where: South Shore
Activities: Surfing, fishing, snorkeling, bodyboarding
Amenities: Parking, lifeguard (seven days a week), restrooms, showers, picnic tables

Popular with visitors and locals alike, this crescent-shaped beach offers crystal-clear waters and occasional Hawaiian monk seal appearances. (If you do spot a monk seal, please be mindful by staying at least 100 feet away and no flash photography as they are currently on the endangered species list.) With lifeguards, picnic facilities, showers and a natural wading pool for young swimmers, it's also a great destination for a family beach day. There's a bodyboarding site directly in front of the park for older children and novice adults, a surfing site for experienced surfers and a good reef for snorkeling. From December through April, you can sometimes spot humpback whales in the distance.

West Side Beaches
Salt Pond Beach Park

Where: West Side, Kauai
Activities: Bodyboarding, fishing, scuba diving, snorkeling, surfing,

swimming, windsurfing

Amenities: Parking, lifeguard, picnic tables, camping area, restrooms, showers

Located near Hanapepe, this inviting beach park is an ideal setting to relax, swim or explore the shallow tide pools. Toddlers will enjoy splashing around in the gentle lagoon.

<u>Hanapepe</u> on the West Side. This inviting park is an ideal setting to relax, swim or explore the shallow tide pools. Lifeguards and facilities are available.

What: Small town, art capital of Kauai
Where: Southwest Kauai, between Koloa and Waimea

Located on the south shore west of Koloa, Hanapepe Town once flourished as one of Kauai's largest communities. From World War I to the early 1950s, West Side Hanapepe was also one of Kauai's busiest towns, alive with G.I.s and sailors who were stationed there for training.

Today, "Kauai's biggest little town" hasn't changed much over the last century at first look. Its historic buildings are so authentic that the town was used as a location for films like "The Thornbirds" and "Flight of the Intruder," and even served as the model for the Disney film

"Lilo and Stitch." But now those plantation-style buildings are home to charming shops, local eateries and more art galleries than any other spot on Kauai.

Hanapepe Town hosts a farmer's market on Thursdays starting at 3 p.m. And it celebrates its artists every Friday from 5-9 p.m., as painters, sculptors and craftsmen open the doors of their galleries and studios to celebrate the arts. Visit the galleries, take a walk on the "Hanapepe Swinging Bridge" which is always an adventure to cross then shop and dine in one of Kauai's most famous small towns.

Kekaha Beach:
Where: West Side, Kauai
Activities: Swimming, surfing, fishing, bodyboarding
Amenities: Parking, lifeguard, restrooms, picnic tables

is a favorite local surf and fishing spot on the far west side Kauai. This long, sandy stretch is also great place to beachcomb and scope out the sunset. At times, strong winds and currents can make Kekaha Beach dangerous for swimming, so be mindful of the conditions.

Kauai Land Activities

Not to be outdone by the famous beaches that ring the island, Kauai's lush landscapes are a feast for the senses. Whether it's a leisurely horseback ride to a remote waterfall or an exhilarating zipline adventure through the jungle, the Garden Isle is a true adventurer's playground.

Hiking is one of the best ways to discover the island, as 90% of Kauai is inaccessible by car. Lace up your hiking boots and explore Kokee State Park and Waimea Canyon on the West Side, with hundreds of trails and breathtaking vistas waiting around every turn.

Adrenaline junkies will find plenty of thrills on mountain biking trails, flying through the rainforest on a zipline safari or traversing rocky ridges on an ATV adventure. There's really no limit to the land activities on Kauai just remember to pack comfortable shoes.

For those seeking a quieter pace, the island offers plenty of additional opportunities to explore local culture, history and more including museums, plantation tours such as Kilohana Plantation, historical landmarks, farmers markets and more.

Outdoor Activities

Biking on Kauai
Flat roads and a lack of big hills make the Ke Ala Hele Makalae trail a leisurely bike ride along parts of Kauai's east shore. The shared-use path stretching along the eastern coast of Kauai was completed in

2009. Ke Ala Hele Makalae is Hawaiian for "The Path that Goes by the Coast." Visitors can now walk, bike or run 4.1 miles between the Lihi Boat Ramp in central Kapaa and Ahihi Point in Kealia, as well as bike through 2.5 miles through Lydgate Park. Ke Ala Hele Makalae creates an uninterrupted bridge between Anahola in the north to Nawiliwili in the south, perfect for biking. On the West Side, you can also take a downhill bike tour 3,600 feet down to sea level along Waimea Canyon. Half-day tours are available.

Remember to always wear a helmet, gloves, appropriate bike shoes, and sunglasses. Travel safely and wear sunscreen. Take a map, water, snacks, sunscreen, bike repair kit and any other accessories that will ensure a friendly, uneventful, but wonderfully scenic ride.

Hiking on Kauai
Since 90% of Kauai is inaccessible by road, hiking is a great way to see the island's natural splendor first-hand.

On the West Side, Waimea Canyon and Kokee State Park offer some of the best hiking trails on the island. Spread over 4,325 acres, Kokee State Park features trails leading to scenic lookouts (like the Awaawapuhi Trail) and hikes for the family (Cliff Canyon and Black Pipe Trail). Visit the Kokee Natural History Museum to plan your hike and to speak to knowledgeable staff members.

There are numerous trails to explore but the most famous hike on Kauai is the challenging 11-mile Kalalau trail along the Napali Coast. Beginning at the end of the road at Kee Beach, most people hike in and stay at least one night before returning. Others limit their hike to the first two miles, which leads to Hanakapiai Beach. Either way, you'll be treated to amazing views of Kauai's North Shore. Permits are required for camping and day hikes past Hanakapiai Valley in the park and may be obtained through the Hawaii State Parks Division.

Kauai Golf

Find the golf course of your dreams on Kauai. From Princeville to Poipu, Kauai is home to some of the world's best golf. Visitors can play beautiful resort courses or affordable independent courses, where the rough is lined with lava rocks while mountain ranges and seascapes frame the greens.

There are nine golf courses at seven locations on Kauai. Princeville on the North Shore offers a challenging option at the Makai Golf Club. PGA legend Jack Nicklaus and Robert Trent Jones, Jr. also designed signature courses in this resort area. You may even see some PGA pros out on the greens during on your visit. After all, they often dream about visiting Kauai, too.

Kauai Gardens & Parks

Kauai is known as "The Garden Isle" for its tropical rainforests, fertile valleys and lush flora. So it's not surprising to find some of Hawaii's most beautiful botanical gardens on Kauai. You can find three of the nation's five National Tropical Botanical Gardens on Kauai: the Allerton Garden and McBryde Garden on the South Shore, and Limahuli Gardens in Haena. McBryde Garden is home to the largest collection of native Hawaiian flora in the world, while Allerton Gardens features amazing landscaping and the giant Moreton Figs made famous in the film "Jurassic Park." The 17-acre Limahuli Gardens offers endangered native plants, taro-filled agricultural terraces and beautiful views of the North Shore.

Other botanical gardens and plantations include Na Aina Kai Botanical Gardens, Smith's Tropical Paradise Botanical Garden and the Kauai Coffee Plantation. You can also take a tour of Hanalei's taro farms to learn about this versatile Hawaiian root starch.

Horseback Riding on Kauai
Get back to nature and discover Kauai on horseback. Ride along bluffs, across foothills toward the coast, past secluded beaches and bays, across sugar cane fields, and even waterfalls. A couple of horseback riding companies offer guided tours ranging from 90 minutes to five hours, which includes stops for snacks, photos, picnics, swimming and time to soak in the views. Many of the tours take you into their privately owned ranches, complete with waterfalls and secret vistas

seen by only few.

Opt for gentle, slower trots, or attempt more strenuous and lengthier journeys. Make sure you wear jeans and sunscreen with a swimsuit underneath, depending on your itinerary. Experience Kauai like a real *paniolo* (Hawaiian cowboy) as you tour the Garden Isle on horseback.

Kauai Water Activities

Kauai is known for its lush scenery on land, but the waters of Kauai offer many additional unique adventures. Kauai is the home of the only navigable rivers in Hawaii. The three rivers are the Hanalei River, Huleia River, and the tranquil Wailua River, which is the most popular for kayakers. The breathtaking cliffs of the Napali Coast are best photographed from the panoramic views of a boat tour. For the less adventurous, Kauai's magnificent beaches offer plenty of activities from swimming, snorkeling and surfing lessons. Be prepared to wear out your bathing suit in the warm waters of Kauai.

Kayaking on Kauai

Kauai is home to the only navigable rivers in Hawaii, so kayaking is an integral part of a unique Kauai vacation.

Relax and take in the exquisite scenery as you paddle down the Wailua River. This popular river for kayaking weaves by lush, jungle landscapes along with island's East Side. Other river routes include the

Huleia River from Nawiliwili Harbor in Lihue, as well as the Hanalei River on the North Shore, the longest on the island.

If you're up for a more difficult challenge, ocean kayaking is a seasonal alternative to experience Kauai by sea. On the South Shore, try the Poipu to Port Allen course with a stop in Lawai Bay. When conditions are calm, kayaking along the 17-mile Napali Coast is unforgettable. "National Geographic" deemed kayaking the Napali Coast the second best adventure in the country. Because this can be a physically demanding activity and the seas can be unpredictable, hiring a guide for this once-in-a-lifetime experience is a must.

Snorkeling and Scuba on Kauai
As amazing as this island is on land, you'll discover even more incredible sights in the waters of Kauai. While flourishing gardens and rainforests get most of the attention on Kauai, the island offers a wide range of snorkeling and scuba spots to explore under the sea.

On the North Shore, fantastic shoreline snorkeling beaches include the reefs off Kee Beach and Haena Beach Park. Anini Beach offers a lagoon great for beginning snorkelers. Makua, or "Tunnels," Beach in Haena also has a wide reef area that's a treat to the senses.

On the East Side, Lydgate Beach Park offers a protected snorkeling lagoon great for keiki (children) snorkelers.

On the South Shore, Poipu Beach State Park offers protected areas for snorkelers. Be sure to check ocean conditions and currents prior to going out, especially during the big north shore swells of the winter.

Scuba

Kauai also offers a variety of scuba sites for beginners and experienced divers. Dive tours offer plenty of tropical fish, reef creatures, dolphins and *honu* (Hawaiian Green Sea Turtles) to discover. Experienced divers will generally find more thrilling spots on the east and west shores, including cave exploration and lava tubes.

Those new to scuba should start on the north or south shores (Hanalei, Kee Beach, or Poipu Beach).

You can rent all the necessary gear and equipment on Kauai, as well as get your certification on the island, but bring your medical paperwork with you if you choose to get certified. Also, keep in mind that if you drive to Waimea Canyon or Kokee State Park, or want to take a helicopter excursion, you need to wait 24-hours due to altitude change.

Kauai Surfing

As any local will tell you, your first taste of surfing, or *hee nalu* in Hawaiian, is something you never forget. From the gentle, beginner-friendly waves of Poipu and Kalapaki to the wild North Shore breaks that attract world champions in the winter months (and should not be attempted by inexperienced surfers because of their extreme danger), Kauai is a surfing paradise set against some of the most majestic scenery on earth.

Believed to have originated in ancient Polynesia, surfing was once reserved for Hawaiian *alii*, or royalty giving it the nickname "the sport of kings." In the 20th century, surfing surged in popularity, spreading from Hawaii's shores around the world.

You can feel the exhilaration of catching a wave by taking a lesson at surf schools and resorts around Kauai. Experienced instructors will take you to safe breaks and get you on your feet during lessons that last 1 2 hours. If you're not quite ready to brave the waves yourself, watch seasoned surfers charge massive swells on the North Shore during big wave season (November February) from the safety of the beach.

Kitesurfing, body surfing and stand-up paddleboarding are other popular activities, and outfitters can be found on many of Kauai's more popular beaches.

Stand-Up Paddleboarding on Kauai

Similar to surfing (but using a longer, wider board), stand-up paddleboarding (SUP) has become an increasingly popular activity over the past several years. On the island of Kauai, you'll frequently find paddlers on the shimmering blue waters of Hanalei Bay, Poipu Beach or Kalapaki Beach. If you didn't have room in your luggage to bring your own board and paddle, you'll find rental places on the islands who can help with gear, and (often-times) lessons as well, if you're new to the sport but want to give it a try during your trip.

Hawaii Regional Cuisine a decades-old cooking movement that focuses on island-grown ingredients can be sampled at restaurants like Merriman's Fish House and Roy's Poipu Bar & Grill, where you'll dine on freshly caught mahimahi, wahoo and other fruits of the sea. In Koloa, Red Salt is another acclaimed, upscale option.

Reserve a night during your trip to feast on kalua pig and taro at an authentic Hawaiian luau, which you can do at several venues from Kapaa to Poipu.

Shave Ice is a distinctly Hawaiian dessert that can be found at stands around the island, while Kauai-based Lappert's Hawaii ice cream shop is among the island's favorite ways to stay cool. And be sure to sample fresh produce and locally made food products at Kauai's Sunshine Markets (the local name for farmers markets), held throughout the island in towns like Lihue and Hanapepe.

Keoki's Paradise

Nestled in sunny Poipu Beach, Keoki's Paradise is famous for its fresh seafood, local island cuisine and exotic drinks served in a jungle-like setting.

2360 Kiahuna Plantation Drive

Koloa, HI 96756

Local Phone: (808) 742-7534

Island:

Kauai

Duke's Canoe Club - Kauai

A tribute to legendary surfer Duke Kahanamoku, this popular restaurant and barefoot bar offers fresh island fish, prime steaks, live Hawaiian entertainment and stunning ocean views.

3500 Rice Street

Lihue, HI 96766

Local Phone: (808) 246-9599

Island:

Kauai

Red Salt

Red Salt's diverse menu by acclaimed Executive Chef and Kauai native Noelani Planas celebrates fresh Hawaiian seafood and produce in a casual, yet sophisticated seaside atmosphere.

2251 Poipu Road
Koloa, HI 96756
Local Phone: (808) 828-4288
US Toll Free: (888) 898-8958
Island:
Kauai

Red Salt's diverse menu by acclaimed Executive Chef and Kauai native Noelani Planas celebrates fresh Hawaiian seafood and produce in a casual, yet sophisticated seaside atmosphere. Modern dinner cuisine including vanilla bean-seared mahi, ahi tartare, and the decadently layered Red Salt burger are served in a contemporary setting. Select nights, the Red Salt Lounge* is host to a sushi bar featuring the day's freshest catch in innovative, isle-inspired rolls. During morning hours, Red Salt offers tropical takes on traditional breakfast dishes, such as lobster benedict and lemon-pineapple soufflé pancakes, recently featured by Food Network. *Lounge and sushi bar seating are not available for reservation and is first come, first served.

Kauai Accommodations

From the moment you arrive on Kauai, the enchanting scenery and generous aloha spirit welcome you. Whether you seek posh resorts with five-star service, a quaint country B&B or a condo rental for the whole family, the Garden Isle has a remarkable range of accommodations waiting to be your home away from home. In fact, the hardest part of staying on Kauai is knowing you'll have to leave at some point.

Three main regions possess the majority of Kauai's accommodations the North Shore, East Coast and South Shore. In the towns of Princeville and Hanalei on the North Shore, luxury resorts like the Princeville Resort Kauai and Westin Princeville Ocean Resort Villas are plentiful, with dining, golf and spa facilities to rival the finest in the world.

The more densely populated East Coast (also known as the Coconut Coast) and South Shore offer a wide variety of hotels, resorts and affordable vacation rentals, plus family-friendly beaches ideal for *keiki* (kids). And while accommodations are more limited on Kauai's West Side, inns and plantation cottages in the charming towns of Waimea and Hanapepe offer convenient access to natural wonders like Waimea Canyonand Kokee State Park perfect for travelers wanting to get the most out of Kauai's incredible landscapes.

Note: *Apartments, condominiums and homes are eligible to operate as short-term rentals if they are located in areas zoned for such use and/or they have obtained the required authorization(s) from the State of Hawaii and/or the relevant County. It is recommended that before* booking a property, you confirm with the owner or manager that the property is operating in compliance with all applicable laws.

Waimea Plantation Cottages

60 restored, plantation-era cottages spread across 27 acres of tropical oasis on Kauai's sunny west shore offer a rare glimpse into Old Hawaii. Full kitchens, private lanais, on quiet, beachfront property at the base of Waimea Canyon State Park. Relax, unwind, and embrace the experience.

9400 Kaumualii Highway

Waimea, HI 96796

Local Phone: (808) 338-1625

US Toll Free: 800-9-WAIMEA

Email: res@waimeaplantation.com

Island: Kauai

A rare gem set in a simpler time and place, this beautiful island oasis with coconut palms, old-growth banyan trees and grassy lawns set right on the beach, offers the peace and serenity truly necessary to recharge, find your center, or simply lose yourself. With spectacular sunsets, starry nights away from city lights, Waimea Plantation Cottages offers an ideal, remote location for an intimate couple's getaway and open spaces to share for family vacations, class reunions, health retreats, business incentives, and wedding celebrations.

Individual 1 to 5 bedroom cottage homes provide a quiet, relaxing ambiance - featuring private, furnished lanais, full kitchens and living areas.

Amenities include: Oceanside swimming pool Hammocks/seating throughout the resort Shuffleboard court, bocce ball, croquet, sand volleyball, board games and beach toys Gas grilling stations Wi-Fi in all cottages Complimentary coffee, chilled juice and water in the lobby Private, drive-up parking spaces Access to weekly cultural activities Computer and printer access Complimentary laundry facilities Located in the laid-back walking town of Waimea with local shops, restaurants, activities & tours. 45 minutes from Lihue Airport. Nearby access to hiking trails and scenic drives at Waimea Canyon State Park, a.k.a. "The Grand Canyon of the Pacific." 5 minute drive (3.5 mi) from a lifeguard station at Kekaha Beach Park.

River Estate

River Estate offers 2 deluxe Kauai vacation rentals which are located in a riverfront botanical garden 2 blocks from the beach that are perfect for honeymoons and a secluded quiet place to relax.

Local Phone: (808) 826-5118 Office
US Toll Free: (800) 390-8444
Email: info@riverestate.com
Island: Kauai

Top Quality Accommodations:

A Completely Unique Central North Kauai Location Tastefully Furnished Homes. Quality Furniture Air Conditioning Ultra Privacy in a Completely Unique Natural Setting

Two Acres of Pristine Riverfront Botanical Gardens * Allergy Free Zones. No Mold or Mildew Inside or Out

Very Close to World Famous Beaches and Landmarks

Float to Beach and Back From the Property Easily * Fully Equipped Large Kitchens With New Appliances

Complimentary Beach Gear and Quality Beach Towels Quality Bedding, Mattresses. High Thread Count Sheets Tile or Chinese Slate Floors in Kitchen and Bathrooms Quality Brazilian Cherry Hardwood Floors (Living Areas) Well Ventilated Homes Cooled by the Trade Winds Flat Panel TVs, DVD Players, Cd Players With iPod Docks Large Master Bedroom Suites with Flat Panel TV's Free Long Distance, WiFi Internet, Wireless Phones Large Collection of DVD's and CD's in each Home Your Host is Nearby 24/7 to Assist (Local 40 Years)

Courtyard Kauai at Coconut Beach

Ocean front resort, centrally located, 15 minutes east of the Lihue Airport. Within walking distance to shopping, restaurants and supermarkets. Delivering hospitality, creating value, every customer, every time.

650 Aleka Loop

Kapaa, HI 96746

Local Phone: (808) 822-3455

Island:

Kauai

Ocean front resort, centrally located, 15 minutes east of the Lihue Airport. Within walking distance to shopping, restaurants and supermarkets. Delivering hospitality, creating value, every customer, every time.

Hanalei Colony Resort

An oceanfront hideaway nestled on a curve of golden beach in Haena on Kauai's lush north shore, offering 48 deluxe two-bedroom suites with fully equipped kitchens. The secluded location and peaceful, laid-back ambiance set amidst stunning natural beauty provide a one-of-a-kind getaway for travelers.

5-7130 Kuhio Hwy

Haena, HI 96714

Local Phone: (808) 826-6235

US Toll Free: (800) 628-3004

Email: aloha@hcr.com

Island: Kauai

Hanalei Colony is an oceanfront hideaway nestled on a curve of golden beach in Haena on Kauai's lush north shore. The sprawling five-acre property offers 48 deluxe two-bedroom suites, all with fully equipped kitchens and private lanais. Hanalei Colony's secluded location and peaceful, laidback ambiance set amidst the North Shore's stunning natural beauty provide a one-of-a-kind getaway for travelers. Unspoiled. Unplugged. Unforgettable.

Hanalei Inn

A quaint four unit Inn located in the heart of Hanalei Town and only one block to Hanalei Bay. The units have a full kitchen, queen bed, HD cable T.V., private bath, air conditioning, private deck and free wireless internet. Coffee is available each morning under the outdoor lanai.

5-5468 Kuhio Highway

Hanalei, HI 96714

Local Phone: (808) 826-9333

US Toll Free: (877) 769-5484

Email: info@hanaleiinn.com

Island: Kauai

A quaint four unit Inn located in the heart of Hanalei Town and only one block to Hanalei Bay. The units have a full kitchen, queen bed, HD cable T.V., private bath, air conditioning, private deck and free wireless internet. Coffee is available each morning under the outdoor lanai.

Kauai Vacation Home Rental

Private Kauai Vacation Home Rental in Princeville, near all North Shore beaches, the Town of Hanalei and Princeville Golf! WiFi, mountain bikes, golf clubs, private tropical garden setting, full kitchen, outdoor shower, outdoor living space and many extras! Great Value for couples or families!

3818 Makani Kai Place
Princeville, HI 96722
Local Phone: (716) 923-3996
Email: Kapuahale@hotmail.com
Island: Kauai

Private Kauai Vacation Rental Home in Princeville; walk to Sea Lodge Beach, free WiFi, golf at The Makai or Prince courses, walking paths throughout Princeville, shopping center close by. We get rave reviews from our guests, come to Kauai and experience our deluxe tropical home! Experience the North Shore of Kauai in comfort! 2 bedrooms have queen beds for 2 masters, 1 bedroom has 2 twins with a surfer decor!

Fully equipped kitchen with 2 lanais for outdoor dining. Some of our amenities include: mountain bikes, beach chairs, beach towels and umbrellas, snorkel gear, coolers, washer and dryer, fully equipped kitchen, Free WiFi, outdoor shower, area guide books for hiking, kayaking and touring, book library for the beach, and DVD library.

Tropical gardens surround the house bringing the "Garden isle" to your doorstep! Perfect location with quick access to all the North Shore beaches of Kauai!

Kauai Banyan Inn

Kauai Banyan Inn has private bed & breakfast vacation rental suites - beautifully appointed with everything you need for a peaceful, relaxing visit to Kauai. Hillside location affords sweeping panoramic mountain and distant ocean views.

3528 B Mana Hema Place
Lawai, HI 96765
Local Phone: (808) 645-6527
Email: kauaibanyan@gmail.com
Island: Kauai

Kauai Banyan Inn's beautifully-appointed bed and breakfast vacation suites are the perfect alternative to expensive resort accommodations. Perfect for honeymoons, romantic getaways for two and as a peaceful retreat, you will find everything you need for a perfect Kauai vacation. Each meticulously cared for suite is fully equipped and features high-quality craftsmanship, unique wood finishes and bathroom and lanai. The sweeping panoramic views from the Kauai Banyan Inn are breathtaking. In addition to ocean views, there are views of the century old Banyan Tree that graces the property, mountains and pasture lands as well as Black Mountains and the southern Kauai coastline. Such a sweet place, you won't want to leave! Just minutes to Poipu Beach and resort amenities.

Kauai Shores Hotel

Set oceanfront along Kauai's Coconut Coast guests enjoy newly remodeled guestrooms and public areas, new pool deck and hot tub, and a variety of amenities including nightly entertainment, complimentary yoga, bicycle rental, and more. Dine on the sand at award-winning Lava Lava Beach Club.

420 Papaloa Road

Kapaa, HI 96746

Local Phone: (808) 822-4951

US Toll Free: (800) 222-5642

Email: hhr@hawaiihotels.com

Island: Kauai

Set on six acres of tropical gardens along a pristine, mile-long stretch of beach on Kauai's Coconut Coast, the Kauai Shores Hotel has recently completed a $10 million renovation. Featuring 206 fully remodeled guestrooms, a beautiful new lobby, two fresh water pools, a new pool deck and hot tub, the property is also home to Kauai's only "toes in the sand" dining experience at the new Lava Lava Beach Club restaurant and lounge.

The fresh design approach of Kauai Shores Hotel captures a timeless charm while offering a contemporary design element and modern decor. Upgraded exterior grounds showcase the award-winning property's picturesque scenery and guests enjoy a wide range of amenities including nightly live entertainment, complimentary yoga classes, use of resort bicycles, a business center, and a full service activities desk. Each of the hotel's comfortable guestrooms features a private lanai, island-style decor, mini refrigerator, WiFi, and in-room safes.

Located adjacent to the open-air Coconut Marketplace shopping village, and just a mile from Kapaa Town and the Wailua River, the Kauai Shores Hotel provides a central location from which guests can explore all of Kauai's wonderful attractions and landmarks.

Grand Hyatt Kauai Resort & Spa

Oceanfront in sunny Poipu renovated rooms, each with its own lanai, welcome you to relax and unwind. Enjoy a water wonderland of pools and lagoons. Savor the flavors at the resort's six restaurants. Play Championship golf. Refresh at Anara Spa.

1571 Poipu Road
Koloa, HI 96756
Local Phone: (808) 742-1234
US Toll Free: (800) 554-9288

Email: res@hyatt.com

Island: Kauai

Discover paradise at the Grand Hyatt Kauai Resort & Spa where nature's spectacular setting is its legacy. Set on 50 acres fronting a soothing white sand beachin sunny Poipu, the resort unfolds among lush gardens and pristine lagoons. Celebrate the sun while floating in a meandering saltwater lagoon, splash through cascading waterfalls, or torpedo down a waterslide into free-form riverpools. Enjoy the many free cultural activities available from lei making to ukulele lessons.

Camp Hyatt provides a day (or night) filled with fun activities for kids. When it's time for dining our chefs will delight you with outstanding fare and unusual ambiance. Imagine enjoying the freshest seafood or a succulent steak in a thatched roof bungalow over a tropical lagoon. Play where champions play at Poipu Bay Resort golf course, designed by Robert Trent Jones, Jr. and for the ultimate pampering, visit Anara Spa to take full advantage of nature's own soothing powers to relax mind and body.

Aqua Kauai Beach Resort

Escape to paradise at the Kauai Beach Resort, a breathtaking oceanfront resort on a 3-mile beach on Kauai's eastern Coconut Coast.

4331 Kauai Beach Drive

Lihue, HI 96766

Local Phone: (808) 245-1955

US Toll Free: (866) 406-2782

Email: kbrreservations@aquaresorts.com

Island: Kauai

Escape to paradise at Aqua Kauai Beach Resort, a breathtaking oceanfront resort on a 3-mile beach on Kauai's eastern Coconut Coast. Located just minutes from the town of Lihue, this beachfront resort features 25 magnificent acres of Kauai's longest beach. Guest room accommodations each include spacious rooms with WiFi internet access. On-site amenities include 2 restaurants, a bar/lounge, car rental services, a business center, meeting rooms, ballroom, activities desk, fitness center, wellness spa, and multiple swimming pools with a water slide and a poolside bar. Aqua Kauai Beach Resort offers an idyllic Hawaiian getaway with a modern plantation-style experience.

Transportation

At just 25 miles long and 33 miles wide, Kauai is relatively easy to explore. In the span of a few miles, you might pass by palm-fringed beaches, vivid green taro fields and soaring, verdant mountains. No matter how you get around the Garden Isle, prepare to be treated to some of the most spectacular scenery in all of the Hawaiian Islands.

Arriving On Kauai

Most visitors arrive on Kauai at Lihue Airport (LIH) on the island's East Side. Many airlines offer nonstop service, though some visitors may choose to fly to Honolulu International Airport on Oahu first, then connect to Kauai (depending on times and prices). Ground transportation includes rental cars (every major rental company is represented here), taxis and limited bus service. Several companies provide guided tours aboard motor coaches, mini-buses, vans and limousines. If you're staying at a hotel on Kauai, check to see if airport transportation is offered, as many provide complimentary pick-up and drop-off service.

Getting Around Kauai
A rental car is your best bet if you want to really explore the island. There is one major highway that nearly circles the island; beginning in Lihue and going north, Kuhio Highway (Hwy. 56) goes to Kee Beach past Hanalei. Beyond the Napali Coast on the West Side, Kaumualii Highway (Hwy. 50) travels to Kekaha and then cuts inland, leading all the way back to Lihue.

Drivers on Kauai follow "aloha" traffic customs: drive slowly, yield to others and don't tailgate. At one-lane bridges, yield to oncoming traffic. If you approach a bridge and there is a line waiting on the other side, stop and let your neighbors cross. Driving here is much more laid-back than the mainland, so relax, enjoy the scenery and drive safely and plan on making plenty of impromptu stops along the way for photos and adventures.

Alaska Airlines

Alaska Airlines, together with Virgin America, offers low fares and the most nonstop flights from Hawai'i to the West Coast. Learn more about Alaska's award-winning service and unmatched reliability at newsroom.alaskaair.com and blog.alaskaair.com.

Local Phone: (800) 252-7522

US Toll Free: (800) 252-7522

Email: sales@alaskaair.com

Islands: Hawaii, Kauai, Maui, Oahu

Alaska Airlines, together with Virgin America, offers low fares and the most nonstop flights from Hawai'i to the West Coast. Learn more about Alaska's award-winning service and unmatched reliability at newsroom.alaskaair.com and blog.alaskaair.com.

Hawaii Car Rentals

At Hawaii Car Rentals we pass our Corporate Discount Rates, Specials and Waivers on to you. Rent from major national brand car rental companies and get our pre-negotiated discount rates. No Pre-Payment, No Cancellation Fees, No Booking Fees. Free Driver(s), Reduced Young Driver Surcharge.

Email: reservations@hawaiicarrentals.net

Islands: Hawaii, Kauai, Maui, Oahu

Hawaii Car Rentals is an authorized Wholesale Corporate Discount Vendor of car rentals for Advantage, Avis, Budget, Dollar, Enterprise, Hertz and Thrifty rental cars. And as such, we are able to offer cheap & discount rental cars on Maui, Kauai, Oahu and the Big Island. We have Pre-negotiated rates, specials, bonuses and waivers available such as: No Pre-Payment, No Cancellation Fees, No Booking Fees, Unlimited Mileage, Free Additional Driver(s) (depending on company) and Reduced Young Driver Surcharge. These are all passed on to our customers at no additional charge.

Aloha Rents Hawaii Car Rental

Discount Kauai car rental service for the Island of Kauai. With locations at the Kauai Lihue Airport (LIH), Popui, Princeville Airport (HPV) and Nawiliwili Port near Lihue. Specially negotiated rates through national rental agencies. FREE mileage and no penalty to cancel or change your reservations.

Email: information@aloharents.com

Island: Kauai

Discount Kauai car rental service for the the Garden Isle. Specially negotiated rates through national Rent-A-Car brands. Why pay more through a large online travel agency? FREE mileage and no penalty to cancel or change your reservations. Vehicle rental locations at the airport in Lihue (LIH), Princeville (HPV) and in the Poipu (K3H) beach area. Check Kauai Rates Today for Jeep Wranglers 4WD, convertibles, vans, SUVs, and cars. FREE mileage and no penalty to cancel or change your reservations. We have vehicle rental locations across Kauai.

Kauai Luxury Transportation

Offering Island-wide, luxury, chauffeured transportation services in sedans, SUVs and Mercedes Sprinter vans. We specialize in weddings, VIP & airport transfers, corporate events and private tours.

Local Phone: (808) 634-7260
Email: bret@kauailuxurytransportation.com
Island: Kauai

Offering Island-wide luxury chauffeured transportation services in sedans, SUVs, and Mercedes Sprinter vans. We specialize in VIP transportation, weddings, airport transfers and corporate events. Serving all of Kauai's airports, resorts, hotels, and event locations, Kauai Luxury Transportation & Tours transports you wherever you want to go while you relax in style.

Our highly-rated Best of Kauai Tour takes visitors on a visual and cultural journey of Kauai to scenic beaches, waterfalls, Kilauea Lighthouse and other Kauai landmarks with a Wailua River boat cruise to Fern Grotto and breath-taking views from the Air in a small airplane flight around the island. Private luxury tours of Kauai are also available.

Polynesian Adventure Tours

Polynesian Adventure Tours provides the best tour and transportation services in the Hawaiian Islands, offering visitors truly unique and memorable experiences. We offer land, one day flyaway tours and more. Our charter department specializes in custom tours and services.

2880 Kilihau Street Honolulu, HI 96819

Local Phone: (808) 833-3000

US Toll Free: (800) 622-3011

Email: sales@polyad.com

Islands: Hawaii, Kauai, Maui, Oahu

Polynesian Adventure Tours, LLC (Poly Ad) was established on Oahu by Bob George and Don Brown in 1977. The company began with the innovative idea that utilized drivers as both narrators and guides. Poly Ad's Maui operation opened in 1987, and shortly after the business was expanded to the Big Island and Kauai. Norwegian Cruise Line acquired Poly Ad in 2004 in order to service its shore excursion requirements throughout its port calls state-wide. Through the growth in the shore excursion segment as well as charter and tour business, Poly Ad has since increased its fleet and now has 177 vehicles statewide. The company transports half a million people a year on 105 motorcoaches, 65 mini buses, and 7 open-air double-decker buses.

Today, Poly Ad provides the best tour and transportation services in the Hawaiian Islands, offering visitors truly unique and memorable experiences. With fleets on the four major Hawaiian Islands, Poly Ad is ready to service groups looking to visit all of the islands during their stay. Every island is a unique experience waiting to be explored. Our charter department specializes in custom charters to must-see-sites and even to locations off the beaten-path. Our charter services include airport transfers, baggage services, greeting services and regularly scheduled sightseeing tours.

On Oahu, we have the best selection of Pearl Harbor sightseeing tours that range from comprehensive all day tours to combo tours which include Honolulu's most famous locales. Our guests explore the source of creation on the Big Island of Hawaii at Volcanoes National Park where they stroll through an ancient lava tube and observe Halemaumau Crater with its billowing steam cloud. On Kauai, the Garden Isle, guests marvel at the steep valleys of the Waimea Canyon and cruise down the Wailua River on an open air boat. The Movie Adventure tour visits the film locations of many Hollywood Blockbusters. On Maui, Poly Ad offers three tours showcasing majestic Haleakala at sunrise, sunset and a Best of Hawaii combo tour that includes central Maui.

As Hawaii's sole licensee of Gray Line Worldwide, Poly Ad also operates under the brand name of "Gray Line Hawaii" and benefits from the extremely high name recognition of the affiliation. Gray Line has a 117-year reputation for offering enjoyable and reliable sightseeing tours throughout the world. Our tours are promoted and sold on PolyAdHawaiiTours.com, GrayLineHawaii.com as well as the worldwide GrayLine.com site.

Luau Kalamaku, a truly Hawaiian experience on the island of Kauai operates under Poly Ad's management. The theatrical luau held on Tuesday and Friday evenings at historic Kilohana Plantation, features a captivating theatrical performance, a delicious buffet of local favorites and so much more!

Roberts Hawaii

Looking for the best tour and transportation company in Hawaii? A business committed to the highest level of service with a genuine Aloha spirit? Look no further than Roberts Hawaii, Inc..

80 Iwilei Road, Suite 700 Honolulu, HI 96817

Local Phone: (808) 539-9451

US Toll Free: (800) 767-7551

Email: reservations@robertshawaii.com

Islands: Hawaii, Kauai, Maui, Oahu

Roberts Hawaii Inc. is a full service company that will deliver first class Transportation, personalized Sightseeing Tours and Excursions, and an exciting variety of Attractions and Activities for your clients. As Hawaii's largest tour and transportation company, Roberts represents activities and attractions ranging from the Magic of Polynesia to the Waikiki Ocean Thriller.

Our offices are located in the Dole Cannery Office Building in Honolulu; we're open daily from 7am - 9pm HST and 7am - 5pm HST on Holidays. The costs of Roberts' services vary depending on the size of the group, type of transportation, selection of tours, etc.

Discount Hawaii Car Rental

Discounted rates on Jeep Wranglers 4WD, convertibles, SUVs, vans and cars from major national companies on Maui Lahaina and Kahului, Kauai Lihue and Princeville, Big Island Kona and Hilo, Oahu Waikiki and Honolulu airport. Toll Free 1-800-292-1930.

US Toll Free: 1-800-292-1930
Email: office@discounthawaiicarrental.com
Island: Kauai

Discounted rates on Jeep Wranglers 4WD, convertibles, SUVs, vans and cars from major national companies on Maui Lahaina and Kahului, Kauai Lihue and Princeville, Big Island Kona and Hilo, Oahu Waikiki and Honolulu airport. Toll Free 1-800-292-1930.

Hawaiian Airlines
Hawaiian has led all U.S. carriers in on-time performance for each of the past 10 years (2004-2013) as reported by the U.S. Department of Transportation. Consumer surveys by Condé Nast Traveler, Travel + Leisure and Zagat have all ranked Hawaiian the highest of all domestic airlines serving Hawai'i

Hawaiian has led all U.S. carriers in on-time performance for each of the past 10 years (2004-2013) as reported by the U.S. Department of Transportation. Consumer surveys by Condé Nast Traveler, Travel + Leisure and Zagat have all ranked Hawaiian the highest of all domestic airlines serving Hawai'i.

Now in its 85th year of continuous service, Hawaiian is Hawai'i's biggest and longest-serving airline, as well as the largest provider of passenger air service from its primary visitor markets on the U.S. mainland. Hawaiian offers nonstop service to Hawai'i from more U.S. gateway cities (11) than any other airline, along with service from Japan, South Korea, China, Australia, New Zealand, American Samoa, and Tahiti. Hawaiian also provides approximately 160 jet flights daily between the Hawaiian Islands.

Enterprise Rent-A-Car - Kauai
Enterprise Rent a Car provides a wide selection of quality vehicles for your leisure or business car rental needs from economy and compact

car models, to convertibles, Jeeps, SUV's and minivans as well as specialty Cars and trucks.

073 Aukele Street Lihue, HI 96766

Local Phone: (808) 543-1509

US Toll Free: (800) 325-8007

Email: samira.mansouri@ehi.com

Island: Kauai

Enterprise Rent a Car provides a wide selection of quality vehicles for your leisure or business car rental needs from economy and compact car models, to convertibles, Jeeps, SUV's and minivans as well as specialty Cars and trucks. Enterprise bring exceptional rental car rates and variety to every car rental reservation. www.enterprise.com

Weddings on Kauai

Wafting trade winds help keep the bride and groom cool. Fresh local flowers adorn the venue. The ocean methodically peeks into the ceremony, then slowly retreats. Here on Kauai, it's as if you have the island's blessing as well.

Say your vows under the North Shore sun, on the sands of the South Shore or on a historic estate like Kilohana. Perform a traditional ceremony or do something unique that speaks to you. The beautiful "Hawaiian Wedding Song" made famous by Elvis in the movie "Blue

Hawaii" (which was filmed on Kauai) is often sung at Kauai ceremonies..

Arrange your wedding on your own or get help from Kauai's wedding planners, the Kauai Wedding Professionals Association or resort specialists. Choose a ceremony at a beautiful resort, or select from unique sites throughout the island. Contact the Kauai Office of the State Department of Health for license information. Now that you've found that special someone, get married in a truly special place that will forever be etched in your memories. Think of it as Kauai's wedding gift to you. Learn more about Kauai wedding photographers, planners and venues.

Honeymoons
With your wedding complete, it's time to relax and start your lives together on the island paradise of Kauai. Whether you want to get away to a luxurious Kauai resort, pampering yourselves with spa treatments and fine dining, or you want to share an unforgettable adventure together, Kauai is home to the honeymoon of your dreams.

Kayak together down the Wailuku or Wailua River or explore one of Kauai's lush and sprawling gardens. Share unforgettable views along the Napali Coast, within Waimea Canyon and on the cliffs of the Kilauea Lighthouse. Take a mid-morning drive to Opaekaa Falls or witness other incredible sights like the 80-foot Wailua Falls and the

Spouting Horn blowhole at sunset. Your new beginning deserves a special celebration, and Kauai offers an unforgettable place to start.

Legacy Events Kauai
Legacy Events Kauai is a full-service wedding & event planning company based on Kauai. We specialize in destination weddings, intimate elopements, and private and corporate events. We believe a great planning experience is equally important to a having a great event.

Local Phone: (808) 652-8186

Email: Marie@legacyeventskauai.com

Island: Kauai

Legacy Events Kauai is a professional full-service wedding & event planning company based on the island of Kauai. We specialize in destination weddings and intimate elopements but we also enjoy planning private and corporate events. Our mission is to design and plan custom beautiful events unique to each client. We believe a great planning experience with clear communication and planning tools is equally important to a having a great event. We invite you to find out more about our services.

Island Weddings & Blessings
The Island wedding of your dreams-personalized ceremonies in lush settings. Island-wide on Kauai. All associated services are available.

Island Weddings & Blessings provides the most excellent and experienced service on Kauai.

Local Phone: (808) 828-1548

US Toll Free: (800) 998-1548

Email: wedding@aloha.net

Island: Kauai

Providing Custom Weddings, Vow Renewals, Special Blessings and Celebrations on Kauai for over 15 years, Fern and Michael are the most experienced wedding planners on Island. They will work with you to create the type and style of wedding that fulfills "your dream." Choose from select tropical locations island-wide, which include private ocean-side or overlook estates, quaint churches, waterfall gardens with exotic flowering plans, or quiet beaches with expansive sunset views. You can trust in the most competent and experienced Officiates, Photographers, Videographers, Florists, Musicians and Caterers. Whether very simple or with luxury options, each ceremony is a special and unique experience, individually designed for each couple.

Wedding Venues and Services
Kauai Wedding Venues
Kauai's sapphire-blue waters, long sandy beaches and verdant tropical landscapes make the "Garden Isle" a dreamy destination to tie the knot. Whether you're seeking an intimate garden wedding or a

ceremony overlooking the sea, partner with local professionals who'll infuse your wedding with the spirit of aloha and facilitate an exquisite affair to remember. Your wedding warrants a special setting and, as you might expect, you have an endless variety of incredible Kauai wedding venues, sites, and locations from which to choose. A favorite of Hollywood filmmakers, the Island of Kauai is home to many of the world's most beautiful and dramatic landscapes, seascapes, gardens, hotels and resorts, and each and every setting is filled with the romantic spirit of aloha. Kauai offers the a wonderful selection of locations and wedding professionals to make your big day as easy as it is memorable.

Alohana Weddings
Our experience & attention to detail will take the stress out of organizing your own wedding. We provide professional advice,have local knowledge and will work with your budget to ensure that your wedding is a success!

Local Phone: (808) 823-0077

US Toll Free: (800) 387-2407

Email: alohawedding@msn.com

Island: Kauai

Our experience & attention to detail will take the stress out of organizing your own wedding. We provide professional advice,have local knowledge and will work with your budget to ensure that your wedding is a success!

Contemporary Flavors, Inc

Contemporary Flavors Catering is the largest and finest full-service licensed catering company on the island of Kauai. We will work with you to custom-design menus and event plans to fit any occasion from weddings to birthdays, luaus, business events, intimate gatherings, and formal affairs.

1610 Haleukana Street Lihue, HI 96766

Local Phone: (808) 245-2522

Email: info@contemporaryflavorscatering.com

Island: Kauai

Contemporary Flavors Catering is the largest and finest full-service licensed catering company on the island of Kauai. We will work with you to custom-design menus and event plans to fit any occasion from weddings to birthdays, luaus, business events, intimate gatherings, and formal affairs.

Kauai Island Weddings

Kauai Island Weddings is a full service wedding company in Kauai providing wedding coordination, minister, photography, and videography services, in addition to arranging flowers, musicians and Limo services for our clients.

6440 Olohena Road Kapaa, HI 96746

Local Phone: (808) 822-5381

Email: martina@kauaiislandweddings.com

Island: Kauai

Kauai Island Weddings is a full service wedding company in Kauai providing wedding coordination, minister, photography, and videography services, in addition to arranging flowers, musicians and Limo services for our clients. Romantic, intimate and affordable. We offer the best photography package in Kauai! Get 300 high resolution digital photos instead of 24. Plus you'll get full copyright at no extra costs! If you are looking for an intimate, romantic wedding ceremony on a beautiful Hawaiian beach look no further.

Tropical Paradise Weddings by Smith's

Cruise the Wailua River in your private wedding boat to the jungle wedding location called the Fern Grotto. The wedding ceremony takes place in a shallow cave with ferns hanging from the top of the cave.

Wailua Marina 3-5971 Kuhio Highway

Kapaa, HI 96746-1455

Local Phone: (808) 821-6895

Email: smiths@aloha.net

Island: Kauai

Cruise the Wailua River in your private wedding boat to the jungle wedding location called the Fern Grotto. The wedding ceremony takes place in a shallow cave with ferns hanging from the top of the cave.

Kauai Marriott Resort - Weddings

The Kauai Marriott is the place to experience lush exotic gardens, newly renovated guestrooms and restaurants featuring local cuisine. The resort is a short five-minute drive from Lihue airport or use our complimentary shuttle.

3610 Rice Street Lihue, HI 96766

Local Phone: (808) 245-5050
US Toll Free: (800) 220-2925
Email: kauai@marriott.com
Island: Kauai

Kauai is one of the most stunning places on earth. The Kauai Marriott Resort is the perfect place to relax, recharge and experience the Island of Discovery's timeless charm. Discover inner-peace as you relax in our newly renovated guestrooms or in one of our private beach cabanas. See how time with family and friends can float gently by when relaxing at the island's largest pool. The golden sands of serene Kalapaki Beach are only steps away, Jack Nicklaus designed oceanfront golf, local cuisine and botanical gardens await your arrival.

Oahu

Welcome to Oahu

Home to world famous Waikiki Beach

From ancient stone heiau (temples) to 21st-Century high-rises, Oahu is an island of endless contrasts. Geographically only the third largest of the inhabited Hawaiian Islands, it is nonetheless home to nearly three-quarters of the state's 1.2 million residents 370,000 of whom are concentrated in urban Honolulu, the ultra-modern, south-coast cityscape kamaʻaina (residents) refer to simply as "Town."

But take a 45-minute drive to "Country" the famed surfing Mecca on the island's north shore and you'll find sleepy Haleʻiwa Town (pop. 2,225) existing much as it has since it was established by missionaries in 1832.

Geography

Like the other islands, islets and shoals that make up the 1,600-mile Hawaiian Island chain, Oahu is believed to be the product of a single "hot spot" in the earth's mantle. Over the course of millions of years, the earth's crust drifted to the northwest across this hot spot, giving rise to each island. The bulk of Oahu was created nearly four million years ago, by two now-extinct shield volcanoes the remains of which are today visible as the Koʻolau and Waiʻanae mountain ranges, running parallel to each other along the length of the island's eastern and western coasts, respectively. As with the rest of the Hawaiian Islands, these mountain ranges separate the wetter windward shore from the drier leeward side, forcing rain clouds blown in off the ocean to leave their water on the east side of the island before gaining passage to the west.

Points of Interest

More recent volcanic activity also created several of Oahu's most visible landmarks: 761-foot-tall Diamond Head, located on Waikiki's eastern border, is a "tuff cone," formed some 100,000 years ago when an eruption of volcanic ash eventually hardened into solid rock. Southeast Oahu's Koko Head and downtown Honolulu's Punchbowl (the latter of which houses the National Memorial Cemetery of the Pacific in its crater) are also tuff cones.

Vastly influenced by its reputation as a world-class travel destination, Oahu offers more of everything than the other Islands combined. Shopping, dining and entertainment opportunities here far eclipse those of neighbor islands. And visitor traffic, drawn to the island by its enticing beaches, big winter waves, super-sized collection of scenic golf courses and signature attractions   Waikiki, Pearl Harbor, the Polynesian Cultural Center   continues to exceed any neighbor island.

Still, Oahu's storied past is very much alive. Hawaii achieved statehood less than 50 years ago, leaving its history as a U.S. territory and before that, a Hawaiian monarchy, very much in evidence. Walking tours of downtown Honolulu, Waikiki or Chinatown, as well as a visit to Pearl Harbor, are a good way to get in touch with the island's unique past.

Many of Oahu's most popular attractions are located outside the city. Hanauma Bay, a world-renown snorkeling destination, is a short drive from Waikiki, just past Hawaii Kai. Sea Life Park is not far from Hanauma Bay. The Polynesian Cultural Center, a unique and perennially popular attraction, is located in La'ie, more than an hour's drive from Honolulu. Kualoa Ranch, near Kaneohe, Hawaiian Waters Adventure Park, near Kapolei, and the Arizona Memorial, the biggest visitor draw in the state, are all outside the city of Honolulu.

Tour operators provide transportation to and from Waikiki, making it easy to see the countryside on your way to adventures like helicopter and glider tours, ultra light and skydiving experiences, kayaking tours, shark excursions, ATV and horseback rides. If you want to take a drive, Hale'iwa is a good bet. A surfers' mecca, it has retained the character of its more than 100-year history.

Fun Facts

- ✓ Oahu's political history is as varied as its geological past. It was on this island's southern shore, near present-day Waikiki, that Kamehameha the Great began a decisive battle in his campaign to unite the Hawaiian Islands for the first time, defeating the forces of Kalanikupule then the high chief of Maui and Oahu in the spring of 1795. It was in Honolulu, also, that a coalition of sugar planters and missionary descendants would overthrow the Hawaiian Monarchy in 1893. After Statehood was declared in 1959, Honolulu became the state capitol.

- ✓ Oahu's largest city, Honolulu ("protected bay" in Hawaiian), is also the largest city in Hawaii, the county seat, the state capitol, and the center of business and industry in the Islands
- ✓ Honolulu is also the only U.S. city to be founded by royalty, and hosts the only royal residence on U.S. soil ('Iolani Palace)
- ✓ 'Iolani Palace featured electricity before even the White House in Washington, D.C.
- ✓ The City and County of Honolulu encompasses the entire island of Oahu
- ✓ Oahu's size is said to be 607.7 square miles
- ✓ The island's highest point is the summit of Mt. Ka'ala in the Wai'anae Range (4,020 feet)
- ✓ Honolulu Harbor serves as a lifeline for all the Islands. Most of Hawaii's food and manufactured goods must be imported and distributed through this busy port
- ✓ Average temperatures on Oahu range from 68 to 85 degrees Fahrenheit, year-round. Coastal rainfall averages 23 inches per year.

- ✓ Oahu hosts several major festivals throughout the year, which fully illustrate Hawaii's famed ethnic diversity: Chinese New Year is celebrated on the lunar new year, usually in late January or early February; the Honolulu Festival, which celebrates Hawaii's ties with Japan, takes place in March; the week-long We Are Samoa celebration is in May; the King Kamehameha Day Floral Parade takes to the streets in June, and the month-long Aloha Festivals celebration kicks off in September.
- ✓ Oahu's official flower is the 'ilima
- ✓ The island's official color is yellow

Oahu Regions

Honolulu

If Oahu is the heart of Hawaii, then Honolulu is its racing pulse. In this cosmopolitan capital city, you'll find everything from historic landmarks to fine dining to world-class shopping. Home to the majority of Oahu's population, Honolulu stretches across the southeastern shores of the island, from Pearl Harbor to Makapuu Point, encompassing world-famous Waikiki Beach along the way..

Arts & Culture in Honolulu

Bishop Museum
What: The largest collection of Hawaiian artifacts in the state
Where: West of Waikiki at the base of the Likelike Highway

Honolulu's Bishop Museum is Hawaii's largest museum dedicated to studying and preserving the history of Hawaii and the Pacific. Originally designed to house the extensive collection of Hawaiian artifacts and royal family heirlooms of Princess Bernice Pauahi Bishop, a descendant of King Kamehameha I, the museum is now the premier natural and cultural history institution in the Pacific. One of Oahu's most historic places, the museum holds millions of artifacts, documents and photos about Hawaii and other Polynesian cultures.

Visit the newly renovated Hawaiian Hall, which immerses you in Native Hawaiian culture and history by showcasing a variety of important artifacts. In the planetarium, kids can learn how voyagers navigated the Pacific using the stars. In the Science Adventure Center, children can see Hawaii's unique natural environment like never before through a variety of interactive exhibits.

The museum is open seven days a week (excluding some holidays) with regular hours from 9 a.m. to 5 p.m.

Honolulu Museum of Art and Shangri La
What: Hawaii's largest fine arts museum
Where: Located near Downtown Honolulu

Not far from Downtown Honolulu, the Honolulu Museum of Art has been sharing the arts with Hawaii since 1927. With a permanent collection of more than 60,000 pieces, this is Hawaii's largest general fine-arts museum.

Stroll from gallery to gallery past open-air courtyards and ponds. Explore one of the finest collections of Asian art in the world as well as impressive collections of Western, European and Polynesian art. If you feel like seeing a film, visit Doris Duke Theatre, which plays an impressive slate of foreign and independent films. After browsing the galleries, take a break to have lunch in the open-air HoMA Cafē or recharge with an energizing drink at the Coffee Bar.

From January to October, the Honolulu Museum of Art even mixes a little nightlife with the arts at its monthly ARTafterDARK event. Guests dance and mingle with young professionals and art lovers on a night that looks like an art gallery opening but feels like a block party. Browse the extensive exhibitions, listen to live music, and grab food and drinks from vendors at stations throughout the museum. Each ARTafterDARK has a fun art-inspired theme, often focusing on an exhibition, and features music and performances. Open from 6-9 p.m. on the last Friday of the month, ARTafterDARK is a fun way to experience the museum in a new way.

Shangri La Museum of Islamic Art, Culture & Design

Shangri-La is a center for Islamic arts and cultures, offering guided tours of what was formerly the home of American heiress and philanthropist Doris Duke. Built in 1937, Shangri La was inspired by Duke's extensive travels throughout North Africa, the Middle East, and South Asia. With an impressive seaside view of Leahi (Diamond Head), Shangri La is home to such Islamic treasures as rich Iranian tilework, Indian jewelry and an entire wood-paneled room from Damascus. Tours are held Wednesdays through Saturdays and are often booked weeks in advance. All tours leave from the Honolulu Museum of Art.

Iolani Palace
What: Former residence of the Hawaiian monarchs
Where: Downtown Honolulu

A national historic landmark and the only official state residence of royalty in the United States, from 1882 to 1893 Downtown Honolulu's Iolani Palace was the official residence of the Hawaiian Kingdom's last two monarchs: King Kalakaua and his sister and successor, Queen Liliuokalani.

The palace was a symbol of promise for the Hawaiian Kingdom built by King David Kalakaua, "The Merrie Monarch." Influenced by European architectural styles, this royal residence included Hawaii's first electric light system, flush toilets and intra-house telephones. The rich interior features a beautiful koa staircase, dramatic portraits of Hawaiian royalty, ornate furniture and royal gifts and ornaments from around the world.

In 1893, a provisional U.S. government was established after opposition forces overthrew the Hawaiian monarchy. The Hawaiian Islands were eventually annexed as a United States Territory in 1898. Hawaii became the 50th state in 1959 and during this time Iolani Palace was used as the capitol building until 1968. After falling into disrepair over the years, the Iolani Palace was renovated and opened to the public in 1978.

Tour through this American Florentine-style palace's throne room, reception and dining room and envision the magnificent state dinners and balls held here. View the private living quarters of the royal family and listen to the tragic story of Liliuokalani's imprisonment in an upstairs bedroom following the overthrow. On the basement level view the ancient regalia of Hawaiian royalty from swords and precious jewelry to the two golden crowns of the King and Queen. On the spacious grounds of the palace, see the Iolani Coronation Pavilion, where in 1883 Kalakaua was crowned king.

Also note that Iolani Palace sits in the center of a vital area that is worth a walking tour. Across South King Street you'll find Aliiolani Hale and the King Kamehameha I statue. Right behind Iolani Palace is the State Capitol building and Washington Place, home to the governor. To the east are the historic Kawaiahao Church, Honolulu Hale (home to the City Council and offices of the Mayor) and the Hawaiian Mission Houses Historic Site and Archives. To the west you'll discover the Hawaii State Art Museum as well as Oahu's main financial and arts district in Downtown Honolulu and Chinatown.

You can take a guided tour or a self-guided audio tour of the Palace Tuesday through Saturday. If you're facing the Palace, the ticket office is to the left on the State Capitol side of the building. One of Oahu's most important historical places, Iolani Palace plays an integral part in understanding the history and culture of Hawaii. Learn more about the Iolani Palace.

Note: *Iolani Palace is also a venue for private events, such as weddings.*

Oahu Restaurants
Oahu Dining
Oahu is home to the metropolitan center of Hawaii, and its vibrant dining scene means that it's an excellent place to find creative and delicious food representing diverse cultures. Splurge on dinner at one

of the buzzworthy high-end spots in Honolulu, or save your vacation funds by finding tasty fare at casual spots, coffee shops and food trucks. On Oahu, you can eat like a local in smaller neighborhoods like Kapahulu or dine in high style at Hawaii's top-rated restaurants in neighborhoods like Waikiki, Kaimuki and Chinatown.

Oahu is home to some of the best chefs in the world. Alan Wong (Alan Wong's Restaurant), Roy Yamaguchi (Roy's Waikiki), George Mavrothalassitis (Chef Mavro Restaurant) and Phillippe Padovani (Elua) were some of the founding chefs of the Hawaii Regional Cuisine movement 25 years ago, and their legacy has continued to spark Oahu's restaurant renaissance today. These local legends take the freshest local produce and ingredients to create flavorful dishes, combining traditional Hawaiian cooking with influences from Japan, China, the Philippines and classic American cuisine among many others.

You'll also find delicious modern interpretations of Hawaiian and Asian cuisines from the next generation of great chefs as well, who carry on the traditions of using local ingredients and creative preparations at Honolulu restaurants like The Pig and the Lady, Lucky Belly and Mud Hen Water.

On the North Shore, you'll find a distinctly laidback vibe as well as a focus on fresh seafood. Fish tacos are a staple in surfer-friendly towns like Haleiwa. Shrimp trucks (food trucks whose menu offers a variety of shrimp-centric plates) are a local staple as well, along with the frozen Hawaiian treat shave ice (similar to a snow cone), which is a perfect way to cool off on a hot day.

Landmarks & Attractions

Waikiki
What: Historic gathering home to the majority of Oahu's hotels and resorts
Where: South shore of Honolulu

Located on the south shore of Honolulu, the world-famous neighborhood of Waikiki was once a playground for Hawaiian royalty. Known in Hawaiian as "spouting waters," Waikiki was introduced to the world when its first hotel, the Moana Surfrider, was built on its shores in 1901. Today, Waikiki is Oahu's main hotel and resort area and a vibrant gathering place for visitors from around the world. Along the main strip of Kalakaua Avenue you'll find world-class shopping, dining, entertainment, activities and resorts.

Waikiki is famous for its beaches and every hotel room is just two or three blocks away from the ocean (if it's not directly on the beach). With Mount Leahi (Diamond Head) as your backdrop, the calm waters of Waikiki are perfect for a surfing lesson. In fact, legendary Hawaiian waterman Duke Kahanamoku grew up surfing the waves of Waikiki. With other reknown Waikiki Beach Boys, this Olympic gold medalist in swimming taught visitors how to surf at the turn of the century. "Duke" was instrumental in sharing the values and sport of surfing to the world and came to be known and respected globally as "the father of modern surfing." Today, surf instructors in Waikiki perpetuate Duke's legacy by teaching visitors how to surf and canoe. The Duke Kahanamoku Statue, located on Waikiki Beach, has become an iconic symbol of Waikiki and the surf culture of Oahu.

But there's more to Waikiki than just the beach. Attractions of Waikiki like the Honolulu Zoo and the Waikiki Aquarium offer fun for the whole family. You can learn about the history of Waikiki by reading the surfboard markers along the Waikiki Historical Trail. Among the various things to do, high-end boutiques, shops, and restaurants can be found all along Kalakaua and Kuhio Avenues and at gathering places like the Royal Hawaiian Center, the Waikiki Beach Walk and the newly transformed International Market Place. After the Waikiki sunset, the fun continues with amazing nightlife and live music.

Best of all, Waikiki is within a half hour of a variety of Oahu attractions, including Pearl Harbor, Iolani Palace, the Nuuanu Pali Lookout and Hanauma Bay. Other notable points of interest nearby include Ala Moana Center (a massive outdoor shopping center), the local neighborhood of Kapahulu and the arts district of Chinatown.

From Hawaiian royalty to Hawaii Regional Cuisine, Waikiki continues to be an evolving expression of the ancient spirit of aloha. On these famous shores, the past and the future are uniting in fresh and surprising ways.

Leahi (Diamond Head)

What: Iconic state monument with a panoramic view of Honolulu
Where: Five minutes east of Waikiki

The iconic silhouette of Diamond Head State Monument sits along the Honolulu skyline just beyond Waikiki. This 760-foot tuff crater is one of Hawaii's most famous landmarks.

History of Leahi

Known as Leahi (brow of the tuna) in Hawaiian, the crater was named Diamond Head by 19th century British sailors who thought they discovered diamonds on the crater's slopes. These "diamonds" were actually shiny calcite crystals that had no value. Formed more than 100,000 years ago, the crater was used as a strategic military lookout beginning in the early 1900's and was named a National Natural

Landmark in 1968. Today, Diamond Head is a popular hiking destination with panoramic views of Waikiki and Oahu's south shore.

Visiting Leahi

It only takes a short drive or bus ride to get to Diamond Head Crater from Waikiki. This moderately challenging trail includes two sets of stairs, totaling 175 steps, as well as dark, underground tunnels and old military bunkers that require a flashlight. The stunning views that greet you at the top of Diamond Head are well worth the effort.

If you plan to hike on Saturday morning, don't forget to stop by the Kapiolani Community College Farmer's Market Oahu's premier farmers market showcasing locally grown food and produce across the street from the monument entrance on Monsarrat Avenue. In fact, there are a few notable cafes and restaurants lining Monsarrat that will make for a great pre- or post-Diamond Head meal.

Leahi Visitor Information
[NOTICE: *Complete closures of Diamond head summit trail are taking place between late October into late November 2017 due to rockfall mitigation work. For more information,*

Open daily, 365 days a year, from 6 a.m. to 6 p.m., including holidays. Parking at Diamond Head State Monument is limited. To avoid the crowds, visit the monument in the afternoon between the hours of 1 and 4 p.m. Last entrance to hike the trail is 4:30 p.m. Admission is $5 per cars and $1 per pedestrian.

Downtown Honolulu
What: Oahu's historic center for government and business
Where: Roughly 15 minutes west of Waikiki

Downtown Honolulu is home to some of Oahu's most historic places. Next to the skyscrapers of the island's main business district you'll find important landmarks like the Iolani Palace, the King Kamehameha I statue, the Kawaiahao Church and the Aloha Tower. This area is also the seat of Hawaii's government, home to the Hawaii State Capitol, Washington Place (the governor's mansion) and Honolulu Hale (Honolulu's City Hall). Clustered within blocks of each other, these important cultural landmarks and architectural wonders can be experienced on a leisurely walking tour.

Kapahulu, Oahu
What: Local neighborhood with a variety of restaurants
Where: Five minutes away from the eastern end of Waikiki

Looking for local flavor near Waikiki? Take a short trip down to Kapahulu Avenue and discover some of Honolulu's most unique shops and restaurants. Bailey's Antiques & Aloha Shirts boasts racks upon racks of vintage aloha shirts, some worth thousands of dollars. But the real find in this busy neighborhood is some of Honolulu's best *ono* (delicious) local food.

It may take just five minutes to drive through Kapahulu Avenue, but in that time you'll pass a restaurant for every appetite. In the mood for sushi or gourmet burgers? Japanese, Chinese or Thai? A massive plate of Hawaiian food at Ono Hawaiian Foods or a plate lunch at the Rainbow Drive In? Eat like a local in Kapahulu with a hot malasada from Leonard's Bakery or cool down with a colorful shave ice from Waiola Bakery and Shave Ice. From fine restaurants to fast food, you'll have plenty of reasons to bring your appetite on your next visit to Kapahulu.

National Memorial Cemetery of the Pacific Oahu
What: Prominent national cemetery honoring American Veterans
Where: North of Downtown Honolulu
Additional Info: Open Daily

Located just north of Downtown Honolulu in a long-extinct volcano called Punchbowl Crater, the National Memorial Cemetery of the Pacific is the resting-place for almost 53,000 veterans (and eligible family members). The memorial, placed on the National Register of Historic Places, stands in honor of the sacrifices and achievements of the American Armed Forces and commemorates the soldiers of 20th century wars, including those who were lost during the attack at Pearl Harbor.

Medal of Honor recipients and other notable Hawaii heroes are buried here, including Ellison Onizuka, Hawaii's first astronaut, and Stanley Dunham, World War II veteran and President Barack Obama's grandfather. The engraved names of almost 29,000 heroes from World War II and the Vietnam and Korean wars who were designated Missing In Action, Lost or Buried at Sea are honored in the ten "Courts of the Missing." Serene and poignant, the memorial also offers a panoramic view of Honolulu from the top of Punchbowl's crater rim.

Informative, free walking tours are sponsored by Veterans of the American Legion.

Shopping in Honolulu

Whether you're looking for Hawaiian-made handicrafts to remember your trip by or high-end fashion labels you can't find at home, Honolulu is a shopper's paradise; you may even want to pack an extra suitcase for all the treasures you'll find.

Honolulu

Waikiki

The shopping has become almost as famous as the beach at Waikiki. Shopping centers like DFS Galleria, the Royal Hawaiian Center and Waikiki Beach Walk offer everything from ukulele and Hawaiian arts and crafts to designer fashion and jewelery. On Luxury Row, browse haute couture labels like Chanel, Coach and Gucci. And all along the main strips of Kalakaua and Kuhio Avenues, you can explore a multitude of shops and boutiques as you treasure hunt for the perfect memento to remember your trip.

Ala Moana Center

Just west of Waikiki, Ala Moana Center is the largest open-air shopping mall in the world. Free trolleys shuttle visitors between Waikiki and Ala Moana, where there are more than 290 shops and 80 dining options.

More Oahu Shopping

Shopping venues beyond Waikiki include Ward Centers, Aloha Tower Marketplace and Kahala Mall in Honolulu; Pearlridge Center and the Waikele Premium Outlets in Central Oahu; and Windward Mall on the Windward Coast.

More Places to See in Honolulu
Duke Kahanamoku

The Father of Modern Surfing

What: Iconic Waikiki statue of "The father of modern surfing"
Where: On Kuhio Beach in Waikiki

On Kuhio Beach, a bronze statue of Duke Kahanamoku welcomes you to Waikiki with open arms. Duke was a true Hawaiian hero and one of the world's greatest watermen, a master of swimming, surfing and outrigger canoe paddling.

Duke Paoa Kahanamoku was born on August 24, 1890. He grew up swimming and surfing in Waikiki near the current Hilton Hawaiian Village Waikiki Beach Resort. Discovered as a swimming sensation, Duke's legend began when he broke the world record in the 100-yard freestyle during his very first competition. The prodigious Duke went on to win Olympic gold in the 100-meter freestyle and silver in the relay in 1912. He also won two gold medals in 1920 and won a silver medal at age 34 in the 1924 Olympics.

He was instrumental in helping to spread the sport of surfing and the spirit of aloha around the world which eventually earned him the nickname "the father of modern surfing." Duke was one of the pioneers of the Waikiki Beach Boys, watermen who earned their livings teaching visitors how to surf and canoe at Waikiki Beach; if you look, you can still find real Waikiki Beach Boys showing visitors a great time in the Waikiki surf today. The amiable Duke also acted in Hollywood, served as Hawaii's first ambassador of goodwill, was eventually elected sheriff and was the first person to be inducted into both the Surfing Hall of Fame and the Swimming Hall of Fame. To see authentic photos and memorabilia of Duke and the Waikiki Beach Boys grab a bite at Duke's Canoe Club in the Outrigger Waikiki overlooking Waikiki Beach.

Note: *Tossing lei onto outstretched arms is discouraged due to the acidity of the flowers on the bronze material.*

Aloha Tower
What: A historic landmark and port with a shopping and dining marketplace
Where: 15 minutes east of Waikiki near Downtown Honolulu and Chinatown

Located on the Honolulu Harbor in Downtown Honolulu, about 15 minutes west of Waikiki, Aloha Tower is an iconic symbol of Hawaii. Built in September of 1926, this was the tallest building in the islands for four decades and its clock was one of the largest in the United States. The tower stood as a welcoming beacon for visitors since travel to Oahu was done entirely by sea. Duke Kahanamoku set his first swimming world record here at Pier 7 and the wharf was also known for Boat Days, a lively celebration to welcome the arrival of visiting ships.

Today, Aloha Tower is still a docking port for Oahu's cruise ships, including The Star of Honolulu. But this historic place has also transformed into the revitalized Aloha Tower Marketplace: a mixed-use space now part of Hawaii Pacific University, featuring student residences, meeting spaces, community event areas and a variety of restaurants. Enjoy an ocean-view lunch, listen to live music at night and explore unique shops or walk just a couple of blocks to Chinatown's art district. You can also visit the Observation Deck, located on the 10th floor of Aloha Tower and dine at Gordon Biersch or Hooters, or dance at the night away at Nashville Waikiki all with beautiful views of the harbor on one side and the cityscape of Honolulu on the other.

Kawaiahao Church, Oahu
What: First Christian Church built on Oahu in 1842
Where: Downtown Honolulu near Iolani Palace

Known as the "Westminster Abbey of the Pacific," Kawaiahao Church was the first Christian Church built on Oahu. Dedicated on July 21, 1842, "The Great Stone Church" is made of 14,000 coral slabs from ocean reefs that were hauled from the sea by native laborers and missionaries. The church and the grounds were named a National Historic Landmark in 1962.

As you stroll the streets of Downtown Honolulu, you may hear the sound of bells from the tower clock. "Kauikeaouli clock," donated by King Kamehameha III in 1850, still tolls the hours to this day. To the right of the entrance you'll find the peaceful tomb of King Lunalilo. This popular King ruled for just a little over one year and he wished to be buried "among his people" at Kawaiahao Church rather than in the Royal Mausoleum. To the left of the church you'll also find the Kawaiahao Fountain. The High Chiefess Hao bathed in this sacred spring, giving the church its name: Ka Wai a Hao, or the water of Hao.

Kawaiahao Church still serves as a center of worship for Hawaii's people, with services conducted every Sunday in Hawaiian and English. Portraits of the royal family adorn the walls of the second floor. In this historic section of Honolulu you'll also find the Iolani Palace, the King Kamehameha I Statue, the Hawaiian Mission Houses Historic Site and Archives and the State Capitol nearby.

Central Oahu

The most important landmark in Central Oahu sits to the south in historic Pearl Harbor, the largest natural harbor in Hawaii. This active naval base is home to five Pearl Harbor Historic Sites that you can visit:

The Pacific Historic Parks, the USS Battleship Missouri Memorial, the USS Bowfin Submarine Museum & Park, the Pacific Aviation Museum and the USS Oklahoma Memorial. These special monuments commemorate the historic events that changed the course of history during World War II.

The fertile central valley between the Waianae Mountains and Koolau range offers a peek back to Oahu's history. Agriculture on the island was booming in the late 19th century, attracting immigrants from around the world to work on plantations. On your way from Honolulu to the North Shore, you'll pass the Leilehua Plateau in Wahiawa and see sprawling fields of pineapples. Get a closer look by stopping at the Dole Plantation, where you can learn about the spiky-but-sweet fruit's legacy on Oahu and cool down with a delicious frozen Dole whip treat. Kids will love running through the huge three-acre shrub maze. At the Hawaii Plantation Village, explore a living history museum of restored and replica sugar-cane plantation homes to get a sense of how people lived and worked more than 100 years ago.

In Central Oahu, you can also take a tour of famous Aloha Stadium, home of the University of Hawaii Warriors as well as many other events throughout the year.

Pearl Harbor

Five historic sites honoring the events occurring at this National Historic Landmark in Central Oahu, about 30 minutes from Waikiki

Known the world over as a "date which will live in infamy," the devastating events of December 7, 1941 changed the course of history. It was here that a surprise air attack by the Japanese plunged the United States into World War II, claiming thousands of lives.

At Pearl Harbor, that tragic history is never too far in the past. Hear first-hand stories from survivors describing the chaotic scene on Battleship Row. Walk through an airplane hangar that still bears the scars from that fateful morning. And peer into the shallow harbor where the sunken hull of the USS Arizona rests, still leaking oil that pools on the water's surface like black tears, as they've been described. Visiting Pearl Harbor is an experience that will be etched into your soul forever and will offer you a new perspective on World War II.

December 7, 2016 marked 75 years since that fateful day. A large-scale 11-day commemoration event to celebrate the survivors of the attack and honor those who lost their lives commenced in Oahu. The intent of this was to find a way to bridge the gap of generations and set the ground work for what is ahead of us for the future. The theme of this event that carries on today was "Honoring the Past, Inspiring the

Future." "As we look to the future, we each have an opportunity and a personal responsibility to invest in and commit to inspiring the leaders of tomorrow, using history to help empower choices that negate fateful outcomes," said Admiral Thomas Fargo in a statement.

The Hawaiian name for Pearl Harbor was *Puuloa* (long hill). Later named Pearl Harbor for the pearl oysters that were once harvested from the waters, the natural harbor is the largest in Hawaii. *Ulu* (breadfruit) was said to be brought here from Samoa.

Attractions at Pearl Harbor

Immerse yourself for a part or more of the day in five historic sites that comprise Pearl Harbor today: the WWII Valor in the Pacific (USS *Arizona* Memorial - *see note below* on temporary closure), Battleship *Missouri* Memorial, USS *Bowfin* Submarine Museum & Park, USS *Oklahoma* Memorial and the Pacific Aviation Museum.

The site of the most devastating loss of life, the USS *Arizona* was hit by a 1,760-pound armor-piercing bomb at 8:06 a.m. on December 7, 1941. The catastrophic explosion that resulted sank this massive battleship in nine minutes, killing 1,177 crewmen.

Today, the USS *Arizona* Memorial (part of the World War II Valor in the Pacific National Monument) is a place of somber beauty and quiet reflection. Begin at the Visitor Center, where you can watch a film about the attack and view plaques honoring lives lost on that fateful day. You'll then take a boat shuttle to the floating memorial built overtop the sunken hull of the *Arizona*, the final resting place for many of the ship's crew. In the shrine room, a marble wall exhibits the names of the men who lost their lives. Poignant and powerful, this is a place where visitors come face to face with the devastating effects of war.

Visiting the USS *Arizona* Memorial is free, but visitors must reserve a time slot for the boat tour in advance. You can do this online (a $1.50 fee will be charged) up to two months in advance. Alternately, 1,300 tickets are released each morning at the Pearl Harbor Visitor Center; the memorial sees an average of 4,000 visitors per day, so show up early (doors open at 7 a.m.) to reserve your same-day time slot in person, fee free. For $7.50, you can add a self-guided, narrated tour for a more immersive experience.

Battleship Missouri Memorial

General Macarthur accepted the unconditional Japanese surrender that ended World War II on September 2, 1945, on the Surrender Deck of the Battleship *Missouri*. Now located at Pearl Harbor's Battleship Row, the massive "Mighty Mo" is a living museum, with exhibits spanning three wars and five decades of service.

Explore the decks of this 60,000-ton battleship, three football fields long and 20 stories tall. Stand on the Surrender Deck and view the documents that ended the war. Take a tour and get special access to restricted areas. Don't miss the ship's most stunning feature: towering 16-inch guns that could fire a 2,700-pound shell 23 miles.

More Details: TOUR OPTIONS and Purchase Tickets: Call 808-455-1600 (x251)

Hours: Daily 7 a.m. - 5 p.m.

Duration: Plan between 2-3 hours

USS *Bowfin* Submarine Museum & Park

Also known as the "Pearl Harbor Avenger," the USS *Bowfin* (SS-287) is one of 288 U.S. submarines that carried out the war in the Pacific. Start at the submarine museum and learn about the battle beneath the seas. A tour of the grounds will take you to a Waterfront Memorial honoring submariners lost in World War II. Then, step aboard the *Bowfin* and descend below deck to tour its torpedo room, engine room and sleeping quarters.

More Details: TOUR OPTIONS and Purchase Tickets: Call 808-455-1600 (x251)

Hours: Daily 7 a.m. - 5 p.m.

Duration: Plan between 1-2 hours

Pacific Aviation Museum

The Museum is home to two WWII era hangars which survived the December 7, 1941 attack on Pearl Harbor, and the Ford Island Control Tower. The hangars and surrounding tarmac still bear the scars of the attack in the form of bullet holes, strafe marks, and bomb craters.

As you step into the hangars, you cross the threshold of time and walk into the pages of history. Up first is a short introductory film in the 200-seat theater that sets the tone with memories from survivors recounting the day of the Japanese attack. Then, it's on to the vintage aircraft.

With 50 aircraft on display, including the instantly recognizable Curtiss P-40 Warhawk and its nemesis, the Mitsubishi Zero, the 1942 Stearman Biplane flown by President George H.W. Bush and the remnants of the "Niʻihau Zero," which crash landed on Niʻihau Island after the Pearl Harbor attack. Among the other aircraft on exhibit are some of aviation's most iconic military aircraft, like the B-17 "Swamp Ghost" Flying Fortress, F-15 Eagle and AH-1 Cobra. From propeller planes to the jets of the Korean War and the Vietnam War, the Museum offers a compelling visual timeline of aviation history as advancements led to ever faster and deadlier aircraft.

More Details: TOUR OPTIONS and Purchase Tickets: Call 808-423-1341

Hours: Daily 9 a.m. - 5 p.m.

Duration: Plan between 1-2 hours

USS *Oklahoma* Memorial

Dedicated on December 7, 2007, the USS *Oklahoma* Memorial honors the 429 crewmen who lost their lives in the Pearl Harbor attack. Approximately nine torpedoes hit "The Okie," capsizing this 35,000-ton battleship in just 12 minutes. Some crewmen were actually trapped in compartments below deck after the ship capsized. They used hammers and wrenches to signal rescue crews on the surface; two days after the attack, 32 men were rescued from the ship's overturned hull.

More Details: To visit the memorial purchase shuttle tickets at the USS Bowfin ticket counter, just north of the USS Arizona Memorial Visitor Center. You can combine the Oklahoma Memorial with visits to the Battleship Missouri Memorial Museum or the Pacific Aviation Museum, also located on Ford Island.

Hours: Daily 8 a.m. - 4 p.m. (summers open until 5 p.m.)

Duration: Plan approximately an hour

More Planning Your Visit Info

Pearl Harbor is still an active U.S. naval base. Due to increased security, the following items are prohibited: purses, backpacks, fanny packs, diaper bags, camera bags, luggage and any other items that provide concealment. Bag storage is available for an extra fee.

North Shore, Oahu
Haleiwa
What: Historic surf town that is the cultural hub of the North Shore
Where: North Shore roughly an hour from Waikiki

Your first stop along the North Shore will be charming Haleiwa, about a one-hour drive from Waikiki. More than the laid-back surf town it seems, Haleiwa is filled with local style and country ambiance, as well as cool surf shops and boutiques, charming art galleries and understated restaurants housed in plantation-era buildings.

Rich with island history, Haleiwa is now the social and artistic hub of the North Shore. Here you'll find surfers fueling up on shrimp or other delicacies at one of the town's abundant food trucks before hitting the famous beaches of Waimea Bay, Ehukai (Banzai Pipeline) and Sunset Beach. You'll also find locals and visitors winding down with a shaved ice after a day in the sun or shopping at boutiques filled with unique gifts that will allow you to bring back a piece of Hawaii with you.

Haleiwa is a far cry from the excitement of Waikiki, and that's exactly how the people of the North Shore like it.

Leeward Coast, Oahu

The sunny and dry Leeward Coast of Oahu lies at the foot of the Waianae mountain range just 30 miles from Waikiki, but the contrast between the regions is striking. Where Waikiki offers urban hustle and bustle, the Leeward side of Oahu is less developed, with picturesque towns, beautiful off-the-beaten-path beaches and rural landscapes to explore.

If you plan to stay on the Leeward Coast, you'll have two major resorts to choose from in the beautiful Ko Olina resort area. Home to the luxurious Four Seasons Oahu and Aulani, A Disney Resort & Spa, this 43-acre marina offers stretches of postcard-worthy shoreline with ample opportunities for water sports and championship golf. Other fun and family-friendly attractions in the area include the Paradise Cove Luau and the Wet n' Wild Hawaii water park. Local beaches include Makaha Beach, one of the first spots where surfers began big wave surfing, and Yokohama Bay.

At the very end of the road, you can hike to Oahu's western-most point at sacred Kaena Point for incredible Pacific Ocean views. If you hike to Kaena Point, be sure to stay on the trail because the area is also a bird sanctuary, and bring water and other supplies with you because the remote area doesn't offer amenities. Leave no trace, and pack out whatever you brought with you in order to respect the land and maintain the pristine natural area for others.

Kaena Point

What: State park, bird sanctuary and hike at the western tip of Oahu
Where: Two trail heads from Waianae (south) or Mokuleia (north)

On the western tip of Oahu is Kaena Point. This dramatic lava shoreline is said to be the place where the souls of ancient Hawaiians would jump off into the spirit world and meet the souls of their ancestors. With scenic views of the Waianae coast to the south, Mokuleia to the north, and the vast Pacific, it's easy to see why this point was deemed so sacred.

The only way to get to Kaena Point is by hiking. There are two trailheads: From the north side, or Mokuleia side, drive to the very end of Farrington Highway and park at the trailhead. This is a long and notoriously hot hike, so bring plenty of sunscreen and water. Hazardous conditions make any water activities extremely dangerous and are highly discouraged. From the south side, or Leeward Coast side, the trail starts at the end of the road past Yokohama Beach and its three "dips," or breaks. This west side Oahu icon offers white sand beaches, diving and the possible sight of dolphins.

Windward Coast

As you drive over the sloping Pali Highway, skyscrapers and the sprawling city of Honolulu give way to lush valleys and country landscapes. Exiting the tunnels east of the Koolau Mountain Range, it feels as if you're entering a different world and a turquoise ocean shimmers in the distance. A trip to the Windward Coast reveals a slower-paced side of Oahu, and some of the most stunning natural beauty anywhere in Hawaii.

From Kailua town, you can head in two directions. Go clockwise down the coast to Sea Life Park, Makapuu Point Lighthouse and eventually Leahi (Diamond Head) and Waikiki. Or drive north spend a day exploring the Windward Coast as it winds lazily around the island toward the North Shore, offering interesting stops along the way, like the serene Valley of the Temples, which is home to a stunning Japanese Buddhist temple.

Driving along the two-lane highway you can't miss Mokolii, the tiny island fondly known as "Chinaman's Hat." Stop at the park and stretch your legs or have a picnic. Just across the highway you'll find one of Hawaii's most seen but least-recognized locations: Kualoa Ranch. A generations-old family-owned ranch, its scenic valley has provided the backdrop for countless movies and TV shows, including "Jurassic Park" and "Lost". Fortunately, it's not just for the stars; visitors can enjoy horseback riding, ziplining, ATV tours and host of other activities. From here, Kamehameha Highway meanders past Kaaawa ("Ka-ah-ah-vah"), gentle Kahana Bay and around the northernmost tip of the island to Oahu's North Shore, home of the best surf spots in Hawaii and some say the world.

Makapuu Point Lighthouse
What: A moderately easy hike to a scenic viewpoint
Where: Eastern most point of Oahu overlooking the Windward Coast
More Info: Parking lot, no restroom facilities

On the eastern most point of Oahu sits the Makapuu Point Lighthouse, a shining beacon built in 1909 on a 600-foot sea cliff overlooking Makapuu Beach a stretch of sand known as one of Oahu's best bodysurfing beaches and family-friendly Sea Life Park.

Fifteen minutes past Hanauma Bay and beyond Sandy Beach (another popular local beach) you'll find the large parking lot that leads to the 2-mile paved trail overlooking the lighthouse. Renovations were recently made to the lighthouse and the trail was recently repaved and additional lookout points were added. This moderately easy hike pays off with breathtaking views of the indigo ocean and Oahu's eastern, or Windward Coast. You can even see the island of Molokai in the distance. Two other smaller islands, Manana (the larger of the two, also known as Rabbit Island) and Kaohikaipu are also visible just offshore.

The Molokai Channel runs right past the Makapuu Lighthouse, so this is also a great place to spot whales using on-site telescopes during whale watching season between December and May. The Makapuu Tide Pools, including a small blowhole, are quite popular and can be found just down from the first set of whale information signs. A word of warning: never go out past the tide pools near the ocean, be careful of big surf crashing into the tide pools, and don't visit if there are strong winds. If you're looking to swim, Alan Davis Beach over by Pele's Chair is a beautiful swimming area with a small secluded beach that is almost always safe for swimming and diving.

Nuuanu Pali Lookout, Oahu
What: Historical landmark and scenic spot with panoramic views
Where: Pali Highway between Honolulu and Kailua
Additional Info: More Info: No entry fee, $3 for cars

Just a five-mile drive northeast of Downtown Honolulu, the Nuuanu Pali Lookout offers panoramic views of the sheer Koolau cliffs and lush

Windward Coast. Driving up the Pali Highway through tall trees and dense forests to get to the lookout, you'll see the city disappear and the tranquil beauty of Hawaii's natural landscape emerge.

Perched over a thousand feet above the Oahu coastline amid mountain peaks shrouded by clouds, the stone terrace overlooks the areas of Kaneohe and Kailua, Mokolii (a pointy island locals call Chinaman's Hat) and the University of Hawaii's marine biology research center, Coconut Island. Other notable landmarks that can be seen are Hawaii Pacific University's Windward campus, Kaneohe Marine Corps Base and the Hoomaluhia Botanical Garden, which is part of the Honolulu Botanical Gardens.

After you've soaked in the view, continue through the Pali Tunnels to Windward Oahu. As you near the bottom you'll face a "tough" decision: go straight to the buzzing beach town of Kailua or turn left through Kaneohe and follow the lush coastline to Haleiwa and Waimea Bay on Oahu's famed North Shore.

The Pali Lookout is a site of deep historical significance. Named "Pali" meaning "cliff" in Hawaiian, the Pali Lookout is the site of the Battle of Nuuanu, where in 1795 King Kamehameha I won the struggle that finally united Oahu under his rule. This fierce battle claimed hundreds of soldiers' lives, many of which were forced off of the Pali's sheer cliffs.

Note that the Pali Lookout is also known for its strong and howling winds. You'll understand why the Nuuanu Pali Lookout is one of Oahu's best scenic points when you feel the wind push up against you, hear the winds whistle through the mountains and see the breathtaking views of Oahu's lush Windward Coast.

Byodo-in Temple
What: A scale replica of a temple in Uji Japan
Where: Off the beaten path on the Windward Coast

Deep in a lush valley along the 2,000-foot Koolau Range lies the Valley of the Temples. The resting place for many of Hawaii's departed, Valley of the Temples' hilly landscape is scattered with hundreds of freshly placed tropical flowers, like torch ginger and bird of paradise, to remember loved ones.

The main attraction in the Valley of the Temples is a Japanese temple called Byodo-in, which translates to the "Temple of Equality." A scale replica of a temple in Uji Japan and made entirely without nails, Byodo-in was dedicated in 1968 as a centennial commemoration of the first Japanese immigrants in Hawaii. Famed Kyoto Landscaper Kiichi Toemon Sano planned the Japanese garden complex that houses

Byodo-in with extreme attention to detail, from the gravel's ripple-like design to the small bridges over the fishpond.

The deep drone of the sacred bell (bon-sho) fills the tranquil temple grounds, as it is customary for visitors to ring the bell before entering the temple for happiness and longevity. To sound the five-foot, three-ton brass bell, you must pull and release a wooden log called a shu-moku. Inside the Byodo-in sits an 18-foot gold leaf-covered Buddha where visitors are welcomed to light incense and offer a prayer. Outside, peacocks and black swans roam the garden grounds and turtles lounge beside the pond. The temple's pond is also filled with koi, a Japanese decorative fish that is a symbol of love and friendship.

The Valley of the Temples is truly a hidden gem in Hawaii found off the beaten path on the Windward Coast. There is no other place where you can see an authentic Japanese temple situated against the gorgeous backdrop of Oahu's soaring Koolau Mountains.

Things to Do on Oahu
Oahu Surfing
Surfing literally began as the "Sport of Kings" in Hawaii, when ancient Hawaiian royalty would show off their skills on Waikiki Beach and other surf spots around Oahu. In the early 20th century, legendary surfer, Olympic swimmer and Waikiki native Duke Kahanamoku

introduced the sport to the world. He was one of the pioneers of the Waikiki Beach Boys, who earned their living teaching visitors how to surf and canoe at Waikiki Beach. In the 1950s, surfers started riding the huge waves in the North Shore's Waimea Bay, now widely regarded as the birthplace of big wave surfing. Oahu has many options for you to experience surfing, either by watching the pros on the major waves or by trying it out yourself on the gentler ones.

Learning How to Surf on Oahu

If you're ready to learn, the calm waters of Waikiki Beach are a great place to get your feet wet. You can still find real Waikiki Beach Boys showing visitors a great time and giving surfing lessons today. Sign up for a lesson at the seaside booths along Kuhio and Waikiki beaches. Some of these instructors have been teaching surfing and outrigger canoe paddling for generations.

You'll find surf schools taught at gentler breaks in town at Ala Moana, the North Shore and various other spots around Oahu. Lessons run between 1-2 hours and are taught by more experienced surfers. Longboards are used to make it even easier for first-timers and a push from your instructor will help you get started. Lessons are highly recommended for your safety and the safety of your fellow beachgoers.

Watching Big Wave Surfing on Oahu

To see the professional surfers in action, take a drive to the North Shore during the winter and watch surfers from around the world ride Hawaii's most famous big waves. The North Shore's legendary winter waves attract the best surfers in the world. The Vans Triple Crown of Surfing, considered the Super Bowl of surfing, is held on its shores every year in November and December at Waimea Bay, Haleiwa Beach and Ehukai Beach (Banzai Pipeline).

"The Eddie" is considered the ultimate Hawaii big wave surfing event since it honors legendary Hawaiian waterman Eddie Aikau. Unlike other competitions, "The Eddie" does not have a set date, but rather, a holding period from December through February and occurs on one day only if the waves hit a face height of 40 feet or more. Since its inception in 1984, this invitation-only event has only been held a handful of times. The opening ceremony brings together surfers from around the world in celebration of the aloha spirit of Eddie Aikau, the legendary lifeguard of Waimea Bay and one of the best big wave riders in the world. He was a legend on the North Shore, and the phrase "Eddie would go" refers to how he pulled surfers out of the raging waters when no one else would or could. Visit Waimea Bay and you'll find Eddie's memorial watching over the surfers as he did in life.

Scuba & Snorkeling

Colorful coral heads. Bright yellow tang. Rainbow runners. And of course, the state fish of Hawaii, the *humuhumunukunukuapuaa*. With 1,200 miles of coral reef fringing the Hawaiian Islands, snorkeling and scuba diving are two of our most popular water activities. On Oahu, a dip beneath the waves reveals a whole new world.

Don't let the name scare you away from Shark's Cove on the North Shore this rocky bay with clear, shallow waters is one of the top snorkeling and shore-diving spots in the world (and no, sharks aren't common here). Shark's Cove is best explored during the summer months, as winter brings massive swells for big wave season.

Oahu also has a variety of other beautiful beaches with calm waters to explore, including Sans Souci near Waikiki and the Ko Olina lagoons on the island's Leeward Coast, a perfect place for *keiki* (kids) just starting out. You can also hop on a snorkel tour or boat charter and let guides help you discover what lies beneath the waters offshore.

Oahu Accommodations

Oahu offers a taste of everything Hawaii has to offer, including a spectrum of places to stay. You'll find five-star resorts with lots of onsite amenities as well as smaller hotels, condos and rentals with a more local feel. Depending on your budget and the adventures you want to have on Oahu, it's easy to find just the right accommodations to fit your trip.

The majority of Oahu's accommodations are in Waikiki. This vibrant Honolulu neighborhood is located in the heart of great shopping and beautiful beaches. It also offers visitors the most lodging choices, including wallet-friendly options like Waikiki Beachside Hostel and well-established beachfront resorts with deluxe ocean views like The Royal Hawaiian, Hilton Hawaiian Village Waikiki and Outrigger Reef Beach Resort Waikiki. Waikiki also has some newer boutique hotel options, including the Modern Honolulu, that offer luxury in a more intimate atmosphere.

Beyond Waikiki, you'll find another luxury resort in east Honolulu (The Kahala Hotel & Resort), one on the North Shore (Turtle Bay Resort) and two on the Leeward Coast in the Ko Olina Resort area (Four Seasons Oahu and Aulani, A Disney Resort & Spa). A condo or bed and breakfast in Kailua can be a great choice for proximity to Kailua's gorgeous beaches on the windward side. North Shore vacation rentals and condos, particularly in the area of the legendary surf town Haleiwa, can be a more peaceful alternative to Waikiki, if you want to experience a different side of the island.

Camping is a low-cost possibility at specified locations five days a week, from 8 a.m. on Friday to 8 a.m. on Wednesday. Some campsites are only open during weekends, and other sites are only open or closed during specific times of year.

Aston at the Waikiki Banyan

Child friendly Hawaii hotel features 1 bedroom suites, w/ fully equipped kitchens making dining affordable. Facilities include mini-playground, heated swimming pool, 10 bbq grills, tennis, sauna, and two hot tubs. Near Waikiki beach and family attractions.

201 Ohua Ave Honolulu, HI 96815

Local Phone: (808) 922-0555

US Toll Free: (866) 774-2924

Email: info@aqua-aston.com

Island: Oahu

Located just over a block from Waikiki Beach, Aston at the Waikiki Banyan combines spacious accommodations with a great location near Waikiki's best attractions and activities. This family-friendly condominium resort boasts the largest recreational deck in Waikiki, offering added amenities such as a heated swimming pool, jet spas, barbecue facilities and a tennis court. Guests can relax in one-bedroom suites with fully-equipped kitchens, separate living areas and bedrooms, and private lanais with sweeping views of Waikiki, the Koolau Mountains, and the blue Pacific.

Paradise Bay Resort

Paradise Bay Resort offers panoramic views of the Ko'olau Mountains laced with magnificent waterfalls after a rain, with awesome views of the Bay, Islands, Ocean and the Ancient Hawaiian Fishpond. The resort is a short drive to the airport or Waikiki usually less than 30 minutes.

47-039 Lihikai Drive Kaneohe, HI 96744

Local Phone: (808) 239-5711

US Toll Free: (800) 735-5071

Email: info@paradisebayresort.com

Island: Oahu

Paradise Bay Resort offers panoramic views of the Ko'olau Mountains laced with magnificent waterfalls after a rain, with awesome views of the Bay, Islands, Ocean and the Ancient Hawaiian Fishpond. The resort is a short drive to the airport or Waikiki usually less than 30 minutes. Experience Oahu's Windward side and escape the hustle, bustle and crowds of Waikiki. The crystal clear, turquoise water of Kualoa, Kailua and Lanikai Beach are just minutes away. Paradise Bay Resort offers kayaking, stand-up paddle boarding, boat excursions, sport fishing and private boat packages.

Each suite offers a full kitchen or kitchenette and most suites offer a spacious and private-covered lanai, with ocean/bay and mountain views. Included in your stay is a deluxe continental breakfast with fresh local fruits . Free Wi-Fi and free parking is available for guests.

OHANA Waikiki Malia by Outrigger

OHANA Waikiki Malia features renovated Malia Tower guest rooms, lobby and common areas, offering fresh surroundings in the heart of Waikiki. Hotel includes an IHOP restaurant and is conveniently located near shopping and dining on Kalakaua Avenue.

2211 Kuhio Avenue Honolulu, HI 96815-2830

Local Phone: (808) 923-7621

US Toll Free: (800) 462-6262

Email: reservations@ohanahotels.com

Island: Oahu

OHANA Waikiki Malia features renovated Malia Tower guest rooms, lobby and common areas, offering fresh surroundings in the heart of Waikiki. The hotel offers 48 sets of connecting rooms and many rooms with two double beds, providing flexible lodging for families and groups. Also available are one-bedroom kitchenettes suitable for four guests. Hotel includes an IHOP restaurant, Rivals Waikiki sports bar, and is conveniently located near shopping and dining on Kalakaua Avenue and the exciting Waikiki Beach Walk.

Shoreline Hotel Waikiki

Just about everything on Waikiki Beach has been discovered, except maybe Shoreline Waikiki Hotel. In the heart of Waikiki, and only seconds from Waikiki Beach, this peaceful hotel is your hidden sanctuary in Honolulu's premier shopping and dining district.

342 Seaside Avenue Honolulu, HI 96815

Local Phone: (808) 931-2444

US Toll Free: (877) 793-8534

Email: ricko@filamenthospitality.com

Island: Oahu

Just about everything on Waikiki Beach has been discovered, except maybe Shoreline Waikiki Hotel. In the heart of Waikiki, and only seconds from Waikiki Beach, this peaceful hotel is your hidden sanctuary in Honolulu's premier shopping and dining district.

DESIGN INTENT: Influenced by the local spirit and nature of Honolulu, this new hotel offers an experience that is inviting, intriguing, fresh, and relaxing, where simplicity and practicality are key. Surrounded by natural grandeur, the hotel offers a match of luxury and balance with tasteful sophistication, complimented by modernistic intention.

OHANA Waikiki East by Outrigger

OHANA Waikiki East is conveniently located in central Waikiki and features guest rooms and suites with kitchenettes and three restaurants. The full-service hotel is minutes from Waikiki Beach and adjacent to the International Market Place.

2375 Kuhio Avenue Honolulu, HI 96815

Local Phone: (808) 921-6656

US Toll Free: (800) 462-6262

Email: michelle.wee@outrigger.com

Island: Oahu

OHANA Waikiki East is a 441-room hotel conveniently located in central Waikiki and is minutes from Waikiki Beach and adjacent to the International Market Place. Guest rooms and suites feature warm earth tone carpeting and anthurium-patterned bedspreads all designed to create a pleasant, relaxing environment. Rooms with convenient kitchenettes are also available. All guests receive an incredible free amenities package called the OHANA Waikiki Connection that includes high-speed Internet access, phone calls to the U.S. & Canada (first 15 minutes), rides on the Waikiki Trolley's Pink Line throughout Waikiki and Ala Moana Center, use of in-room safe, and in-room coffee and tea daily. Well suited for leisure or business travelers, the hotel offers three restaurants, three moderate size meeting rooms, espresso cafe, room service, fitness room, swimming pool, self-service laundry, travel agency, rental car desk, and video arcade.

Hilton Hawaiian Village Waikiki Beach Resort

Located on the widest stretch of beach this is Waikiki's only true oceanfront resort. The resort offers 22 lush acres with 5 pools, a refreshing salt water lagoon, a wide variety of shopping and dining, activities and Friday night fireworks.

2005 Kalia Rd Honolulu, HI 96815-1999
Local Phone: (808) 949-4321
US Toll Free: (800) HIL-TONS
Island: Oahu

Hilton Hawaiian Village Waikiki Beach Resort is Waikiki's only true resort destination, offering the perfect mix of exceptional resort accommodations and classic Hawaiian hospitality, all nestled on 22 beachfront acres. Imagine the widest stretch of white sand on Waikiki, a serene beachfront lagoon, lush tropical gardens and cascading waterfalls, majestic views of Diamond Head and stunning seaside sunsets. Discover 90 shops and boutiques and a diverse, international selection of restaurants. The resort offers five pools including the Paradise Pool with water slides and the Super Pool which on Friday nights becomes the stage for a celebration of Hawaiian culture and entertainment, ending with a spectacular Fireworks show! Hilton Hawaiian Village stands as the premier meeting center of the Pacific with more than 150,000 square feet of meeting, convention and outdoor function space. Oahu's most prestigious and productive place to mix business and pleasure.

The Royal Hawaiian, a Luxury Collection Resort

The most coveted spot on Waikiki Beach is at The Royal Hawaiian, within the billowing sanctuary of private beachfront cabanas or from luxurious guest rooms showcasing unrivaled panoramic views of Diamond Head and the sparkling Pacific Ocean - we offer Hawaii's most majestic experiences.

2259 Kalakaua Ave. Honolulu, HI 96815-2578

Local Phone: (808) 923-7311

US Toll Free: (800) 782-9488

Email: scott.kawasaki@luxurycollection.com

Island: Oahu

The Royal Hawaiian, known for its brightly-colored exterior, has welcomed celebrities, heads of state and influential figures to Waikiki since 1927. Waikiki's most iconic landmark is located within the excitement of Waikiki yet buffered by serene tropical gardens. Abhasa Spa features massages in garden cabanas. Choose from two outdoor pools; The Malulani Pool provides a tranquil setting while the more adventurous explore Helumoa Playground's waterfalls, waterslides, and hot tubs. Additional amenities include valet, concierge service, laundry services, limousine service, and more. Dining offers Azure's fresh seafood, Mai Tai Bar for oceanfront fresh cocktails and nightly entertainment, and Surf Lanai for breakfast and lunch. Guestrooms feature bakery items from the Royal Hawaiian Bakery, 24-hr room service, luxury bath amenities, flat-panel TVs, newspapers, desks, irons, ipod compatible cd clocks, and safes.

Oahu Activities

Oahu is called the "Heart of Hawaii," so it's the appropriate home to Hawaii's widest range of popular activities and famous sights. You'll find an activity and attraction for every inclination, from the North Shore to the Makapuu Lighthouse on the island's southeast tip.

Oahu Water Activities

With endless golden beaches, inviting blue waves and balmy weather, you can play in the water all year long on Oahu. If you've always dreamed of hanging ten on a long board, Waikiki Beach is the spot to learn. Duke Kahanamoku and the Waikiki Beach Boys popularized the art of *hee nalu* (wave sliding) in the waters of Waikiki Beach during the early 1900s, and it's still a perfect place to take your first surfing lesson today.

Beyond surfing, you can explore the ocean by taking a group outrigger canoe ride off of Waikiki Beach. If you're looking for something fun for the whole family to do, try snorkeling and swimming at one of Oahu's many beautiful beaches. Take a sunset cruise or sailing excursion and you might spot a humpback breach during whale watching season (December through May). Sports fisherman can also charter a boat and fish for Pacific Blue Marlin, Ahi (yellowfin tuna), Ono (wahoo) or Mahimahi.

Satisfy your sporty side with other water activities in Oahu, including jet-skiing, parasailing, wind surfing, kite surfing, wakeboarding and bodyboarding (boogie boarding). Stand up paddle boarding (SUP) where surfers stand on a larger board using a paddle to maneuver has also become a popular alternative to surfing in the islands. With so many exciting activities, you'll understand why adventure thrives in the deep blue Pacific surrounding Oahu.

Fishing on Oahu
Oahu is a great place to sport fish, with charter boats available to tackle some of the state's biggest fish swimming just off its shores. Types of fish that can be reeled in include marlin, *ahi* (yellow fin) and *mahimahi* (dolphinfish, unrelated to the dolphin). The largest sports-fishing marlin ever caught was reeled in from Oahu's coast at 1,805 pounds.

Start from one of Oahu's harbors where experienced crew members can take you to the best fishing areas and can provide you with rods, tackle and bait.

Snorkeling & Scuba on Oahu

Colorful coral heads. Bright yellow tang. Rainbow runners. And of course, the state fish of Hawaii, the *humuhumunukunukuapuaa*. With 1,200 miles of coral reef fringing the Hawaiian Islands, snorkeling and scuba diving are two of our most popular water activities. On Oahu, a dip beneath the waves reveals a whole new world.

Don't let the name scare you away from Shark's Cove on the North Shore this rocky bay with clear, shallow waters is one of the top snorkeling and shore-diving spots in the world (and no, sharks aren't common here). Shark's Cove is best explored during the summer months, as winter brings massive swells for big wave season.

Oahu also has a variety of other beautiful beaches with calm waters to explore, including Sans Souci near Waikiki and the Ko Olina lagoons on the island's Leeward Coast, a perfect place for *keiki* (kids) just starting out. You can also hop on a snorkel tour or boat charter and let guides help you discover what lies beneath the waters offshore.

Oahu Surfing
Surfing literally began as the "Sport of Kings" in Hawaii, when ancient Hawaiian royalty would show off their skills on Waikiki Beach and other surf spots around Oahu. In the early 20th century, legendary surfer, Olympic swimmer and Waikiki native Duke Kahanamoku introduced the sport to the world. He was one of the pioneers of the

Waikiki Beach Boys, who earned their living teaching visitors how to surf and canoe at Waikiki Beach. In the 1950s, surfers started riding the huge waves in the North Shore's Waimea Bay, now widely regarded as the birthplace of big wave surfing. Oahu has many options for you to experience surfing, either by watching the pros on the major waves or by trying it out yourself on the gentler ones.

Learning How to Surf on Oahu

If you're ready to learn, the calm waters of Waikiki Beach are a great place to get your feet wet. You can still find real Waikiki Beach Boys showing visitors a great time and giving surfing lessons today. Sign up for a lesson at the seaside booths along Kuhio and Waikiki beaches. Some of these instructors have been teaching surfing and outrigger canoe paddling for generations.

You'll find surf schools taught at gentler breaks in town at Ala Moana, the North Shore and various other spots around Oahu. Lessons run between 1-2 hours and are taught by more experienced surfers. Longboards are used to make it even easier for first-timers and a push from your instructor will help you get started. Lessons are highly recommended for your safety and the safety of your fellow beachgoers.

Watching Big Wave Surfing on Oahu

To see the professional surfers in action, take a drive to the North Shore during the winter and watch surfers from around the world ride Hawaii's most famous big waves. The North Shore's legendary winter waves attract the best surfers in the world. The Vans Triple Crown of Surfing, considered the Super Bowl of surfing, is held on its shores every year in November and December at Waimea Bay, Haleiwa Beach and Ehukai Beach (Banzai Pipeline).

"The Eddie" is considered the ultimate Hawaii big wave surfing event since it honors legendary Hawaiian waterman Eddie Aikau. Unlike other competitions, "The Eddie" does not have a set date, but rather, a holding period from December through February and occurs on one day only if the waves hit a face height of 40 feet or more. Since its inception in 1984, this invitation-only event has only been held a handful of times. The opening ceremony brings together surfers from around the world in celebration of the aloha spirit of Eddie Aikau, the legendary lifeguard of Waimea Bay and one of the best big wave riders in the world. He was a legend on the North Shore, and the phrase "Eddie would go" refers to how he pulled surfers out of the raging waters when no one else would or could. Visit Waimea Bay and you'll find Eddie's memorial watching over the surfers as he did in life.

Whale Watching on Oahu

From December to May, you may catch a glimpse of a majestic *kohola*, or humpback whale, in Oahu's southern seas. The gentle giants come to the warm Hawaiian waters every year to breed and give birth to new calves.

Schedule a tour or charter a boat to spot these magnificent creatures. Treat yourself to scenic ocean views as expert guides take you to the best spots to observe whales playfully surfacing, tail slapping or blowing spouts in the air. Regulations prohibit boats from approaching within 100 yards of a whale and you should never swim with or touch whales or any other marine mammals.

You can also spot whales from Oahu's many beaches and from southeastern Oahu spots like the scenic Makapuu Lighthouse, Hanauma Bay, and along the seaside overlooks near Leahi (Diamond Head). Whale watching tours and cruises depart from various ports along Oahu's southern and western harbors.

Beaches of Oahu

Oahu's beaches are a true taste of paradise whether you're looking for high adventure on the sea, gentle waves for your first surfing lesson, a romantic sunset view or a family-friendly swimming spot. While you might already be familiar with world-famous Waikiki Beach and the high-octane winter waves of the North Shore, there's even more to discover along the island's 112 miles of coastline. Explore Oahu's beaches below by region below.

North Shore Beaches

Sunset Beach spans from Ehukai Beach (Banzai Pipeline) to Sunset Point, encompassing a dozen different reef breaks. This two-mile stretch of sand is considered one of the longest rideable surf spots in the world, and it's also a venue for the Vans Triple Crown of Surfing (November-December).

Waimea Bay Beach Park is notorious for producing monstrous winter waves, so it's one of the first places surfers began to ride big waves in the '50s. In the summer, the swells subside for great swimming and snorkeling. With full facilities, this is a popular beach for locals and visitors alike.

Ehukai Beach (Banzai Pipeline) is known for powerful waves that break over a sharp reef no more than a few feet from the surface. These massive tubes make this one of the most dangerous surf spots in the world and one of the venues for the Triple Crown of Surfing.

Haleiwa Alii Beach State Park is popular with surfers with waves that can reach over 25 feet in the winter months.

Haleiwa Beach Park has some of the calmer waters of the North Shore beaches.

Chun's Reef a great beach for all ages and features a freshwater pond which is perfect for keiki (children).

Ke Waena Beach is not as well-known as other North Shore beaches, but is largely popular with surfers and known for big waves during the winter that only professionals should attempt. Summer brings calmer waters for swimming.

Kawela Bay/Turtle Bay is located on Oahu's northeastern tip, past Haleiwa and near Kahuku. It's protected from large waves and surf, making it a great place to snorkel. You might even catch a glimpse of a honu (Hawaiian green sea turtle).

Windward Coast Beaches (Eastside)

Kualoa Regional Park is across from Kualoa Ranch. This beautiful beach park offers spectacular views down the east coast of Oahu as well as Mokolii, an islet off the Windward Coast.

Makapuu Beach Park is sea cliffs and is very popular with bodyboarders and bodysurfers alike. Around the corner is the Makapuu Lighthouse.

South Shore Beaches

Waikiki Beach is one of the most popular beaches in the world, boasting more than four million visitors every year and breathtaking views of Leahi (Diamond Head). The Duke Kahanamoku statue welcomes you to Waikiki, one of the best places in Hawaii to learn how to surf or paddle a canoe thanks to its small but long-lasting wave break. Waikiki is actually made up of a few beaches, including Fort DeRussy Beach to the west, Waikiki Beach (fronting the Royal Hawaiian Hotel and Westin Moana Surfrider), Kuhio Beach (along Kalakaua Avenue) and Queen Surf Beach, home to quieter stretches on the Diamond Head side of Waikiki.

Waikiki - Duke's Beach is named in honor of the Olympic swimmer, Duke Paoa Kahanamoku and is one of the smaller beach strips in Waikiki that makes up a larger beach.

Waikiki - Kuhio Beach is nick-named "Kuhio Ponds" as the beach is divided by two walls. This is a smaller beach strip in Waikiki that makes up a larger beach.

Waikiki - Queen's Surf Beach is popular among bodyboarders and surfers and is also a smaller strip of beach that makes up a larger Waikiki beach.

<u>Waikiki - Sans Souci/Kaimana Beach Park</u> is shallow and sandy and free of strong currents - perfect for families!

<u>Ala Moana Regional Park</u> is just minutes west from Waikiki. This half-mile beach is protected by a fringing reef for calm waters. Tables are available for picnics.

<u>Magic Island Lagoon</u> extends out from Ala Moana Regional Park beach, a manmade peninsula with large seawalls and a shallow lagoon, making it a perfect place for keiki (children) to swim.

Leeward Coast Beaches (Westside)

<u>Depot Beach Park</u> is a locals favorite with a wide stretch of white sand.

<u>Makaha Beach</u> has the best surfing on Oahu's west coast and is one of the places where big wave surfing was pioneered. Beware of the sloping sand beachhead that can cause backwash and catch unsuspecting visitors off-guard.

<u>Keawaula Beach (Yokohama Beach)</u> is the last sandy stretch on the <u>Leeward Coast</u>. Its curvy beach and turquoise waters are a great spot to sunbathe and watch surfers and dolphins. If you're an avid hiker, nearby Kaena Point offers a trail with rewarding ocean views.

Ko Olina Resort and Marina is where you'll find man-made lagoons created for the Ko Olina Resort, home to the J.W. Marriott Ihilani Resort & Spa and the Aulani, A Disney Resort & Spa. With parking, restrooms and showers available, this is a perfect beach for families.

Oahu Land Activities

Oahu's diverse tropical terrain, unmatched ocean views and wide range of activities will bring out your adventurous side. Hike to the top of the iconic volcanic crater Leahi (Diamond Head) for a panoramic view of Waikiki. Crisscross the picturesque countryside on horseback or on an all-terrain vehicle (ATV) at Kualoa Ranch. Play golf well into the evening on a long Hawaiian summer day. Stroll or run the popular paths of Ala Moana Beach Park, Kapiolani Park in Waikiki or the Diamond Head Loop from the Waikiki Bandstand to Leahi via Monsarrat Avenue. Whether you're hiking, biking, driving, golfing or riding, you can hit the ground running on your visit to Oahu. And, last, but definitely not least experience a luau during an evening celebrating Hawaiian and Polynesian traditions along with a feast of traditional foods like Kalua pig and *poi* (taro).

Local Culture

Farms Tours on Oahu

From Waialua to Waimanalo, farmland is nearly as abundant on Oahu as its beaches. The contemporary idea of "eating Hawaii" is actually grounded in our Native Hawaiian roots, and there are many ways you can experience it yourself.

Stop for a bite to eat at any of Oahu's trendy eateries and you're sure to see a note on the menu about locally grown products. Restaurants ranging from high-end bistros to cool hole-in-the wall dives proudly tout their farm-to-table ingredients, like Kahuku sweet corn, specialty cheeses from Naked Cow Dairies and fresh fish direct from the Honolulu Fish Auction.

Farmers markets have been around almost as long as farms themselves, and on the island of Oahu, they're more abundant than ever. Several times a week, in a variety of locations, food producers and local culinary stars gather in parks and parking lots to sell fresh produce and other agricultural products. It's the perfect opportunity for residents and visitors alike to enjoy locally grown Oahu products, including aqua-cultured seafood, North Shore beef, Manoa honey, Kahuku corn, Waialua chocolate and Waimanalo greens (that's just for starters).

You can also follow the farm-to-table process by strolling through Oahu's plantations, farms and gardens. Or drive to Oahu's North Shore and sample the fresh fruit at Kahuku Farms or savor Waialua Estate's award-winning chocolate.

Oahu Historic Places

Oahu was the home of the Hawaiian monarchy, the birthplace of modern and big-wave surfing and the tipping point in the United States involvement in World War II. Explore the historic places of Oahu and see why there's more to Hawaii than just sun, sand and surf.

Brief History of Oahu

From the Hawaiian monarchy to the attack on Pearl Harbor, an exploration of Oahu's history reflects the key influences that have impacted all of Hawaii. In 1795, King Kamehameha I led his forces in the legendary Battle of Nuuanu, which resulted in the conquering of Oahu and the eventual unification of the Hawaiian Islands under one rule in 1810.

Seven Hawaiian monarchs followed after Kamehameha the Great. King Kamehameha III (Kauikeaouli) permanently established the Hawaiian Kingdom's government on Oahu. Queen Liliuokalani was Hawaii's last reigning monarch after American colonists overthrew the Hawaiian Kingdom in a controversial coup in 1893. In 1898, Hawaii became a territory of the United States.

As agriculture boomed in the late 19th century, plantation owners found themselves in the midst of a labor shortage. Immigrants from Japan, China, Korea, Puerto Rico, Portugal, Russia and the Philippines arrived to work in the plantations. Today, this mix of ethnicities is the source of Hawaii's multicultural population. Visitors can step backward in time to explore this era at Waipahu's Plantation Village. You can also still see the smoke stack of the old Waialua Sugar Mill as you drive toward historic Haleiwa town.

Hawaii's visitor industry began to grow in the early 1900s. In 1901, the Moana Hotel opened on the beach in Waikiki. Today, the Westin Moana Surfrider is Hawaii's oldest resort still in operation. The <u>Aloha Tower</u> opened in 1926, and was the tallest building in Hawaii for four decades. It's now a historic Honolulu landmark and home to an outdoor shopping and dining marketplace. In 1927, the iconic Royal Hawaiian Hotel opened and was nicknamed the "Pink Palace."

On the morning of December 7, 1941, the Imperial Japanese Navy attacked Pearl Harbor pushing America into World War II. In 1959, Hawaii became the 50th state of the United States. Completed in 1969, the Hawaii State Capitol is located in Downtown Honolulu, behind <u>Iolani Palace</u>.

Oahu Heritage Sites
There are nine Heritage Sites of Hawaii on Oahu, serving as destinations that showcase significant historical, cultural and environmental contributions and encapsulate Native Hawaiian

customs, beliefs and practices.

Diamond Head (Leahi) State Monument

One of Hawaii's most recognized natural landmarks, you can hike to the top of the crater for panoramic views of Waikiki and Honolulu.

Pearl Harbor

Five Pearl Harbor Historic Sites honor this National Historic Landmark with amazing memorials and living museums. WWII Valor in the Pacific National Monument is where the attack of Pearl Harbor took place on December 7, 1941, marking the beginning of U.S. involvement in World War II.

Best known for the USS *Arizona* Memorial, there are four other Pearl Harbor Historic Sites to experience, including the Battleship *Missouri* Memorial, the USS *Bowfin* Submarine Museum & Park, the Pacific Aviation Museum and the USS *Oklahoma* Memorial.

Today, you can also walk in the footsteps of Hawaii's rich military past at locations throughout Oahu. In Waikiki, the U.S. Army Museum of Hawaii chronicles the history of warfare in Hawaii from King Kamehameha to today. Two of Waikiki's most historic hotels, the Moana Surfrider and the Royal Hawaiian Hotel were popular rest and recreation stops for soldiers during WWII. Even iconic Leahi (Diamond

Head) was used for the coastal defense of Oahu. A total of five military batteries were built atop Diamond Head State Monument between 1910 and 1943, the remains of which are still visible.

National Memorial Cemetery of the Pacific

Located at Punchbowl Crater, this is one of the nation's most prominent national cemeteries, with more than 49,000 internments including more than 13,000 soldiers and sailors who died during World War II. Over 5 million visitors come to pay their respects here each year. The memorial lookouts also offer panoramic views of Honolulu.

Iolani Palace State Monument

King Kalakaua, also known as the Merrie Monarch, built the majestic Iolani Palace in Downtown Honolulu. Dedicated in 1882, it is the only official state residence of royalty in the United States. The palace's grounds and galleries are now open to the public as a museum. The iconic King Kamehameha I statue stands just across the street.

Nuuanu Pali State Wayside (Pali Lookout)

Overlooking the lush Windward Coast and the majestic Koolau mountain range, the Nuuanu Pali Lookout was the site of the Battle of Nuuanu. It was here, high atop these sheer cliffs, that King Kamehameha I won a decisive battle that helped him conquer the island of Oahu.

Ka Iwi State Scenic Shoreline (Makapuu Trail)

Hike the one-mile **Makapuu Point Lighthouse Trail** to this scenic point on Oahu's eastern-most tip for incredible views and whale watching during the winter.

Queen Emma Summer Palace

Known as Hanaiakamalama, the summer retreat in the Nuuanu Valley of Queen Emma wife of King Kamehameha IV is now a museum that houses a collection of her belongings, furnishings and artifacts.

Bishop Museum

The premier natural and cultural history institution in the Pacific region, Bishop Museum is known through the world for its research projects, public education programs and cultural exhibits including a unique and unparalleled collection of Hawaii cultural artifacts.

Washington Place

Most commonly known as the home of Queen Liliuokalani, Hawaii's last reigning monarch, this storied mansion sits in Downtown Honolulu in the heart of the Hawaii Capital Historic District and is a registered National Historic Landmark.

Nearby, you'll find modern landmarks like the Hawaii State Capitol and

Honolulu Hale, home to the city council and mayor's office. Just east of Kawaiahao Church, the Hawaiian Mission Houses Museum displays three missionary homes built in New England and shipped to Oahu.

Hula on Oahu

Hula is a uniquely Hawaiian dance accompanied by chant or song that preserves and perpetuates the stories, traditions and culture of Hawaii. You can see hula throughout Oahu at live performances at hotels and resorts and seasonal festivals and competitions like the King Kamehameha Hula Competition (June), the Prince Lot Hula Festival (July) and the World Invitational Hula Festival (November). The Kuhio Beach Hula Show by Hawaii's finest *halau hula* (hula school) and Hawaiian performers is held every Tuesday, Thursday and Saturday (weather-permitting) from 6:30 pm to 7:30 pm (6 pm to 7 pm Nov. Jan.) at the Kuhio Beach Hula mound on Kalakaua Avenue. This is a free event to the public!

A luau is another fun and festive place to watch the hula and learn about Hawaiian and Polynesian culture. Fantastic luau venues can be found throughout Oahu including the Alii Luau at the Polynesian Cultural Center on the North Shore, the Paradise Cove Luau in the Ko Olina area of the Leeward Side of Oahu, and the Royal Luau at the Royal Hawaiian Hotel, one of many luau events in Waikiki.

Hula is taught by a *kumu hula* (hula teacher) in a *halau hula* but visitors can get free lessons at select Oahu hotels and resorts and places like the Royal Hawaiian Center.

Hula in the Hawaiian Islands

Hula is Life
More than just a dance, more than just a way of life... Hula is life itself.

History of Hula in Hawaii
In ancient Hawaii, a time when a written language did not exist, hula and its chants played an important role in keeping history, genealogy, mythology and culture alive. With each movement a hand gesture, step of foot, swaying of hips a story would unfold. Through the hula, the Native Hawaiians were connected with their land and their gods.

Before the arrival of Western missionaries, the hula was danced for protocol and social enjoyment. The songs and chants of the hula preserved Hawaii's history and culture. Many believe hula was born on the island of Molokai, but other legends tell of hula originating on Kauai. For many years following the arrival of missionaries, the hula as well as the Hawaiian language and music were suppressed. The hula, specifically, was even outlawed. It wasn't until King David Kalakaua came to the throne in 1874 that Hawaiian cultural traditions were restored. Public performances of hula flourished and by the early 1900s, the hula had evolved with modern times.

Today, this unique art form, deeply rooted in culture, has become a worldwide symbol of Hawaiian culture, and one that you can experience on your trip to the islands.

The Art of Hula

There are two types of hula *Hula Kahiko* and *Hula Auana*.

Hula Kahiko is the traditional or ancient style of hula tied to hula lineage with motions, voice and choreography that comes from an old place, patterned after ancient hula. It can also be ancient hula still being danced today. This unique style of hula is performed to chants and is accompanied by percussion instruments such as the *pahu* or *ipu* (different types of drums). Hula Kahiko requires much training and dedication and is regarded as being a dance of spiritual connection to ancient Hawaii.

Hula Auana is the modern style of hula, usually coming from a school of hula that has a genealogy, but with new choreography and music. Influenced by contemporary times but with old knowledge, this style of hula is accompanied by modern instruments such as the ukulele, guitar, steel guitar, bass or piano.

Where Can I See Hula?

You can see hula throughout the Islands at a number of festivals and events as well as at hotels and resorts. If you want to see the best of the best in hula, head to Hilo on the island of Hawaii in the spring for the Merrie Monarch Festival. Dedicated to King David Kalakaua, known as the Merrie Monarch, the week-long festival features the world's premier hula competition and includes art exhibits, craft fairs, demonstrations, performances and a parade. Tickets for the festival can be tough to get so planning ahead is suggested.

The Prince Lot Hula Festival (July), as well as the Kauai Mokihana Festival (September) also showcase hula. Molokai, which is especially proud of its hula traditions, celebrates the artform every May at the Molokai Ka Hula Piko Festival.

Museums of Oahu
Oahu is home to some of Hawaii's largest and most extensive museums and collections featuring art, artifacts and heirlooms from Hawaii and the Pacific.

Explore these Oahu museums:
Bishop Museum
Hawaii's museum of natural and cultural history, the Bishop Museum was originally designed to house the extensive collection of Hawaiian artifacts and royal family heirlooms of Princess Bernice Pauahi Bishop. The Museum has since expanded to include millions of artifacts,

documents and photos about Hawaii and other Pacific cultures. Daily programs allow visitors to discover more about Hawaiian and Polynesian cultures through live, interactive presentations and exhibit tours.

Hawaii State Art Museum (HISAM)

Located in Downtown Honolulu across the street from the Iolani Palace and State Capitol, the Hawaii State Art Museum Hawaii (HISAM) is dedicated to exhibiting and interpreting the art and culture of Hawaii. Through Enriched by Diversity, a semi-permanent installation reflecting Hawaii's rich ethnic and cultural traditions, as well as a dynamic changing exhibition program, the museum honors and inspires artistic excellence and promotes educational enrichment. Located in the historic No. 1 Capitol District Building, a Spanish-Mission style structure built in 1928, the museum is comprised of three spacious galleries, an outdoor tiled lanai, a 70-seat multi-purpose room and a volunteer resource center: WWW.HAWAII.GOV/SFCA

Honolulu Museum of Art

Located near Downtown Honolulu, the Honolulu Museum of Art (formerly known as the Honolulu Academy of Arts) was chartered in 1922 by Mrs. Charles Montague Cook (Anna Rice), who desired to share her love for the arts with the children of Hawaii. Since the doors opened on April 8, 1927, the Museum has steadily grown to become Hawaii's largest private presenter of visual arts programs, boasting a permanent collection of over 38,000 works of art from cultures around the world. From the Museum of Art you can also take a tour of Shangri La, one of Hawaii's most architecturally significant homes. you can also take a tour of Shangri La, one of Hawaii's most architecturally significant homes.

Honolulu Museum of Art   Spalding House

Visit Oahu's Honolulu Museum of Art   Spalding House (formerly known as the Contemporary Museum) for a stimulating look at the Museum's outstanding art collection and a light lunch at its gourmet cafe. The dramatic Mount Tantalus serves as the backdrop for the Museum's artist gardens and outdoor exhibits of contemporary art.

Iolani Palace

Located in Downtown Honolulu and one of Hawaii's most historic places, Iolani Palace is the only the only official state residence of royalty on U.S. soil. Journey through the times of happiness and tragedy of King Kalakaua and Queen Liliuokalani as you view their two-story American Florentine style palace.

Hawaiian Mission Houses Historic Site and Archives

Nearby Iolani Palace, take an escorted historical walking tour into the life and work of the Protestant missionaries who settled in Hawaii in 1820. Hawaiian Mission Houses Historic Site and Archives displays three original frame homes that were built in New England and shipped to Hawaii to house the missionaries. Nearby you'll see the island's original schoolhouse and the printing house where the first alphabet book and Hawaiian hymnal were printed.

Queen Emma Summer Palace

Located on the drive to the Nuuanu Pali Lookout, visit the secluded summer retreat of Queen Emma, King Kamehameha IV and their son, Prince Albert. Following the tragic death of the 4-year old prince in 1862 and the king in 1863, Hawaii's Queen lived a life of mourning at the Palace. Inside the Queen Emma Summer Palace you can find royal antiques and furnishings stand in their original places, including the koa wood cradle of Prince Albert and gifts from his Godmother, Queen Victoria.

Hawaii Plantation Village

Located in Central Oahu, escape the present day and explore Oahu's plantation heritage and culture at the Hawaii Plantation Village in Waipahu. You'll learn how more than 400,000 immigrants who arrived between 1852 and 1947 to work on Oahu's plantations actually shaped Hawaii into the vibrant multiethnic community it is today.

Explore a sugar plantation village and botanical garden featuring historic homes and plants reflecting the cultural diversity of the islands.

Pearl Harbor

Named for the pearl oysters once harvested there, Pearl Harbor, located in the Ewa District of Central Oahu, is the largest natural harbor in Hawaii and the only naval base in the United States to be designated a National Historical Landmark. Explore the living museums of one of Oahu's most well known landmarks at the Pacific Historic Parks, the USS *Arizona* Memoria, the Battleship *Missouri* Memorial, the USS *Bowfin*Submarine Museum & Park, the Pacific Aviation Museum and the USS *Oklahoma* Memorial.

Hula on Oahu

Hula is a uniquely Hawaiian dance accompanied by chant or song that preserves and perpetuates the stories, traditions and culture of Hawaii. You can see hula throughout Oahu at live performances at hotels and resorts and seasonal festivals and competitions like the King Kamehameha Hula Competition (June), the Prince Lot Hula Festival (July) and the World Invitational Hula Festival (November). The Kuhio Beach Hula Show by Hawaii's finest *halau hula* (hula school) and Hawaiian performers is held every Tuesday, Thursday and Saturday (weather-permitting) from 6:30 pm to 7:30 pm (6 pm to 7 pm Nov. Jan.) at the Kuhio Beach Hula mound on Kalakaua Avenue. This is a free event to the public!

A luau is another fun and festive place to watch the hula and learn about Hawaiian and Polynesian culture. Fantastic luau venues can be found throughout Oahu including the Alii Luau at the Polynesian Cultural Center on the North Shore, the Paradise Cove Luau in the Ko Olina area of the Leeward Side of Oahu, and the Royal Luau at the Royal Hawaiian Hotel, one of many luau events in Waikiki.

Hula is taught by a *kumu hula* (hula teacher) in a *halau hula* but visitors can get free lessons at select Oahu hotels and resorts and places like the Royal Hawaiian Center.

Get Outdoors
Hiking on Oahu
Take a hike on Oahu and reward yourself with panoramic ocean views and lush mountain scenery. One of Oahu's most famous landmarks and most accessible hikes is up the slopes of Leahi (Diamond Head). Just minutes from Waikiki, this moderately challenging trail includes two sets of stairs as well as dark tunnels and old military bunkers that open out to stunning panoramic vistas of the Pacific Ocean and Honolulu.

On the eastern tip of Oahu is the Makapuu Lighthouse Trail, which features breathtaking views of the indigo Pacific Ocean and whale watching in winter months. For a more off-the-beaten-path hike, travel to the western tip of the island to Kaena Point. This sacred area offers a dramatic lava shoreline and views of the Waianae coast. For a lush hike not far from Waikiki, take a short drive to Manoa Valley and hike through beautiful rainforests full of bamboo trees and native flora, ending at a beautiful Manoa Falls. In Central Oahu, the challenging Aiea Loop Trail offers phenomenal views of Halawa Valley and the majestic Koolau mountains.

Enjoy a leisurely afternoon stroll with a Botanical Collections Specialist as they take you on a journey through Waimea Valley on the North Shore, highlighting beautiful blooming plants and fruits along the way. This walk is offered on Thursdays at 12:00pm starting at the ticket booth. Discover stunning views as guides help you identify native and exotic plants, showcase the valley's indigenous birds and lead you to various streams including the beautiful Waimea Waterfall. Back in Honolulu, venture to lush Makiki and go on a tropical forest hike at the Hawaii Nature Center. See and learn about some of the most varied tropical plant life in the Islands as you and your guide trek along this moderate loop hike.

Horseback Riding on Oahu

On the Windward side of the island, you'll find one of Hawaii's most seen but least recognized locations: Kualoa Ranch. A generations-old family-owned ranch, its scenic valley has provided the backdrop for countless movies and TV shows, including LOST and Hawaii Five-O. Fortunately, it's not just for the stars. Visitors and locals alike enjoy horseback riding and host of other activities there. You'll discover some of the island's most breathtaking scenery on a day's adventure here.

Oahu Golf
The Koolau mountains tower in your sightline. Palm trees line the green. The white of your golf ball pops against the deep blue sky. Even a bad game of golf on Oahu is still pretty darn good.

With more golf courses than any other island, golfers of every skill level from around the world head to Oahu. Choose from 40 public and private courses, ranging from casual municipal links to elegant resort courses. Spectacular scenery awaits you no matter which course you choose. If you prefer to watch the pros play, Oahu hosts the PGA TOUR's Sony Open at the Waialae Country Club every January.

You may also want to make a few adjustments to your game in the islands. Most notably, Hawaii's trade winds can exaggerate mistakes in your swing on a windy day. Luckily, most Oahu courses have wide, forgiving fairways. Bermuda greens can also be harder to read than traditional bentgrass greens. All these factors help make for some fun and challenging rounds on the golfer's heaven of Oahu.

Royal Hawaiian Golf Club

Daily Fee Golf Course just 20 minutes from Waikiki. Designed by Perry Dye includes a fully stocked pro shop as well as a venue for your golf event, wedding, meeting or any special occasion. We offer attractive locations, exquisite cuisine & excellent service.

770 Auloa Road Kailua, HI 96734

Local Phone: (808) 262-2139

Email: gyamamoto@royalhawaiiangc.com

Island: Oahu

At Royal Hawaiian, legendary Pete Dye and his son Perry have integrated crafty golf holes into tumbling terrain framed by ancient jungle trees upwards up of 100 feet tall at the foot of the Ko'olau Mountains in Oahu. The back nine builds to an exciting finish as it winds through leafy corridors to fast bentgrass greens; players are presented with tantalizing risk-reward scenarios, exemplified by the 386-yard par-four 6th and the 218-yard par-3 7th. With the lush tropical surroundings and few signs of civilization, locals refer to Royal Hawaiian as Jurassic Park, and it's a hit with most everyone who plays it.

Ko Olina Golf Club

Ko Olina Golf Club is recognized as one of the top resort courses in the US with an award winning golf shop and spectacular water features, generous fairways and challenging greens.

92-1220 Aliinui Dr Kapolei, HI 96707

Local Phone: (808) 676-5300

US Toll Free: (808) 686-9050

Email: chris.domaloan@koolina.com

Island: Oahu

Ko Olina Golf Club, designed by renown architect Ted Robinson, offers an experience for all with spectacular water features, generous fairways and challenging greens. Ko Olina Golf Club has hosted Champions Tour and LPGA events, including the LPGA LOTTE Championship from 2012 - 2014.

The Ko Olina Golf Club is home to a world-class golf academy and helps golfers of all skill levels learn to play the game better. Practice facilities include an all-grass driving range, putting greens, the finest short game practice area on the island along with an award winning golf shop, ProLink hands-free GPS system with yardage, scoring and food & beverage ordering capabilities. The locker rooms are equipped with full size lockers, showers, steam room, and Jacuzzi.

Known as the "Best 19th Hole in Hawaii", Roy's Ko Olina provides Hawaiian Fusion Cuisine using fresh local ingredients with European sauces and bold Asian spices. Roy's Ko Olina is open for lunch and dinner.

Turtle Bay Golf

Turtle Bay is situated along acres of majestic coastline on Oahu's North Shore. Though the area is primarily known for its spectacular surf, two legends of golf - Arnold Palmer and George Fazio - have boldly chosen to leave their indelible mark as well. With 36 holes of championship golf, two complete practice facilities with professional instruction, and a restaurant as identifiable with North Shore surf culture as Pipeline itself (Lei Lei's), Turtle Bay beckons you.

57-049 Kuilima Drive Kahuku, HI 96731

Local Phone: (808) 293-8574

Email: golfshop@turtlebaygolf.com

Island: Oahu

Turtle Bay is situated along acres of majestic coastline on Oahu's North Shore. Though the area is primarily known for its spectacular surf, two legends of golf - Arnold Palmer and George Fazio - have boldly chosen to leave their indelible mark as well. With 36 holes of championship golf, two complete practice facilities with professional instruction, and a restaurant as identifiable with North Shore surf culture as Pipeline itself (Lei Lei's), Turtle Bay beckons you.

From Golf Digest to the Champions Tour to the LPGA Tour to Golf Channel's The Big Break, those who make their living seeking out the world's best golf destinations have consistently chosen Turtle Bay. The Palmer Course Consistently regarded as the best course on Oahu (and among the very best on all the islands), the Arnold Palmer Course is an absolute must-play. Set along the fabled North Shore, the course is consistently ranked among the best courses in Hawaii by Golf Digest and Golf Week. The George Fazio Course

The original course on property and is generally more forgiving than the Palmer Course. The design meanders among traditional Hawaiian Palms while skirting the North Shore coast on numerous occasions. The Fazio Course is an experience well worth having, and for those enjoying multiple days at the resort, a great complement to the Palmer experience. Following are the essential terms of HVCB membership. Please review these terms carefully.

By clicking the checkbox below and obtaining or renewing HVCB membership, you agree to be bound by these terms. "You" refers to the company or individual completing this form and seeking or renewing HVCB membership. "HVCB" refers to the Hawaii Visitors & Convention Bureau and its island chapters, the Oahu Visitors Bureau, Maui Visitors Bureau, Island of Hawaii Visitors Bureau, and Kauai Visitors Bureau.

Oahu Parks & Gardens

Discover the colorful flowers and tropical plant life of Oahu's various botanical gardens. The Honolulu Botanical Gardens feature five diverse sites including the Foster Botanical Garden near Downtown Honolulu and the 400-acre Hoomaluhia Botanical Garden on the lush Windward Coast. The Waimea Valley on the North Shore not only offers gardens to explore, but also allows you and your family to experience Hawaiian games and crafts.

Learn about Hawaii's farm-to-table process which is so important to Hawaii Regional Cuisine by taking a farm tour of places like Kahuku Farms. Visit Dole Plantation for a taste of some fresh pineapple and learn about Jim Dole's pineapple legacy in Hawaii. While you're there, lose yourself in the plantation's 1.7-mile pineapple maze.

Kahuku Farms

Take a Fun Filled Wagon Ride through one of Oahu's most Beautiful Farms and learn about the history, people and crops of this special place! Visit our Farm Café for Fine Country Gifts, Fresh Island Fruit and Tasty Treats from our Fields!

56-800 Kamehameha Hwy Kahuku, HI 96831

Local Phone: (808) 628-0639

Email: reservations@kahukufarms.com

Island: Oahu

Take a Fun Filled Wagon Ride through one of Oahu's most Beautiful Farms and learn about the history, people and crops of this special place! Visit our Farm Café for Fine Country Gifts, Fresh Island Fruit and Tasty Treats from our Fields! Our Menu offers Farm-Harvested Vanilla Bean Ice Cream, Tangy Lilikoi Sorbet, Fresh Fruit Smoothies, Wholesome Farm Fresh Soup, Salads, Panini and Pizza. Take Home a jar of our Home-Made Lilikoi Butter and Pineapple Papaya Jam.

Waimea Valley

This beautiful treasure is rich in Hawaiian history and cultural sites, nestled in a stunning botanical garden. Experience more than 5,000 botanicals along a paved path to the 45-foot waterfall. Along the way there are cultural practitioners and artisans sharing various native Hawaiian practices.

Waimea Valley Road Haleiwa, HI 96712

Local Phone: (808) 638-7766

Email: rpezzulo@waimeavalley.net

Island: Oahu

Located on Wamiea Valley Road, across from Waimea Bay, this beautiful treasure is rich in Hawaiian history and cultural sites, nestled in a stunning botanical garden. Experience more than 5,000 botanicals along a paved path to the 45-foot waterfall. Along the way there are cultural practitioners and artisans sharing various native Hawaiian practices. Waimea Valley is a lush 1,875 acre privately owned property and a non-profit organization. Open daily 9am to 5pm from September to May and 9am to 5:30pm in the summer.

Relax and Unwind
Spa & Wellness
Rejuvenation & Relaxation on Oahu

World-class spas can be found throughout Oahu, most in the resorts of Waikiki or at business in and around Honolulu. Oahu's unique spa services offer rejuvenating treatments found only in the islands. Succumb to the rhythmic strokes of a *lomilomi* massage. Add heated *pohaku* (stones) to relieve sore muscles. Renew your skin with a facial using unique local ingredients like papaya, *ti* leaf, honey ginger and *poi*, helping to stimulate and increase circulation.

Soothing weather and therapeutic surroundings also make Oahu a place to rejuvenate the spirit as well. Take a yoga class or go on an outdoor retreat. Discover holistic medicine and acupuncture. Explore natural and organic products that stimulate wellness and good health. Make your visit to Oahu more than a vacation make it a time to heal your body, mind and spirit.

Still & Moving Center

Still & Moving Center is the most comprehensive mind body movement center in Honolulu. An international training facility, we offer corporate or private, wellness & Hawaiian cultural packages and retreats, movement classes/workshops/performers, personalized coaching and bodywork services.

1024 Queen St. Honolulu, HI 96814

Local Phone: (808) 397-7678

Email: info@stillandmovingcenter.com

Island: Oahu

Still & Moving Center is a local and global hub for mindful movement. An international training facility, the Center offers corporate wellness and retreat programs for groups, wellness and cultural activities packages for individuals, mind-body movement classes and workshops, as well as personalized coaching and treatment services both onsite, in a beautiful, fully equipped, 6,000 square foot, two-story facility in the heart of Kakaako, downtown Honolulu, as well as offsite in a location of your choice.

Focused on wellness arts and cultivating the rich cultural and educational exchanges that occur in retreat settings, the Center provides immersive experiences in various movement forms. Traditional practices are offered, honored and enjoyed authentically through the expertise of our in-house Kumu Hula, Malia Helela. The Center hosts talented master teachers from across the globe as they share their expertise while their students experience the true aloha of Hawaii. Still & Moving Center has a solid and varied roster of movement and wellness practitioners that can meet every need and inspire healthy sustainable practices for all levels. Our other offerings include massage, a boutique, gorgeous rental rooms and performance space, as well as the services of entertainment, therapists, lecturers and teachers for parties or corporate events.

Waikiki Massage and Foot Spa LLC
Waikiki Massage and Foot Spa offers various massage techniques from our massage therapists trained in Thailand & Hawaii. If you're looking for a healing & relaxing therapeutic massage in a pleasant, comfortable atmosphere, please visit us. We're located steps away from the Hilton Hawaiian Village.

1920 Ala Moana Blvd. #106, Honolulu, HI 96815
Local Phone: (808) 291-9265
Email: waikikimassageandfootspa@gmail.com
Island: Oahu

Waikiki Massage and Foot Spa offers various massage techniques from our massage therapists who are trained in Thailand and Hawaii. If you're looking for a healing and relaxing therapeutic massage in a pleasant, comfortable atmosphere, please visit us at Waikiki Massage and Foot Spa located steps away from the Hilton Hawaiian Village.

Spa Pure Corp.
A luxurious boutique day spa with amazingly unique services: floating massages in a salt pool, granite-saunas with herbal steam domes

anchor our 2.5 hour couples special. For skin care, we feature Phytoceane products for their proven benefits and safety. Open daily, Courtyard by Waikiki Beach Hotel.

400 Royal Hawaiian Avenue. Honolulu, HI 96815

Local Phone: (808) 924-3200

Email: spawaikiki@gmail.com

Island: Oahu

A luxurious, boutique day spa feature amazingly unique services: floating massages in a warm salt pool, personal granite-saunas with herbal steam domes anchor our 2.5 hour couples special. For skin care, we choose to feature Phytoceane products for their proven benefits and safety. Open daily in the Courtyard by Waikiki Beach Hotel.

All our massages are performed on sheets so soft they induce sighs, using massage oils handmade with farm-fresh ingredients from Hilo. And all massages can be tailored to your needs.

Please feel free to discuss your health and massage goals with your therapist. Choose any of the following or a combination of techniques. A pure relaxation massage? With pleasure. Deep-tissue work on your neck and shoulders, followed by a sports massage? No problem.

Swedish

Shiatsu

Lomi Lomi Massage

Sports Massage

Pregnancy Massage

Reflexology

Foot Massage

Just Perfect Massage

Four Hands Massage

Massages for Spa Connoisseurs

For those accustomed to conventional massages, Spa Pure has connoisseur-level offerings that go beyond the traditional spa repertoire.

Rhythm into Space

Now That's What I Was Looking For

Salt & Pepper

Spa for Couples

Deluxe Pair Special

Couples Soak Tub

Spa Party for 8

Ocean Massage

Simple Pleasure

Water to Land

Around the World in 90 Minutes

Around the World in 2 Hours

Facials & Skin Treatments

Head-to-toe package of massage, facial and skin treatments that will leave you relaxed and revitalized from the inside out.

Spa Pure Facial
Beautiful Body, Beautiful Face
Skin Care Extravaganza
Intense Seaweed Anti-Aging
Intense Seaweed Skin Therapy
Ganban Yoku, wrap, & facial.

Body Scrubs, Masks, & Wraps

Luxuriant full-body treatments that cleanse, hydrate and rejuvenate your skin with healing oils, vitamins, minerals and other natural compounds.

Body scrubs come in your choice of sweet or savory and feature Ola products handmade with pure, fresh ingredients grown in the lush volcanic soils on the Hilo side of the Big Island. Choose from a range including tropical passion fruit, coconut, cane sugar and pineapple, or mineral-rich natural sea salts with soothing kukui nut oil. All Spa Pure body scrubs are thorough and gentle.

Body masks and wraps feature your choice of Ola products, created from healing plant extracts and tropical oils from the Big Island, or Phytoceane's Deep Sea Mud Mask, made with potent compounds extracted from the ancient seabed off Brittany.

The Spa at the Modern Honolulu

The Spa at THE MODERN HONOLULU offers massage, body treatments and facials including signatures from advanced-technology oxygen infusions to the ancient Polynesian tradition of Lomi Lomi Massage in addition to nail and waxing services.

1775 Ala Moana Boulevard. Honolulu, HI 96815

Local Phone: (808) 450-3379

Email: spa@themodernhonolulu.com

Island: Oahu

The Spa at THE MODERN HONOLULU offers massage, body treatments and facials including signatures from advanced-technology oxygen infusions to the ancient Polynesian tradition of Lomi Lomi Massage in addition to nail and waxing services. We've developed our Waikiki spa services around some of the purest and most exclusive products in the world, including Ola for body treatments and Éminence Organic Skin Care for facials. Both lines are natural, organic, hand-crafted and sustainably developed. Ola's tropical ingredients are grown, and its end products hand-crafted, on the Big Island of Hawaii.

Na Ho'ola Spa

10,000 square-foot, full-service spa with gorgeous ocean and mountain views. Facials, massages, body treatments, body wraps, waxing and wedding services available.

2424 Kalakaua Ave. Honolulu, HI 96815

Local Phone: (808) 237-6330

US Toll Free: (800) 233-1234

Email: nahoolaspahnlrw@hyatt.com

Island: Oahu

10,000 square-foot, full-service spa with gorgeous ocean and mountain views. Facials, massages, body treatments, body wraps, waxing and wedding services available.

Spa Suites at the Kahala Hotel & Resort

ESPA has created a unique treatment concept which merges philosophies & techniques from around the world, embracing Hawaiian culture & traditional therapies using the highest quality organically grown plants. MAE 2110

5000 Kahala Ave. Honolulu, HI 96816

Local Phone: (808) 739-8938

Email: spa@kahalaresort.com

Island: Oahu

Recognized as AAA Five Diamond 2004 resort and renowned for having the "Best Rooms in the U.S." by Conde Nast Traveler, the beachfront Kahala Hotel & Resort evokes Hawaii's nostalgic era of timeless elegance.

From exotic Hawaiian interiors to its verdant tropical gardens, the 364-room resort offers direct beach access and features panoramic views of the Pacific Ocean, Diamond Head Crater, Ko'olau Mountain Range and a private lagoon with five resident Atlantic Bottlenose dolphins.

A mere 10 minutes away from Waikiki, the resort offers guests a multitude of innovative dining concepts and five exclusive Spa Suites that were voted "Best New Hotel Spa" by Departures magazine in 2003. MAE 2110

Moana Lani Spa
This is a tranquil place where Hawaiian healing traditions and innovative spa rituals inspire the spirit and become one. A spa blessed with history, whose home is the First Lady of Waikiki, the Moana Surfrider, A Westin Resort & Spa.

2365 Kalakaua Avenue. Honolulu, HI 96815
Local Phone: (808) 237-2535
Email: moanalanispa@westin.com
Island: Oahu

Moana Lani Spa, a place where the ocean, heaven and healing meet. This is a tranquil place where Hawaiian healing traditions and innovative spa rituals inspire the spirit and become one. A spa blessed with history, whose home is the First Lady of Waikiki, the Moana Surfrider, A Westin Resort & Spa. Enjoy our peaceful and private men's and women's relaxation lounges overlooking Waikiki beach, separate men's and women's steam rooms, dry saunas and water therapy areas. For the ultimate couple's renewal, Moana Lani Spa has two beautiful oceanfront suites, that cater to those wishing to savor these exquisite moments as a pair.

Ranked one of the Top 100 Spas by Spas of America, named the Readers Choice for Best Spa by Honolulu Magazine and America's 2012 Top 100 spas by spAWARDS.

Arts & Culture
Oahu Arts & Culture

Oahu is home to many art museums and galleries, and Honolulu is the epicenter of Hawaii's art scene, both past and present. The Hawaii State Art Museum (HISAM) and the Honolulu Museum of Art both house extensive collections exhibiting and interpreting the art and culture of Hawaii. Alongside works from the 19th and 20th centuries, you'll find collections of traditional Hawaiian handicrafts, including *kapa* (cloth made from beaten bark), *umeke* (wooden bowls), feather capes and quilts, as well as paintings from the Volcano School (depicting nighttime scenes of Hawaii's volcanoes, most from the late 1800s).

The Bishop Museum boasts millions of artifacts, documents and photographs about Hawaii and other Polynesian cultures, as well as an extensive collection of Hawaiian royal family heirlooms.

Today, the Honolulu neighborhood of Kakaako is ground zero for Hawaii's contemporary art explosion, with colorful murals by global artists that have turned the streets a living gallery. Music, dance, theatre and the arts in general are community treasures on Oahu. Artists and makers from around the world intersect with locals still perpetuating Hawaiian traditions and customs. And while the people of Oahu blend the rich legacy of Hawaiian culture with the world of the 21st century, you'll find the spirit of aloha remains as timeless as ever in the Heart of Hawaii.

Art on the Zoo Fence
Visit us in beautiful Waikiki and discover the richness of Hawaii through the eyes of a variety of artists. The artists will personally introduce you to their work in the splendor of this outdoor tropical setting.

2760 Monsarrat Ave. Along the Honolulu Zoo Fence. Honolulu, HI 96815

Island: Oahu

Since 1953 Art On The Zoo Fence has been one of Hawaii's lasting treasures. Artists personally present their wide variety of art styles in both original works and prints. You can find oils, acrylics, watercolors and photography. Artists participating in Art On The Zoo Fence also contribute to a non profit group called Zoo Fence Artists, which annually donates funds to promote arts education for children.

Every Saturday and Sunday year round, from 9 a.m. to 4 p.m., Art On The Zoo Fence artists present their artwork for viewing and sale in Waikiki along the Honolulu Zoo fence on Monsarrat Avenue, across from the bandstand at Kapiolani Park. We are within view of the Pacific Ocean, in the shade of lovely Banyan trees and within walking distance of Waikiki hotels.

The artists will personally introduce you to their work in the splendor of this outdoor tropical setting. Aloha, and please visit us soon. Featured painting of artists on the zoo fence courtesy Poor Lydia.

Honolulu Museum of Art
Honolulu's culture hub featuring a world-class art collection, theater, cafés, shop, art classes, and art research library on three historic properties.

900 S. Beretania Street. Honolulu, HI 96814-1495
Local Phone: (808) 532-8700

Email: frontdesk@honolulumuseum.org

Island: Oahu

One of the world's premier art museums, the Honolulu Museum of Art presents international caliber special exhibitions and features a collection that includes Hokusai, van Gogh, Gauguin, Monet, Picasso and Warhol, as well as traditional Asian and Hawaiian art. Located in two of Honolulu's most beautiful buildings, visitors enjoy two cafés, gardens, and films and concerts at the theater. Tuesday-Saturday 10am-4:30pm; Sunday 1-5pm. $10 general admission; $5 students, military and seniors; children 12 and under free. FREE DAYS: First Wednesday and third Sunday of every month. Special features: Theater, Cafes, Shop, Robert Allerton Art Research Library, Art School.

Hawaiian Mission Houses Historic Site and Archives
DISCOVERY: In three historic buildings guests can see and feel the dramatic changes the New England Missionaries brought to Hawaii starting in 1820.

553 S. King Street. Honolulu, HI 96813

Local Phone: (808) 447-3910

Email: info@missionhouses.org

Island: Oahu

DISCOVERY: In three historic buildings guests can see and feel the dramatic changes the New England Missionaries brought to Hawaii starting in 1820.

Visitors discover how a small group of New England missionaries who came to the islands in 1820 worked with the Native Hawaiians to introduce Christianity, to develop a written language, public education, western medicine and representative government.

Tours at 11:00 a.m., 12:00 p.m., 1:00 p.m., 2:00 p.m., and last tour at 3:00 p.m. Tuesday Saturday. General Admission $10, Seniors, Military, Kamaʻaina $8, Students (6-college) $6.

Mahinalani Gift Shop at the Polynesian Cultural Center
In the Polynesian Cultural Center is our Mahinalani Gift Shop, displaying the finest traditional arts and crafts from Samoa, New Zealand, Marquesas, Fiji, Tonga, Tahiti, and the Hawaiian Islands. Take with you a piece of Polynesia.

55-370 Kamehameha Hwy. Laie, HI 96762

Local Phone: (808) 293-3058

Email: internetrez@polynesia.com

Island: Oahu

The Mahinalani Gift Shop is part of the Polynesian Cultural Center's new shopping experience. Come and take a piece of ancient Polynesian culture home with you. Also, visit us at shop.Polynesia.com and have it sent straight to your home. The store has great gift items including fine jewelry and high-end Hawaiian-style apparel by Tommy Bahama. In addition, Mahinalani offers souvenir caps and t-shirts for men, women, and children. As well as items such as key chains, pencils, and mugs to remind visitors of their island experience. Located on the way to the Polynesian Cultural Center's island villages, you can also pick up snack items and suntan lotion to help start and sustain your day of exploration. The Polynesian Cultural Center is open Monday through Saturday from 11:45 a.m. to 9 p.m.

Malama Loko Ea Foundation
Loko Ea is a 400-year-old fishpond in heart of Haleiwa. The Holole'a tour is a cultural based experience where you and your families can participate in activities that include fishing, a walking tour, and a chance to give back to the land through restoration of the pond. Mahalo nui for your support.

P.O.Box 553. 62-540 Kamehameha Hwy. Haleiwa, HI 96712
Local Phone: (808) 637-3232
Email: info@hololeatours.com
Island: Oahu

Loko Ea is indeed an ancestral place of importance, a significant Wahi Pana, or celebrated place, to the people of Waialua. The site is associated with ancient deities, cultural practices, and historical events. This fishpond once helped to sustain its community by providing aquatic food resources like native fish and seaweed. Overtime the fishpond has been neglected, but today, Loko Ea is on a path to restoration with the help of the Mālama Loko Ea Foundation and the community. Your visit to Loko Ea will directly support the education and restoration efforts of the organization. Our goal is to someday be able to feed our communities once again from the abundance of the land.

The activities included in the Holole'a tour is a walking tour that will educate you on the various aspects of Loko Ea fishpond and look in to the complex history of fishponds in Hawaii. Your tour will also include bamboo pole fishing. This activity will remove the invasive tilapia from our pond. This will allow for more resources for the native fish for which we are cultivating. The tour also includes a chance for us to harvest pohaku, or stone, from the river that feeds Loko Ea fresh water. This gathering of stone is the material necessary for us to rebuild our kuapa or retaining fishpond walls in the ancient uhauhumu, or dry-stack construction technique. We will end our tour with discussion, reflection, and awa.

Hawaii Okinawa Center
The Hawaii Okinawa Center (HOC) is the "home" of the Hawaii United Okinawa Association. The Hawaii United Okinawa Association is a 501(c)(3) non-profit organization whose mission is to promote,

perpetuate and preserve Okinawan culture. For more information, visit www.huoa.org.

94-587 Ukee St. Waipahu, HI 96797
Local Phone: (808) 676-5400
Email: edhuoa@hawaii.rr.com
Island: Oahu

The Hawaii Okinawa Center (HOC) is the "home" of the Hawaii United Okinawa Association. The Center is situated on 2.5 acres in the Gentry Waipio Business Park and stands as a living tribute to the Okinawan immigrant pioneers who began arriving in Hawaii in 1900. It was built with donations from Hawaii's Okinawan and business communities as well as from supporters in Okinawa. The HOC opened in 1990, which marked the ninetieth anniversary of Okinawan immigration to Hawaii.

The Hawaii United Okinawa Association is a 501(c)(3) non-profit organization whose mission is to promote, perpetuate and preserve Okinawan culture. The organization is made up of 50 member clubs, whose combined member total exceeds 40,000 members.

Polynesian Cultural Center
Voted the #1 paid attraction in Hawaii, the Polynesian Cultural Center on Oahu's North Shore offers 6 Pacific Island villages and exhibits. Featuring Hawaii's most authentic luau, and our award-winning show,

"Hā: Breath of Life." Visit us for an unforgettable experience great for the whole family.

55-370 Kamehameha Highway Suite 1010. Laie, HI 96762

Local Phone: (808) 293-2068

US Toll Free: (800) 367-7060

Email: davisc@polynesia.com

Island: Oahu

The Polynesian Cultural Center is Hawaii's #1 visitor attraction, has 6 island villages representing the unique island cultures of Hawaii, Fiji, Aotearoa (New Zealand), Samoa, Tahiti, and Tonga.

Set on 42 acres along Oahu's North Shore, the Polynesian Cultural Center has a lagoon that hosts daily canoe tours and an exciting cultural Canoe Pageant.

Our award-winning Ali'i Luau takes guests on a journey to learn about Hawaii's royalty while enjoying traditional Polynesian food and entertainment.

You can also enjoy our immersive cinema presentation "Hawaiian Journey", a tribute to the splendors of Hawaii.

Visit our Hukilau Marketplace to shop for various Hawaiian and island-themed centered handiworks, clothing, jewelry, and treats.

End your day by attending our show "Ha: Breath of Life", featuring over 100 performers and the thrill of Samoan fireknife dancing.

The Polynesian Cultural Center is open Monday through Saturday from 11:45a - 9:30p.

Hawaii Temple Visitors' Center
Enjoy a tranquil moment during your busy sightseeing schedule. Enjoy the lush gardens on the Laie Hawaii Temple grounds, then come inside the visitors' center to learn more about Jesus Christ and the purpose of temples. We also invite you to visit the nearby Polynesian Cultural Center.

55-600 Naniloa Loop. Laie, HI 96762
Local Phone: (808) 293-9297
Island: Oahu

A trip to Oahu's North Shore is not complete without a visit to a notable landmark, the Laie Hawaii Temple of The Church of Jesus Christ of Latter-day Saints. The peaceful grounds of this spiritual place offer an idyllic setting to explore.

Often called the "Taj Mahal of the Pacific," it was the first temple built outside of the continental US. It was dedicated in 1919 to serve members throughout the Pacific and has a ten-foot marble replica of Thorvaldsen's "Christus" statue. Free trams depart from the

Polynesian Cultural Center to tour Laie, the Temple, and the Brigham Young University-Hawaii campus.

All are welcome to visit the Temple grounds, including its Visitors' Center and Family History Center; but, only members of the Church may enter the temple.

Bishop Museum

Hawai'i's museum of natural and cultural history. Experience daily exhibits, garden tours, planetarium shows and interactive exhibits. Shop for authentic Hawaiian and Pacific gifts. Discover the history of Hawai'i!

1525 Bernice Street. Honolulu, HI 96817

Local Phone: (808) 847-3511

Email: amber.bixel@bishopmuseum.org

Island: Oahu

Hawaii's museum of natural and cultural history. Originally built to house the extensive collection of Hawaiian artifacts and royal family heirlooms of Princess Bernice Pauahi Bishop, the Museum has since expanded to include millions of artifacts, documents and photos about Hawaii and other Pacific cultures. Daily programs from 9am to 5pm (Closed Thanksgiving and Christmas Day) allow visitors to discover more about Hawaiian and Polynesian cultures through live, interactive presentations and exhibit tours.

Planetarium shows showcase Polynesian skies and how voyagers navigated using the stars to sail the Pacific. The Science Adventure Center offers visitors interactive experiences related directly to Hawaii's unique natural environment. Control volcanic eruptions, see lava melting demos, or walk-through the vivid environment of the Hawaiian Origins Tunnel. For more information please call (808) 847-3511 or visit www.bishopmuseum.org.

Hawaii State Art Museum
A venue for the Art in Public Places Program of the Hawaii State Foundation on Culture and the Arts, the Hawaii State Art Museum (HiSAM) features works of art primarily by artists with a connection to Hawaii and exhibits on topics of interest to communities in our state. Admission is always free!

250 South Hotel Street. Second Floor. Honolulu, HI 96813
Local Phone: (808) 586-0300
Email: hawaiisfca@hawaii.gov
Island: Oahu

As a venue for the Art in Public Places Program of the Hawaii State Foundation on Culture and the Arts, the Hawaii State Art Museum (HiSAM) features works of art primarily by artists with a connection to Hawaii (such as born/raised here, went to school here, worked here) with exhibits on topics of interest to communities in our state. Entry and admission are always free and family-friendly.

Current exhibits include "HAWAII: Change & Continuity" telling a story about Hawaii from before human contact to the present through contemporary art. For additional information, including searchable image galleries.

First Fridays at HiSAM: every first Friday of the month (except for major holidays) the museum galleries are open from 6:00 - 9:00 pm and there is live entertainment either in the second floor lobby or courtyard. First Fridays at HiSAM are casual and family-friendly.

Second Saturdays: every second Saturday of the month (except for major holidays), free hands-on art activities for all ages are available from 11:00 am - 3:00 pm. Art Lunch is a "meet the artist" lecture series that takes place on the last Tuesday of each month from 12:00 - 1:00 pm (except for holidays).

Oahu Air Activities

See Oahu from a different point of view. Oahu's pleasant, year round weather is great for helicopter tours, parasailing, paragliding, skydiving and other adventures. Fly over the verdant valleys of the Windward Coast and the majestic cityscapes of Honolulu. Parasail by parachute, up to 800 feet above Waikiki beach. For the ultimate rush, try a tandem sky dive. No matter what you choose, experienced pilots and instructors will guide you through your sky adventure.

If you've always wanted to feel the rush of skydiving, there's no better place to do it than on Oahu's North Shore. Begin your adventure at Dillingham Airfield and take off to one of the world's most beautiful drop zones. Fly thousands of feet above the spectacular North Shore coast. Feel the anticipation build, moments before your tandem jump, your instructor harnessed to your back. Before you know it, you'll be freefalling at 120 miles per hour, taking in a panoramic view of Oahu's green mountains and deep blue waters that few have ever seen. It's an experience you'll never forget.

Please note that skydiving can be very dangerous so please take caution before attempting.

Paradise Helicopters
If you can dream it, we can do it. Paradise Helicopters offers you the opportunity to create memories that will last a lifetime while here in the islands. See volcanoes, waterfalls & more on our helicopter tours, exclusive landings and custom charters departing from Kona, Hilo and Turtle Bay Resort.

73-341 U'u St. Kailua-Kona, HI 96745

Local Phone: (808) 969-7392

US Toll Free: (866) 876-7422

Email: marketing@paradisecopters.com

Island: Oahu

Paradise Helicopters is a locally-owned and operated helicopter tour company offering air adventures departing from Kona, Hilo and Oahu. Whether you dream of doors off tours over Kilauea volcano, descending into a Kona coffee farm or soaring over green sand beaches, our helicopter tours, exclusive landings, air & land adventures and custom charters are crafted to immerse our guests in the awe-inspiring natural beauty of Hawaii and to create memories that will last a lifetime.

Here are a few of our featured tours departing from Oahu:

North Shore Sunset Spectacular
Savor the brilliant hues of the "golden hour" and the Hawaiian sunset from a truly unique vantage on the North Shore Sunset Spectacular. Over thirty minutes, you'll witness how the landscape, laid out below with Oahu's famed North Shore surf breaks and beaches and the rippled Ko'olau Mountains, changes dramatically with the light. You'll cruise past Haleiwa town and secluded Kaena Point before turning back towards Turtle Bay to see the sun sink below the horizon.

Magnum Experience
Covering the island of O'ahu from above, our Magnum Experience will show you all of the island's highlights. See stunning views of the fabled

North Shore, Pearl Harbor, Le'ahi (Diamond Head), Kaliuwa'a (Sacred Falls), and more! You will even fly the same thrilling route seen in the opening sequence of Magnum, P.I., which takes you offshore above the ocean as you cruise past iconic Waikiki. Fly with Paradise and get your moustache on by taking a flight in the only exact replica of Magnum, P.I.'s Chopper!

Valleys & Waterfall Explorer

Explore the serenity and beauty of Oahu's best from the air on Paradise Helicopter's Valleys & Waterfall Explorer Tour. Discover aerial views of the 1000-foot Kaliuwa'a (Sacred Falls), which has been closed to the public since 1999, and the dramatic ridgelines of the Ko'olau Mountains, places completely inaccessible by car. In addition, your aerial expedition will take you above Kane'ohe Bay and the fabled North Shore surf breaks must sees on any adventure!

Novictor Helicopters

Guests enjoy their choice of premium experience aboard a Robinson R-44 helicopter including Daytime, Sunset, and Honolulu City Lights Tours. BOOK NOW

Local Phone: 1(888) 779-7724

Email: info@novictoraviation.com

Island: Oahu

Guests enjoy their choice of premium experience aboard a Robinson R-44 helicopter including Daytime, Sunset, and Honolulu City Lights Tours. Novictor Aviation is also available for aerial photography charters for film and advertising and other private flight instruction. With a warm spirit of Aloha and a friendly multi-cultural staff, everyone who flies Novictor Aviation becomes a member of our Ohana.

Magnum Helicopters
Feel the wind in your hair. Embrace the elements. There's nothing between you and the sky. For a truly great helicopter adventure, fly without doors on the aircraft. Every seat has a great view.

130 Iolana Place. Honolulu, HI 96819

Local Phone: (808) 833-4354

Email: info@MagnumHelicopters.com

Island: Oahu

Feel the wind in your hair. Embrace the elements. There's nothing between you and the sky. For a truly great helicopter adventure, fly without doors on the aircraft. Every seat has a great view.

Honolulu Soaring
Soar the North Shore and experience Hawaii from the air. Come and fly in one of our sleek, high-performance sailplanes and encounter nature

at her most spectacular. Call our reservations desk for prices and further details (808) 637 0207.

Local Phone: (808) 677-3404
Email: mrbill@hawaii.rr.com
Island: Oahu

We are Hawaii's oldest and largest sailplane/glider operation. Experience the serenity of flying in a sailplane: the peaceful majesty of the mountains and spectacular views that only a few have encountered.

Watch the whales as they breach in the warm pacific waters of the North Shore and trace their footprints across the surface of the ocean as they come up for air. This is a breath taking adventure for all of the family.

Earth, Air and Water: Nature at her most dynamic and yours to treasure for the rest of your life.

Enjoy a 20 or 30 minute Scenic Ride for one or 2 passengers, a 'Hands-on' Intro Flying Lesson or an Aerobatic Ride for the thrill of a lifetime!

We are open 10 AM to 5.30 PM, 7 days a week (including holidays). Please call our reservations desk for prices and further details (808) 637 0207.

Blue Hawaiian Helicopters

Frommer's Hawaii 2013 says, "Blue Hawaiian is the Cadillac of helicopter tour companies." Now featuring the incredible, 21st-Century "Eco-Star" helicopter. Daily departures from Oahu, Maui, Big Island and Kauai.

99 Kaulele Place Honolulu. Honolulu, HI 96819

Local Phone: (808) 871-8844

US Toll Free: (800) 745-2583

Email: info@bluehawaiian.com

Island: Oahu

Founded in 1985, and honored by National Geographic as "Hawaii's premiere helicopter tour company," Blue Hawaiian is the only helicopter tour company that serves all of Hawaii Oahu, Maui, Kauai,and the Big Island. Blue Hawaiian was also the first in the world to introduce the incredible EC130-B4 "ECO-Star," the world's first 21st-century touring helicopter. This phenomenal machine sets a whole new standard in environmentally responsible air touring. It's significantly quieter and incorporates all the latest cutting-edge technologies, materials, systems and avionics. Plus it offers incomparable passenger comfort, 23% more interior space, individual "First Class" seats, raised theatre-style platform in the rear, and far more cockpit glass for fantastic sweeping views. Blue Hawaiian also continues to operate a superb fleet of A-Stars the industry standard in touring helicopters, all purchased new and meticulously maintained by Blue Hawaiian's FAA award-winning staff of top A&P mechanics.

Hawaii Activities Discount
Save on Hawaii activities at a discount. Reserve Hawaiian tours and activities such as land tours, luaus, attractions, water activities such as snorkeling and even air adventures like helicopter tours.

Local Phone: (866) 482-9775
US Toll Free: (866) 482-9775
Email: sales@hawaiidiscount.com
Island: Oahu

Save on Hawaii activities tours and places to stay at a discount. Reserve Hawaiian tours and activities such as land tours, luaus, attractions, water activities such as snorkeling and even air adventures like helicopter tours.

HawaiiDiscount.com friendly activity agents offer advice on the best operators and things to do on all the islands which helps you plan the best Hawaiian vacation.

Molokai

Welcome to Molokai
Hawaii's fifth largest island, Molokai is only 38 miles long and 10 miles across at its widest point and is home to the highest sea cliffs in the

world and the longest continuous fringing reef. Molokai remains true to its island roots, with a high percentage of its population being of Native Hawaiian ancestry who continue to preserve their rural lifestyle thanks to their love of the land. Whether you're lead by a guide along the cliffs leading to Kalaupapa National Historical Park or discovering Papohaku Beach, one of Hawaii's largest white-sand beaches, Molokai is truly an island of outdoor adventure where Hawaii's past comes alive!

Regions of Molokai

Central Molokai

The central region of Molokai is also the center of local life on the island. If you arrive by air, you'll fly into Molokai Airport in Hoolehua, which is also where you can try a fresh macadamia nut straight from the branch at Purdy's Macadamia Nut Farm. (Hawaii grows the majority of the world's macadamias.) Sample another famous Hawaiian export at Coffees of Hawaii, a 100-acre coffee farm plantation in nearby Kualapuu.

Head south to Molokai's biggest town of Kaunakakai, where the tallest point is the church steeple. Grab a tasty fresh-baked treat at Kanemitsu's Bakery and check out the local shops on the island's only main street. Take a fishing or boating adventure from Kaunakakai harbor, stroll down the state's longest pier, or explore the nearby landmarks, including historic Hawaiian Fishponds used for aquaculture in the 13thcentury and one of Hawaii's last royal coconut groves at Kapuaiwa Coconut Beach Park.

Along the north coast of Central Molokai is the isolated Kalaupapa Peninsula, home to historic Kalaupapa National Historical Park, where victims of Hansen's disease (commonly known as leprosy) were exiled in the 1800s. St. Damien came to the remote colony in 1873 to care for the residents, and eventually succumbed to the disease himself after 16 years. Today, you can learn about the pain and resilience of Kalaupapa's residents on a tour of the site, which is only accessible by hike or mule ride along the 1,700-foot sheer cliffs.

Before you depart Central Molokai, stop by the Hoolehua Post Office for a fun, only-in-Hawaii experience: Mail home a free coconut from the Post-a-Nut counter far more exciting than a postcard and you just provide the postage.

Molokai Ancient Hawaiian Fishponds

What: Historic Hawaiian fishponds dating back to the early 13th century

Where: Along the south shore between Kaunakakai and Mile Marker 13

One of the Hawaiians' greatest engineering innovations was their use of aquaculture, namely stone and coral fishponds. Molokai has many of these well-preserved fishponds located along its southern coast, most built 700-800 years ago.

The semicircular walls of the ponds were made from lava boulders and coral that would allow the seawater to ebb in and out. The fish ponds had wooden gates that would allow small fish to swim in, providing a haven to reside and feed, and as they grew, the fish would become too large to exit back through the gate. The Hawaiians would then harvest fish responsibly and sustainably.

During this time only royal Hawaiian *alii* (chiefs) were permitted to eat the fish harvested from these ponds. You'll find the most extensive examples of their ingenuity scalloped along 20 miles off Molokai's south and southeastern shores, where more than 60 fishponds were once in use.

Stop a quarter mile after Hotel Molokai to see Alii fishpond, once reserved for royalty. This historic site is easily accessible and is a fine example of Molokai's fishponds. Continue down Kamehameha V Highway east from Kaunakakai to see two fishponds that have been designated national historical landmarks: Keawanui and Ualapue Fishponds. These two ponds are unmarked and can be difficult to find so please contact the Molokai Visitor's Association for detailed directions.

Kalaupapa National Historical Park
What: Historic site accessible by scenic mule ride
Where: On the northern tip of Molokai

It's quiet as you ride on your mule along the 2.9-mile trail to Kalaupapa Peninsula. The sheer cliffs overlook the Pacific, descending from 1,700 feet with Molokai's North Shore Pali just to the east the tallest sea cliffs in the world as recorded by the Guinness Book of World Records, measuring 3,600 to 3,900 feet.

Three miles, 26 switchbacks and 90 minutes of magnificent views later, you're back to sea level in the historic town of Kalaupapa, one of the most remote settlements in Hawaii. It's scenic, isolated and peaceful here, but the story of Kalaupapa National Historical Park is even more compelling.

This special community was once home to Belgian missionary Saint Damien and later, to Saint Marianne Cope. In 1873, Father Damien chose to leave the "outside world" to care for the residents with Hawaii's Hansen's disease who were exiled to this isolated peninsula. After 16 years of faithful service, he too, tragically succumbed to the disease and was laid to rest at historic St. Philomena Roman Catholic

Church in Kalaupapa where you can visit his grave. In October of 2009, Father Damien was canonized as a saint for his selfless dedication.

A few months before Saint Damien's death, a woman of extraordinary spirit came to Kalaupapa to continue his life's work. Mother Marianne Cope had been the head of her religious order, an accomplished hospital administrator at the St. Joseph's Hospital in New York, and oversaw several hospitals and care homes in Hawaii. At Father Damien's request, she and her Franciscan sisters volunteered to live out their lives in the exiled community, operating the Boys' Home he established and the Bishop Home for Girls. The beloved Mother died in 1918 of natural causes. Her remains were buried on the grounds of the Bishop Home and returned to Syracuse, New York in 2005.

Mother Marianne was canonized as Saint Marianne Cope on October 21, 2012. A bronze statue in her honor overlooks the ocean at Kewalo Basin Park in Honolulu.

Today, the serene Kalaupapa National Historical Park is a place of preservation and education and is only accessible by mule ride, hiking tour or airplane from the small commuter Kalaupapa Airport (LUP). Kalaupapa cannot be reached by car. To take a Kalaupapa tour, make a reservation in advance with Damien Tours, (808) 567-6171. For mule ride information, call Kalaupapa Mule Tour at (808) 567-6088. To reserve flights to Molokai, contact Makani Kai Air (877) 255-8532 or Mokulele Airlines (866) 260-7070.

You can also view Kalaupapa Peninsula from the 1,000-foot elevation of Palaau State Park. This 34-acre recreation area offers winding trails among eucalyptus and ironwood trees as well as breathtaking views of Molokai's north coast.

Kapuaiwa Coconut Grove

What: Historic coconut grove
Where: In Kaunakakai across from Church Row

In Kaunakakai across from Church Row, visit Kapuaiwa Coconut Grove, an ancient Hawaiian coconut grove planted in the 1860s during the reign of King Kamehameha V. With hundreds of coconut palm trees, this is one of Molokai's most recognizable natural landmarks.

There is an obvious danger of falling coconuts within the grove, so the safest view of the grove is from the grassy area found off Mauna Loa Highway. It's an amazing spot for a spectacular, sunset view of one of the last royal coconut groves in Hawaii. The still shallow waters will reflect the sky in such a way that you won't know where one starts and the other ends. A great setting for that perfect selfie.

Note: Kapuaiwa Coconut Grove is private property of the Department of Hawaiian Homelands; there is no beach access.

Kaunakakai, Molokai

What: Molokai's central town

Where: 15 minutes southeast of Molokai Airport

In the central town of Kaunakakai, an absence of traffic lights take you back to a simpler time, virtually unchanged since the early 1900s. This charming *paniolo* (Hawaiian cowboy) town is also the island's main harbor, where some locals still fish for their dinner. Stroll down to Kaunakakai Harbor to the end of the state's longest pier, extending well past the reef. It's just you, the local fisherman and the sound of boats slowly jetting out of the harbor.

The town's main strip, Ala Malama Avenue, was named after the nearby house used by King Kamehameha V in the 1860s. You'll find it easy to browse the shops and boutiques of its business district. Brave the crowds at the famous Kanemitsu's Bakery, where locals and visitors alike line up after hours to get piping-hot loaves of fresh bread. Be sure to order their famous onion-and-cheese bread or slather a half loaf with jelly, butter, cream cheese or cinnamon. It's a Molokai must.

Stay the night at the Hotel Molokai, a Kaunakakai landmark located on Kamiloloa Beach, or find a condominium or cottage rental. Then visit the Kapuaiwa Coconut Grove to see palm trees in one of the last royal coconut groves. Across the way you'll discover "Church Row," the site of seven small, missionary-style churches, some dating back to the late 19th century. Other local Kaunakakai eateries and shops include Friendly Market, Mrs. K's Lunch Counter, Imamura's Store, Outpost Natural Foods, Pascua's General Store, Kalele Bookstore and the Molokai Pizza Café. And don't forget the Saturday outdoor market, perfect for a Molokai day trip.

West End

Escape to west Molokai for a quiet retreat. Relax on some of the state's largest and least crowded beaches, including the sweeping white sand expanse of Papohaku Beach and peaceful Kapukahehu Beach (also known as Dixie Maru Beach), a perfect spot to snorkel or gaze at a romantic Molokai sunset. The arid West End faces the Kaiwi Channel. This treacherous 41-mile stretch of Pacific Ocean is the arena for the annual Molokai Hoe canoe competition in October, from Hale O Lono Harbor in Molokai to Waikiki on Oahu.

Visit the small plantation town of Maunaloa, where you'll find unique shopping, including the handmade kites of the Big Wind Kite Factory. Once a resort area, the West End is still a great place to find condominium and cottage rentals. As you make your way down Kaluakoi Road westward, be on the lookout for wild Axis deer. These spotted beauties were given to King Kamehameha V as a gift in the 1860s.

Maunaloa, Molokai

What: Small West End town with unique shopping
Where: 20 minutes west of Molokai Airport

This small, charming plantation village set in the hills above the coast is the only town in West End. The Maunaloa area is nearby two popular Molokai beaches, Papohaku Beach and Kapukahehu Beach (also known as Dixie Maru Beach) on the western coast and is also a great place to find rental condominiums and cottages.

You'll also find a unique shop and galleries in Maunaloa including the famous Big Wind Kite Factory. You'll discover everything from dancing hula girl windsocks to high-performance stunt kites here. Go on a tour of the factory or take a free kite-flying lesson. Many of their kites are handmade right in Molokai and these perfect gifts can only be found in Maunaloa.

Papohaku Beach

What: One of Hawaii's largest white sand beaches
Where: From Maunaloa town, take Kaluakoi Road to the western coast

Visit Papohaku Beach (also known as Three Mile Beach) and discover three miles of soft-sands uninterrupted down Molokai's west end. One of Hawaii's largest white sand beaches at about 100 yards wide, there's plenty of room to spread out and enjoy the "Friendly Island" ambience.

Here you'll find campsites, indoor and outdoor showers, as well as picnic and restroom facilities. What you won't find is a lot of foot traffic. There's ample space to enjoy a beautiful view of Oahu. Over the Kaiwi Channel, just past Leahi (Diamond Head), is Waikiki, which actually took sand from Papohaku years ago to help build up its own shores.

Note that during the winter months, from October through March, it is best to avoid any dangerous shore break. Please heed all posted safety signs on the beach.

East End, Molokai

Undiscovered country and natural wonders abound on Molokai's East End. Take a drive along Kamehameha V Highway, where Kamakou, Molokai's highest mountain, is on your left and Hawaii's longest continuous fringing reef (28 miles) is on your right. Pass by historic sites like St. Joseph's Church, built in 1876 by Saint Damien, and Molokai's first Christian church, Kaluaaha Church, originally built in 1833.

Stop by Kumimi Beach (also known as Murphy Beach) for great snorkeling, or continue to the end of the road for a picnic at peaceful

Halawa Beach Park. Take a guided hike into beautiful Halawa Valley, the only one of Molokai's five epic valleys that's easily accessible.

Follow a different path inland and four-wheel drive to the Kamakou Preserve, a primeval Hawaiian rainforest home to rare endemic plants and animals. Get a gorgeous view of Waikolu Valley at the Waikolu Overlook. Lining the northeast coast are the sky-high cliffs of the North Shore Pali. At 3,600 to 3,900 feet, they're the tallest sea cliffs in the world.

Things to Do on Molokai

Molokai Beaches

For those longing to get away from it all, Molokai's miles of sandy beaches offer amazing unspoiled beauty and seclusion. You won't find resort-studded shores teeming with beach bars and surf schools, as is common on other islands, nor is there an abundance of clear, calm water for snorkeling. But don't be surprised if you have the beach all to yourself (that means no lifeguards, either) a rare luxury that sets Molokai apart.

West Molokai Beaches

Papohaku Beach Park
At three miles long and 100 yards wide, this is one of the largest white-sand beaches in all of Hawaii, offering distant views of Leahi

(Diamond Head) on Oahu and ample space to spread out. There are restrooms, picnic facilities and even campsites, but no lifeguards.

Kapukahehu Beach (Dixie Maru Beach)

There are no facilities at this small, sheltered cove, but the protected waters make it a popular swimming spot for families. High surf can bring strong currents, so use caution.

East Molokai Beaches

Kumimi Beach Park (20 Mile Marker Beach)

This is one of Molokai's snorkeling spots that is easier to access. There are no restrooms here, and the water can become rough at high surf, so be careful.

Kawili Beach

At the mouth of the majestic Halawa Valley, Halawa Beach Park offers two separate beaches on a secluded bay, with sweeping views of lush mountains and distant waterfalls. The beaches are good for swimming on a calm day, and picnic and restroom facilities are available.

Central Molokai Beaches

One Alii Beach Park

Situated just east of Kaunakakai, this favorite beach of Hawaiian alii (royalty) has picnic facilities, restrooms and parking, making it a great place for a day in the sun.

Molokai Water Activities

The waters around Molokai are among the richest in the Pacific. Aside from having some of the more deserted beaches in Hawaii (there's a reason travelers from every island often head here when they want to "get away"), Molokai is a welcome paradise for anglers and divers wishing to explore the living aquarium just beneath the water's surface.

Take a sport-fishing charter from Kaunakakai, or whale watch in the Kalohi Channel during the winter months. Kayaking and stand-up paddleboarding are also amazing off Molokai's pristine shores. Sprawling Papohaku Beach is ideal for a dip in the calmer summer months, while Kumimi Beach (also known as 20 Mile Marker Beach) is known for its great, easy-to-access snorkeling.

Molokai is also home to Hawaii's longest continuous fringing reef, at 28 miles long. Natural "finger" coral and stony coral harbor *honu* (green sea turtles), Hawaiian monk seals and a swirling rainbow of reef fish, making for fantastic snorkeling and scuba diving.

Snorkeling and Scuba of Molokai

Molokai's southern shore is home to Hawaii's longest continuous fringing reef at 28 miles long. Full of natural "finger" coral, stony coral and an abundance of reef fish, this a fantastic place for snorkeling and scuba diving when the waters are calm.

Explore the reef on a scuba diving tour or visit special snorkeling spots with local companies like Molokai Fish & Dive. Or rent some snorkeling equipment and explore the beaches of the south shore. Kumimi Beach (also known as 20 Mile Marker Beach) is one of the island's most popular snorkeling spots. Join the colorful reef fish, *honu* (Hawaiian green sea turtles) and friendly manta rays in the waters of Molokai.

Fishing on Molokai

Cast off from Kaunakakai pier, the longest wharf in Hawaii for a fishing adventure. Experienced fishermen will love the thrills of deep-sea, big-game fishing in Molokai's fertile waters, but first-timers will also be in for some fun as Molokai boat captains will help you with everything.

There is excellent sport fish to be had in Molokai, including marlin, mahimahi, *ahi* (tuna), and ono. Bottom fishing, usually with live bait, can also yield the fruits of the sea. Most charters depart from Kaunakakai Harbor.

Alyce C. Sportfishing

Deep sea sportfishing off of Molokai for Pacific Blue Marlin, Yellowfin Tuna (Ahi), Ono, Mahi Mahi. All gear provided. 1/2, 3/4 and full day charters available. ROUND ISLE TRIPS-WEATHER PERMITTING, WHALE WATCHING IN SEASON(DEC-APRIL)

Kaunakakai Harbor Slip 10. Kaunakakai, HI 96748

Local Phone: (808) 558-8377

Email: ace@aloha.net

Island: Molokai

Deep sea sportfishing off of Molokai for Pacific Blue Marlin, Yellowfin Tuna (Ahi), Ono, Mahi Mahi. All gear provided. 1/2, 3/4 and full day charters available. ROUND ISLE TRIPS-WEATHER PERMITTING , WHALE WATCHING IN SEASON(DEC-APRIL)

Boating on Molokai

Molokai is a great place to cast off for a fishing adventure and a great way to experience Molokai's local lifestyle. You can charter a boat from Kaunakakai. You can also go on snorkeling and scuba dive adventures, rent a kayak to explore Molokai's south shore or go on a boat tour.

You can also take boating day trips between Kaunakakai Harbor and Lahaina Harbor in Maui. You might even spot whales during whale watching season from December to May.

Molokai Land Activities

Only 38 miles long and 10 miles wide, Molokai's small footprint makes it easily accessible by foot, bike or car. Along the way, you'll discover deep jungles, cathedral valleys, windswept beaches and one of the most remote settlements in the world. No matter how you choose to explore this intriguing island, you'll soon see why Molokai is truly Hawaiian by nature.

Some of the most spectacular landscapes in Hawaii can be found in the ancient Halawa Valley on Molokai's East End. This lush cathedral valley can only be explored on a guided hike, which will lead you to sacred heiau (temples), breathtaking vistas and cascading waterfalls, like the 250-foot Mooula Falls. Almost as spectacular as the Halawa Valley itself is the cliffside drive that leads there, with one-lane switchbacks and sweeping views of deserted black-sand beaches along the coast.

Hop on a bike (you can rent one in Kaunakakai) and explore the local shops, eateries and many historic sites of Molokai's south shore, like Kapuaiwa Coconut Grove, Church Row and the Alii Fishpond. Or, head to the three-mile-long Papohaku Beach on the island's west side for a romantic sunset stroll.

Perhaps the ultimate land adventure on Molokai is found at Kalaupapa National Historic Park. Located on a remote peninsula jutting from Molokai's rugged northern coast, this former fishing village became a colony for exiled sufferers of Hansen's Disease (leprosy) in the 19th century. To visit the preserved settlement, you must take a thrilling guided mule tour down the world's tallest sea cliffs, offering bird's-eye ocean views along the winding 2.9-mile trail.

Hiking on Molokai

Hiking is one of the best ways to get a firsthand look at Molokai's natural beauty and untamed wilderness. There are a variety of trails around the island to suit hikers of all ability levels.

Halawa Valley
What: Historic Hawaiian valley with towering waterfalls
Where: Molokai's East End, 1.5 hours from Molokai Airport

Hike into the East End's classic cathedral valley to see the Hawaii of long ago. It's believed ancient Polynesians settled in lush Halawa Valley as early as 650 AD. With many hidden heiau (places of worship) it's easy to see why this spot, half a mile wide, 3-4 miles deep and blessed with beautiful vistas and towering waterfalls, is one of the island's most historic areas.

Roughly two miles up the trail is the impressive, double-tiered 250-foot Mooula Falls. The hike in is moderate, and the only way to explore the area is with a guide, since the trail crosses private property. Anakala Pilipo Solotorio provides guided hiking tours with a unique perspective. His cultural knowledge adds to an extremely engaging and authentic experience. Call (808) 542-1855 to arrange for a guided hike.

The long drive to Halawa Valley (roughly 1.5 hours from Molokai Airport) is an adventure in itself. You'll pass by Hawaiian Fishponds, points of interest like Kumimi Beach (also known as "20 Mile Marker"), Kaluaaha Church (Molokai's first Christian church built in 1833), Halawa Beach Park and Halawa Bay.

Halawa Beach Park has two swimming beaches, called Kaili and Kaiwili, located in Halawa Bay along Molokai's eastern shore. During summer the water is usually very nice, though the beach should be avoided during times of high surf or rough water, especially during the winter months (October March).

Molokai Farms & Gardens

Molokai's natural beauty offers a variety of places to learn about Hawaii's special flora. Taste local beans at the Coffees of Hawaii plantation store, stock up on fresh produce at Kumu Farms or visit Purdy's Natural Macadamia Nut Farm in <u>Central Molokai</u>. Or, explore the 2,774-acre <u>Kamakou Preserve</u>, run by the Nature Conservancy and home to more than 250 rare Hawaiian plants. If you're lucky you may even spot the olomao or the kakawahie, two birds nearing extinction. .

Molokai Golf

The course marshal won't cite you for slow play here. Take your time. Enjoy the view from every tee box. An errant shot? Take another. Nobody's going to ask to play through your group on Molokai.

On the nine-hole Ironwood Hills (Molokai's only golf course), you'll find expansive views, including Oahu and Molokai's towering sea cliffs, from many of the holes due to the course's high elevation. There are no tee times. No golf pros. Not even a clubhouse. So slow it down. The more you relax, the better your swing. And remember, there are always mulligans on Molokai.

Ironwood Hills Golf Course on Molokai

This charming, plantation-style nine-hole course sits on sloping land along central Molokai's north coast mountains, not far from the island's only airport. Ironwood Hills offers a purely fun 'who's-keeping-score' round. Its well-kept, elevated greens give the golfer surprising approach-shot results, especially when the prevailing trade winds are blowing.

Not only is Ironwood Hills easy on the pocketbook, this Molokai golf course also provides a glimpse into Hawaii golf history. This course is the descendant of one of Hawaii's original plantation courses, the Hanekekua Golf Club, which opened in 1938. Anyone who plays

Ironwood Hills should also plan a side trip to nearby Palaau State Park. Just a short walk from the parking area, visitors are afforded dominating vistas of the beautiful Kalaupapa Peninsula, some 2,000-feet straight down. Standing at this elevation, it's not uncommon to see small airplanes below, navigating their way along the incredible scenery of Molokai's northern cliffs, the tallest oceanfront cliffs in the world. Look closely, and it's likely you'll see any number of black mountain goats somehow holding their ground on the vertical cliff faces below.

Molokai Historic Places

With a high percentage of Molokai's population being of Native Hawaiian descent, it's no wonder why Molokai is sometimes known as the "most Hawaiian Island." A visit here is like a journey into Hawaii's past, where historic spots can be discovered today, looking much like they did hundreds of years ago.

Kalaupapa National Historic Park

Here on this isolated and serene peninsula along Molokai's rugged north coast, victims of Hansen's disease were forced into isolation from 1866 to 1969. Yet Saint Damien and Saint Marianne's selfless devotion to treating the people of Kalaupapa has become legendary. In October 2009, Saint Damien was ordained a saint in Rome posthumously and Saint Marianne was canonized posthumously in

2012. Take a memorable mule ride from 1,700 feet to the seaside Kalaupapa National Historical Park, one of the most remote settlements in Hawaii.

Molokai Heritage Site

Molokai is home to one Heritage Site of Hawaii. Kalaupapa Lookout at the Palaau State Park is an overlook that features an amazing view of Molokai's north coast and Kalaupapa National Historical Park.

Hawaiian Fishponds

Molokai has many well-preserved Hawaiian fishponds along 20 miles of its south shore, most built 700 800 years ago. Ancient Hawaiians practiced a very sophisticated form of aquaculture, building some 60 rock-wall fishponds along the south shore. East of Kaunakakai is Alii Fishpond, one of the finest examples of early Hawaiian ingenuity.

Halawa Valley

One of the oldest known Hawaiian settlements on Molokai was in Halawa Valley, an area you can still explore today. Take a guided hike into this cathedral valley, blessed with beautiful vistas and towering waterfalls. Legends say some of the first Polynesian voyagers landed in their canoes at the mouth of the valley.

Kaunakakai

King Kamehameha V built a vacation home in this sleepy town and planted the Kapuaiwa Coconut Grove in the 1860s. Kapuaiwa Coconut

Beach Park is one of Molokai's most recognizable natural landmarks, while One Alii Beach Park was once a favorite of Hawaiian royalty.

Kalaupapa National Historical Park

What: Historic site accessible by scenic mule ride
Where: On the northern tip of Molokai

It's quiet as you ride on your mule along the 2.9-mile trail to Kalaupapa Peninsula. The sheer cliffs overlook the Pacific, descending from 1,700 feet with Molokai's North Shore Pali just to the east the tallest sea cliffs in the world as recorded by the Guinness Book of World Records, measuring 3,600 to 3,900 feet.

Three miles, 26 switchbacks and 90 minutes of magnificent views later, you're back to sea level in the historic town of Kalaupapa, one of the most remote settlements in Hawaii. It's scenic, isolated and peaceful here, but the story of Kalaupapa National Historical Park is even more compelling.

This special community was once home to Belgian missionary Saint Damien and later, to Saint Marianne Cope. In 1873, Father Damien chose to leave the "outside world" to care for the residents with Hawaii's Hansen's disease who were exiled to this isolated peninsula. After 16 years of faithful service, he too, tragically succumbed to the disease and was laid to rest at historic St. Philomena Roman Catholic

Church in Kalaupapa where you can visit his grave. In October of 2009, Father Damien was canonized as a saint for his selfless dedication.

A few months before Saint Damien's death, a woman of extraordinary spirit came to Kalaupapa to continue his life's work. Mother Marianne Cope had been the head of her religious order, an accomplished hospital administrator at the St. Joseph's Hospital in New York, and oversaw several hospitals and care homes in Hawaii. At Father Damien's request, she and her Franciscan sisters volunteered to live out their lives in the exiled community, operating the Boys' Home he established and the Bishop Home for Girls. The beloved Mother died in 1918 of natural causes. Her remains were buried on the grounds of the Bishop Home and returned to Syracuse, New York in 2005.

Mother Marianne was canonized as Saint Marianne Cope on October 21, 2012. A bronze statue in her honor overlooks the ocean at Kewalo Basin Park in Honolulu.

Today, the serene Kalaupapa National Historical Park is a place of preservation and education and is only accessible by mule ride, hiking tour or airplane from the small commuter Kalaupapa Airport (LUP). Kalaupapa cannot be reached by car. To take a Kalaupapa tour, make a reservation in advance with Damien Tours, (808) 567-6171. For mule ride information, call Kalaupapa Mule Tour at (808) 567-6088. To reserve flights to Molokai, contact Makani Kai Air (877) 255-8532 or Mokulele Airlines (866) 260-7070.

You can also view Kalaupapa Peninsula from the 1,000-foot elevation of Palaau State Park. This 34-acre recreation area offers winding trails among eucalyptus and ironwood trees as well as breathtaking views of Molokai's north coast.

Molokai Ancient Hawaiian Fishponds

What: Historic Hawaiian fishponds dating back to the early 13th century

Where: Along the south shore between Kaunakakai and Mile Marker 13

One of the Hawaiians' greatest engineering innovations was their use of aquaculture, namely stone and coral fishponds. Molokai has many of these well-preserved fishponds located along its southern coast, most built 700-800 years ago.

The semicircular walls of the ponds were made from lava boulders and coral that would allow the seawater to ebb in and out. The fish ponds had wooden gates that would allow small fish to swim in, providing a haven to reside and feed, and as they grew, the fish would become too large to exit back through the gate. The Hawaiians would then harvest fish responsibly and sustainably.

During this time only royal Hawaiian *alii* (chiefs) were permitted to eat the fish harvested from these ponds. You'll find the most extensive examples of their ingenuity scalloped along 20 miles off Molokai's south and southeastern shores, where more than 60 fishponds were once in use.

Stop a quarter mile after Hotel Molokai to see Alii fishpond, once reserved for royalty. This historic site is easily accessible and is a fine example of Molokai's fishponds. Continue down Kamehameha V Highway east from Kaunakakai to see two fishponds that have been designated national historical landmarks: Keawanui and Ualapue Fishponds. These two ponds are unmarked and can be difficult to find so please contact the Molokai Visitor's Association for detailed directions.

Kaunakakai, Molokai

What: Molokai's central town
Where: 15 minutes southeast of Molokai Airport

In the central town of Kaunakakai, an absence of traffic lights take you back to a simpler time, virtually unchanged since the early 1900s. This charming *paniolo* (Hawaiian cowboy) town is also the island's main harbor, where some locals still fish for their dinner. Stroll down to Kaunakakai Harbor to the end of the state's longest pier, extending well past the reef. It's just you, the local fisherman and the sound of boats slowly jetting out of the harbor.

The town's main strip, Ala Malama Avenue, was named after the nearby house used by King Kamehameha V in the 1860s. You'll find it easy to browse the shops and boutiques of its business district. Brave the crowds at the famous Kanemitsu's Bakery, where locals and visitors alike line up after hours to get piping-hot loaves of fresh bread. Be sure to order their famous onion-and-cheese bread or slather a half loaf with jelly, butter, cream cheese or cinnamon. It's a Molokai must.

Stay the night at the Hotel Molokai, a Kaunakakai landmark located on Kamiloloa Beach, or find a condominium or cottage rental. Then visit the Kapuaiwa Coconut Grove to see palm trees in one of the last royal coconut groves. Across the way you'll discover "Church Row," the site of seven small, missionary-style churches, some dating back to the late 19th century. Other local Kaunakakai eateries and shops include Friendly Market, Mrs. K's Lunch Counter, Imamura's Store, Outpost Natural Foods, Pascua's General Store, Kalele Bookstore and the Molokai Pizza Café. And don't forget the Saturday outdoor market, perfect for a Molokai day trip.

Halawa Valley
What: Historic Hawaiian valley with towering waterfalls
Where: Molokai's East End, 1.5 hours from Molokai Airport

Hike into the East End's classic cathedral valley to see the Hawaii of long ago. It's believed ancient Polynesians settled in lush Halawa Valley as early as 650 AD. With many hidden heiau (places of worship) it's easy to see why this spot, half a mile wide, 3-4 miles deep and blessed with beautiful vistas and towering waterfalls, is one of the island's most historic areas.

Roughly two miles up the trail is the impressive, double-tiered 250-foot Mooula Falls. The hike in is moderate, and the only way to explore the area is with a guide, since the trail crosses private property. Anakala Pilipo Solotorio provides guided hiking tours with a unique perspective. His cultural knowledge adds to an extremely engaging and authentic experience. Call (808) 542-1855 to arrange for a guided hike.

The long drive to Halawa Valley (roughly 1.5 hours from Molokai Airport) is an adventure in itself. You'll pass by Hawaiian Fishponds, points of interest like Kumimi Beach (also known as "20 Mile Marker"), Kaluaaha Church (Molokai's first Christian church built in 1833), Halawa Beach Park and Halawa Bay.

Halawa Beach Park has two swimming beaches, called Kaili and Kaiwili, located in Halawa Bay along Molokai's eastern shore. During summer the water is usually very nice, though the beach should be avoided during times of high surf or rough water, especially during the winter months (October March).

Kapuaiwa Coconut Grove

What: Historic coconut grove
Where: In Kaunakakai across from Church Row

In Kaunakakai across from Church Row, visit Kapuaiwa Coconut Grove, an ancient Hawaiian coconut grove planted in the 1860s during the reign of King Kamehameha V. With hundreds of coconut palm trees, this is one of Molokai's most recognizable natural landmarks.

There is an obvious danger of falling coconuts within the grove, so the safest view of the grove is from the grassy area found off Mauna Loa Highway. It's an amazing spot for a spectacular, sunset view of one of the last royal coconut groves in Hawaii. The still shallow waters will reflect the sky in such a way that you won't know where one starts and the other ends. A great setting for that perfect selfie.

Note: Kapuaiwa Coconut Grove is private property of the Department of Hawaiian Homelands; there is no beach access.

Molokai Restaurants

Molokai is smaller and less developed than some of the other islands, so it's a great place to seek out fresh island food, local Hawaiian favorites and friendly beachside spots rather than luxurious restaurants. You'll also find Hawaii's cultural diversity represented with Japanese and Filipino options alongside pizza, tasty burger joints and cozy coffee shops. For a memorable taste of Molokai, stop by Kanemitsu's Bakery, an 80-year old island staple known for yummy doughnuts and the must-have late night snack of fresh bread served hot from the oven and out of the bakery's back door.

Molokai Accommodations

Molokai doesn't have a major resort, and that's exactly what visitors love about it. Instead, you'll find towering sea cliffs (the tallest in the world), sweeping Pacific Ocean vistas and a rustic, intimate Hawaiian experience that extends to the lodging options. Molokai has a variety of charming oceanfront hotels, vacation rentals, cottages and bed and breakfasts in the central town of Kaunakakai and the village of Maunaloa in the West End. No matter where you stay on Molokai, you'll be close to pristine beaches and beautiful unspoiled views.

Ka Hale Ola / Ka Hale Kealoha

Our 2 luxurious oceanfront 1bed/1bath non-smoking adults-only condos are immaculate and comparable to a 5-star resort with granite countertops, fully equipped kitchens, Cal king pillow-top mattresses, 1000-count linens, and luxury bath amenities.

Local Phone: (847) 840-1071

Email: dacra@comcast.net

Island: Molokai

Ka Hale Ola (House of Life Wavecrest A304) offers a secluded location in the midst of tropical grounds. From the lanai (just 30 feet from the ocean) view 3 neighboring islands and experience prime whale watching. Tennis courts and a beautiful oceanside pool with adjoining cabana/library are yours to enjoy. Telescope, binoculars, snorkel and tennis equipment are provided.

The view from the lanai of Ka Hale Kealoha (House of Love Molokai Shores A215) encompasses the beautiful oceanside pool, tropical grounds, fish pond, and the island of Lanai. Proximity to town makes it easy to partake in activities on the island and to dine at various restaurants. Snorkel equipment and golf clubs for the putting green at the resort are provided, as well as binoculars for whale-watching.

Both condos are immaculately clean and feature top quality amenities, computers, webcams, and free internet access; both are non-smoking, adults only.

Molokairentals.net

A delightful condominium on the beautiful West end of Molokai at the Kaluakoi Villas and Resort offers breath-taking ocean vistas of Kepuhi Beach. Visit our website at MolokaiRentals.net for more details

Local Phone: (707) 541-6543

Email: orthodong@aol.com

Island: Molokai

One Bedroom Condo with Awesome Ocean view. Upstair-end unit, Full Kitchen with Silstone counter tops, Ceramic flat top Stove with Oven, 22 Cu Ft Refrig, Dishwasher, 37"LCD TV/ DVD/Stero, Cal King Bed. Telephone with Nationwide Long Distance. High Speed Internet

Dunbar Beachfront Cottages

Charming two bedroom beachfront cottages located on the lush east end of Molokai. Each on own secluded beach with safe swimming, snorkeling, fishing year round. Views of Mau'i, Lanai and Kaho'olawe. Whale watching December through April.

9750 Kamehameha V Hwy

Kaunakakai, HI 96748

Local Phone: (808) 558-8153

Email: dunbarbeachfrontcottages@gmail.com

Island: Molokai

Charming two bedroom beachfront cottages located on the lush east end of Molokai. Each on own secluded beach with safe swimming, snorkeling, fishing year round. Views of Maui, Lanai and Kaho'olawe. Whale watching December through April. Located just past the 18 mile marker on Molokai's east end, these cottages offer easy access to the spectacular Halawa Valley with its waterfalls and scenic beauty.

1-888-282-3459 Molokai Rentals

Spacious oceanview, ground floor, one bedroom, privately owned condo at oceanfront Kepuhi Beach Resort, fully furnished with all resort amenities, steps to beaches, pool, BBQ, laundry, TV, DVD. From $59/night (2 persons, 4 night minimum), monthly & longer term bookings starting at $50/night.

Kepuhi Beach Resort. Molokai, HI 96748

Local Phone: (888) 282-3459

US Toll Free: (888) 282-3459

Email: mfpr@bellsouth.net

Island: Molokai

Located at the Kepuhi Beach Resort (formerly Kaluakoi Resort), this one bedroom oceanview condo is fully furnished with all amenities. There are 3 miles of sand beaches with private coves, perfect for watching those fabulous sunsets, a swimming pool overlooking the Pacific and a 15 kilometer jogging course. This is THE perfect place for relieving the tensions of daily life and experiencing all the beauty of an unspoiled Hawaii.

A116 - Wavecrest

Wavecrest is located on five beautiful waterfront acres with lush tropical landscaping 13 miles east of town. This upgraded, quiet, oceanfront, 2 bedroom, 1 bath end unit is available nightly and weekly. Luxury linens decorate the King and Queen bed.

7142 Kamehameha V Hwy. A116. Kaunakakai, HI 96748

Local Phone: (808) 553-8334

US Toll Free: (800) 367-2984

Email: dayna@molokaivacationproperties.com

Island: Molokai

Wavecrest is located on five beautiful waterfront acres with lush tropical landscaping 13 miles east of Kaunakakai. This oceanfront 2 bedroom 1 bath unit is available nightly and weekly. Luxury bedding covers the king bed in the ocean front master bedroom. The guest room queen bed is quietly separated from the master bedroom. The gourmet kitchen has all the amenities for a great meal. You'll feel right at home in this well appointed condo.

Beautiful Condo at Paniolo Hale Unit T2

This spacious open-air condo is located on Molokai's sunny west end at Kaluakoi. The architecture is plantation-style with two tall french doors spanning the length of the main floor. It is two-story with 1,200 sq. ft. of space.

Paniolo Hale. Kaluakoi, HI 96770

Local Phone: (909) 474-5809

Email: plntflwrs@charter.net

Island: Molokai

This spacious open-air condo is located on Molokai's sunny west end at Kaluakoi. The architecture is plantation-style with two tall french doors spanning the length of the main floor. It is two-story with 1,200 sq. ft. of space.

Hotel Molokai

A genuine hideaway from all things mainstream. Located on the exotic beach of Kamiloloa, you'll find our Polynesian village of bungalows replete with kitchenettes and Wi-Fi. Hotel Moloka'i is just five minutes from the island's largest city, Kaunakakai.

1300 Kamehameha V Hwy. Kaunakakai, HI 96748

Local Phone: (808) 553-5347

Email: guestservices@hotelmolokai.com

Island: Molokai

Aloha! Welcome to Hotel Moloka'i, a genuine hideaway from all things mainstream. Located on the exotic beach of Kamiloloa and adjacent to Hawaii's only barrier reef, you'll find our Polynesian village of bungalows replete with kitchenettes and Wi-Fi. Known as the birthplace of Hula and deemed the "Friendly Isle," Hotel Moloka'i is just five minutes from the island's largest city, Kaunakakai. We look forward to your stay!

Molokai Wedding

On Molokai you'll find unique, stress-free alternatives to a larger wedding that can take away from your special day. This is the ultimate destination wedding for intimate weddings. Whether you're saying your vows on the grounds of the Hotel Molokai or saying "I do" on one of Molokai's serene beaches, a personal wedding experience awaits you both on Molokai.

Molokai Honeymoons

Whether it's for a long retreat or for a Maui daytrip, Molokai provides the perfect encore for your wedding festivities. Here, you can both relax, untethered from wedding planning and organizing, in a serene, untouched paradise that promises an unforgettable experience.

Charter a sightseeing boat from Kaunakakai Harbor from December to May and spot magnificent pods of humpback whales together. Experience top-notch snorkeling on Molokai's south shore, along

Hawaii's longest barrier reef. Or take advantage of the island's clear skies that are ideal for stargazing at night.

Whether you choose to explore all that the island has to offer or choose to do nothing at all, Molokai will provide you both with lasting honeymoon memories. Take advantage of our honeymoon resources and start planning the vacation of your dreams.

Relaxation and Romance
Ideas for Couples

Misty waterfalls, sun-kissed beaches, thrilling opportunities for adventure our six Hawaiian Islands invite you to slow down and savor the company of the one you love. One of the world's top honeymoon destinations, Hawaii's alluring landscapes provide an idyllic setting for intimate and relaxing escapes.

Here's a look at the couples' experiences on each island:

Kauai

Take hand-in-hand hikes into Waimea Canyon and Kokee State Park. Soak up unparalleled natural beauty at several botanical gardens and sail along the towering Napali Coast. Savor intimate dinners at romantic restaurants in Kauai's finest resorts, and rejuvenate your mind, body and spirit at the island's spas.

Oahu

Take a couples' surfing lesson on Waikiki Beach, and drive up the Pali Highway to Nuuanu Pali Lookout for spectacular vistas of the Windward Coast. Experience the serenity of a Buddhist sanctuary in the Valley of the Temples or browse the acclaimed collections at the Honolulu Museum of Art.

Lanai

Spot rainbow-colored fishes and protected tide pools at Hulopoe Bay's marine sanctuary. Embark on a short hike along the cliffs to Puu Pehe, also known as Sweetheart Rock. Feel the trade winds as you watch a quiet sunset from Kaumalapau Harbor.

Maui

Watch the sunrise wrapped in a blanket at the top of Haleakala Crater, or admire the sunset as you cruise along the golden Kihei coastline. Hike to one of East Maui's spectacular waterfalls, then enjoy a couples' massage at a resort in Wailea. Browse the charming shops of Lahaina and peruse the Maui Arts and Cultural Center.

Molokai

Sleep in at a cozy bed and breakfast on the island's West End and shop in the charming towns of Kaunakakai and Maunaloa. Catch unobstructed sunsets at Papohaku Beach, Kapukahehu Beach (Dixie

Maru Beach) or Kapuaiwa Coconut Grove also amazing places for stargazing.

Island of Hawaii

Spend the day window shopping and sightseeing together in <u>Historic Kailua Village (Kailua-Kona)</u>, the coffee and art town of Holualoa or beautiful <u>Hawi</u>. Take a road trip along the <u>Hamakua Heritage Corridor</u>, then wander the historic streets of <u>Downtown Hilo</u>. Set up a tee time at a spectacular golf course on the Kohala Coast, and hit the spa at one of the island's luxurious resorts.

Lanai

Welcome to Lanai

Those seeking peace, tranquility and an escape from the busyness of everyday life will find their solace in the serenity offered by Lanai. Hawaii's smallest inhabited island, Lanai offers visitors a lovely reprieve from the fast pace of their usual schedules. Originally an island-wide pineapple plantation, Lanai now is known for its quiet beauty and luxurious five-star resorts. Surround yourself with serenity and decadence at the best spots Hawaii has to offer amid world class resorts like the Four Seasons Resort at Manele Bay. Go window shopping amid charming boutiques in the island's central town of Lanai City or make memories road tripping along the Norfolk pine-lined Munro Trail, a roadway offering sweeping and majestic views of the island's pristine beauty. Also a must, visiting Hulopoe Bay, a protected marine reserve with a wealth of sea creatures including Hawaii's famous spinner dolphins.

The "Most Secluded Island" offers adventure and romance

If you're looking for nightlife, Lanai may not be your best choice. Alternately known as Hawaii's "Most Secluded Island" and "The Pineapple Island" (it once hosted the world's largest pineapple plantation), Lanai is home to a mere 5,000 residents the vast majority of whom live in the cool heights of Lanai City overlooking the vast, red-dirt fields below.

What Lanai lacks in discos it more than makes up for in outdoor adventure. Not far from Lanai City you'll find the Munro Trail, which climbs from the city's 1,600-foot elevation through stands of Norfolk pines (planted in the early 1900s by New Zealand naturalist George Munro) and up to the highest point on the island, Lanaihale ("house of Lanai"). From this point at 3,370 feet five other islands are visible on a clear day, along with much of Lanai including Maunalei Gulch, where the island's defenders were unable to stop the advance of Kamehameha I's warriors in his quest to unite the Hawaiian Islands in the late 18th and early 19th centuries.

Points of Interest

Back on the coast visitors have a number of options, though many require either a four-wheel-drive vehicle or a good set of hiking shoes. In Kaunolu Village, a national historic landmark on the south side of the island, some of the best-preserved ruins and petroglyph carvings from ancient Hawaii are found. To the southeast are the abandoned fishing villages of Lopa, Naha and Keomuku, all of which are rumored to be guarded by the mana (spiritual power) of former residents. (It is said that if you climb the coconut trees here without first saying the proper prayers, you will not come back down.)

On the eastern shore, Shipwreck Beach is a haven for beachcombers and a testament to the island's reputation as an unsafe harbor in a storm. Named for the remains of a World War II liberty ship rusting offshore, this eight-mile strand captures everything from Nautilus shells to timbers and assorted ocean-going debris. While the waters around Shipwreck are generally too rough to swim safely, the southeasterly shore facing Hulopo'e Bay offers crystal-clear waters and some of the best snorkeling in Hawaii.

Although agriculture and ranching are still a vital part of Lanai's economy, the island is these days better known as an upscale tourist destination, offering two five-star resorts the Manele Bay Hotel and The Lodge at Ko'ele.

What's More...

- ✓ Lanai was formed about 1.5 million years ago by the volcano Palawai. The island is currently 140 square miles in size.
- ✓ Southeast Lanai's Kaunolu Point is said to be the birthplace of the modern sport of cliff diving, begun by Hawaiian warriors leaping into the ocean from an 80-foot ledge as proof of their courage. Each August, the Cliff Diving World Championships are held at this same spot.
- ✓ The Lodge at Ko'ele hosts a "visiting artists" program throughout the year, with a varying schedule of lectures and performances by world-renowned musicians, artists, chefs and more.
- ✓ Lanai's official flower is the kauna'oa (yellow and orange air plant)
- ✓ The island's official color is orange

Regions of Lanai

Central Lanai

Wide open plains dotted with Cook pine trees give Central Lanai a more rustic feel than the other Hawaiian Islands. The higher elevations of Central Lanai also make for cooler temperatures similar to Upcountry Maui. If you're traveling to Central Lanai from Hulopoe Bay you'll pass through the Palawai Basin, an area once covered with pineapple fields. To the east, the Munro Trail leads to Lanaihale, Lanai's highest peak.

The geographic and cultural epicenter of the island is in Lanai City. Centered around Dole Park, you'll discover one of a kind shops, local dining and unique art galleries in Lanai City. You'll also find the historic Hotel Lanai, which has welcomed guests since 1923. Just up the street is the lavish Four Seasons Resort Lanai, The Lodge at Koele. The Lodge is unlike any other resort in Hawaii featuring fine dining, horseback riding, tennis, archery, and a clay shooting range.

Lanai City
What: Lanai's central town
Where: Central Lanai, three miles from Lanai airport

Just 3 miles north of the airport, Lanai City was founded in the early 1900s as a plantation town at the center of the island's booming pineapple industry. In its heyday, Lanai was responsible for 75 percent of the world's pineapple production, and the fruit is still celebrated in the city's annual Pineapple Festival. Located in Lanai's central highlands and at an elevation of 1,700 feet, Lanai City is noticeably cooler than coastal areas of the island.

Many of the shops, restaurants and businesses of Lanai City are found near Dole Park. This grassy spot is a popular place for locals to gather, meet and picnic. The towering pines lining the park provide just the right amount of shade on a sunny afternoon.

Lanai City is also a great place for unique shopping and inexpensive dining. Visit the Local Gentry, a small boutique clothing shop with unique finds. The Lanai Art Center displays local artists' works, from ceramics to watercolors. After window-shopping, grab a cup of coffee from Coffee Works, or pull up a chair at the Blue Ginger Café, Café 565 or Pele's Other Garden for a true local dining experience. For entertainment, enjoy the local entertainment and ambiance at Lanai City Grille. You'll also find additional dining and shopping options at the Four Seasons Resort Lanai.

Finally, Lanai City is home to two outstanding hotels. Hotel Lanai is a country inn with charming plantation-style décor secluded amongst the Cook island pines.

Munro Trail
What: 12.8-mile hiking trail with scenic views
Where: Begins just north of Lanai City and ends in the Palawai Basin

The rustic Munro Trail begins just north of Lanai City, past the stables of the Four Seasons Resort Lanai, The Lodge at Koele. Named for George Munro, the naturalist from New Zealand who arrived in 1890, this 12.8-mile, one-lane dirt road offers sweeping vistas among the majestic Cook pine trees introduced by Munro himself.

The trail offers spectacular views and the 1,600-foot elevation takes you through a rain forest filled with ohia lehua, ironwood, eucalyptus and pine trees. Only 2.5 miles into the trail you'll find a scenic lookout. You'll discover stunning canyon views of Maunalei gulch, and on a clear day, you can see all six Hawaiian islands at once. The trail, which can also be biked or hiked, also takes you to the top of Lanaihale (House of Lanai), Lanai's highest peak at 3,370 feet.

Things to Do on Lanai

Lanai Restaurants

With its five-star resorts and discerning clientele, dining on Lanai has become a world-class affair. Between the mom-and-pop cafes of Lanai City and the high-end resort restaurants that turn eating any meal into a special occasion, this tiny island has more than enough dining choices to satisfy any appetite.

For local flavor, head to Lanai City favorites like Blue Ginger Cafe, Cafe 565 and Richard's Market. At the historic Hotel Lanai, the Lanai City Grille is a great option for an intimate, romantic dinner with wine.

The Four Seasons Resort Lanai offers a range of upscale options. One Forty specializes in steaks, seafood and unbeatable ocean views, while trendy Nobu slices up melt-in-your-mouth sashimi and creative Japanese cuisine. Just across the property, Views at Manele Golf Course offers casual pupu (Hawaiian small plates) and as the name suggests stunning views of the beach, golf course and even breaching humpbacks during whale season.

Nobu Lana'i
Set cliffside overlooking a protected marine preserve, Nobu Lanai offers sweeping panoramic views and innovative Japanese cuisine.

One Manele Road. Lanai City, HI 96763

Local Phone: (808) 565-2000

US Toll Free: (800) 321-4666

Island: Lanai

Set cliffside overlooking a protected marine preserve, Nobu Lanai offers sweeping panoramic views and innovative Japanese cuisine. Drawing upon Chef Nobu Matsuhisa's classical training as a sushi chef in Tokyo, his life abroad in South America and his travels around the world, Nobu Lanai showcases the chef's signature new-style Japanese cuisine, as well as new creations infusing local Hawaiian ingredients.

Sports Bar & Grill
This open-air sports bar with dramatic views of the ocean offers a lively social atmosphere to gather and mingle. Guests can enjoy pool and

other table games or relax with their favorite sports program, broadcast on the Lounge's 46-inch LCD television.

Four Seasons Resort Lanai. One Manele Bay Road. Lanai City, HI 96763
Local Phone: (808) 565-2000
US Toll Free: (800) 321-4666
Island: Lanai

This open-air sports bar with dramatic views of the ocean offers a lively social atmosphere to gather and mingle. Guests can enjoy pool and other table games or relax with their favorite sports program, broadcast on the Lounge's 46-inch LCD television.

ONE FORTY, American Steak and Hawaiian Seafood

This ocean-view restaurant offers breakfast and an extensive steak and seafood dinner menu. With an emphasis on local ingredients, Chef Joseph Yaple showcases prime and wagyu beef from Snake River Farms and local Hawaiian catch, prepared to perfection.

1 Manele Bay Rd. Lanai City, HI 96763
Local Phone: (808) 565-2000
US Toll Free: (800) 321-4666
Island: Lanai

This ocean-view restaurant offers breakfast and an extensive steak and seafood dinner menu. With an emphasis on local ingredients, Chef

Joseph Yaple showcases prime and wagyu beef from Snake River Farms and local Hawaiian catch, prepared to perfection. Traditional side dishes from a wide selection complement main courses, while an accomplished wine list features a variety of fine labels.

Lanai City Grille
Lanai City Grille, Hotel Lanai's in-house restaurant, awaits you with fabulous food and a wonderfully fun atmosphere, a place where you truly experience a sense of Aloha.

828 Lanai Avenue. Lanai City, HI 96763
Local Phone: (808) 565-7211
US Toll Free: (800) 795-7211
Island: Lanai

Lanai City Grille, Hotel Lanai's in-house restaurant, awaits you with fabulous food and a wonderfully fun atmosphere, a place where you truly experience a sense of Aloha. Each night features locally caught fish prepared in a variety of innovative ways, prime meats and our signature rotisserie chicken.

VIEWS at Manele Golf Course
The Challenge at Manele Clubhouse specializes in casual, light fare with the distinctive flavors of Lana'i. A sampling of dishes includes:

Grilled Fish Tacos with mahi mahi, cabbage, spicy aoli, sour cream, guacamole and salsa and Fish & Chips.

1 Manele Road. Lanai City, HI 96763

Local Phone: (808) 565-2222

US Toll Free: (800) 321-4666

Email: reservations@lanai-resorts.com

Island: Lanai

The Challenge at Manele Clubhouse specializes in casual, light fare with the distinctive flavors of Lana'i. A sampling of dishes includes: Grilled Fish Tacos with mahi mahi, cabbage, spicy aoli, sour cream, guacamole and salsa and Fish & Chips with crispy fried fresh fish, tartar sauce, and fries.

Malibu Farm

Overlooking the sparkling pool with commanding views of the ocean, The Lounge is located in the lower lobby area and offers an unforgettable setting for guests to enjoy sunset cocktails and after dinner drinks and live entertainment.

One Manele Road. Lanai City, HI 96763

Local Phone: (808) 565-2000

US Toll Free: (800) 321-4666

Island: Lanai

Overlooking the sparkling pool with commanding views of the ocean, The Lounge is located in the lower lobby area and offers an unforgettable setting for guests to enjoy sunset cocktails and after dinner drinks and live entertainment. The elegant lounge features a refined cocktail menu with emphasis on house made ingredients, local produce and handcrafted methods, complimented by a world class selection of wines and sparkling wines by the glass.

Lanai Accommodations

Ever since its days as a Dole plantation drew to a close, Lanai has lured travelers seeking a bygone, off-the-beaten-path Hawaii. This no-stoplight island has just two hotels, but what Lanai lacks in quantity it more than makes up for in quality, not to mention the greatest luxury of all: seclusion.

On the island's south side, The Four Seasons Resort Lanai overlooks pristine Hulopoe Bay, a marine preserve with protected tide pools ideal for snorkeling and swimming.

The 1930s-era Hotel Lanai is a charming in-town hideaway and an affordable alternative to the island's resorts. Originally built as lodging for Dole executives, the property now has 11 guest rooms and an esteemed restaurant, the Lanai City Grille.

Four Seasons Resort Lanai

Discover an ocean-side paradise bordering a marine preserve that teems with colorful reef fish and protected species such as green sea turtles and spinner dolphins. Explore this untouched island playground, and experience your own private Hawaii.

One Manele Bay Road. Lanai City, HI 96763

Local Phone: (808) 353-3062

US Toll Free: (808) 353-3062

Email: kurk.diekhoff@fourseasons.com

Island: Lanai

Welcome to Four Seasons Resort Lanai. Discover an ocean-side paradise bordering a marine preserve that teems with colorful reef fish and protected species such as green sea turtles and spinner dolphins. Laze on the white-sand beach or golf on two world-ranked courses. Explore this untouched island playground, and experience your own private Hawaii.

Hotel Lanai

Hotel Lanai, Hawaii's Best Little Inn, nestled in towering Cook Pines at the top of Lanai City invites you to slow down, step back in time and enjoy a simpler way of life.

828 Lanai Avenue. Lanai City, HI 96763

Local Phone: (808) 565-7211

US Toll Free: (800) 795-7211

Island: Lanai

Hotel Lanai, Hawaii's Best Little Inn, nestled in towering Cook Pines at the top of Lanai City invites you to slow down, step back in time and enjoy a simpler way of life. A historic landmark in Lanai City, the hotel has ten plantation-style rooms featuring Hawaiian quilt bedcovers, ceiling fans and hardwood floors. All rooms feature original art by local artist Mike Carroll. The hidden gem is the one bed room cottage, the only accommodation with a TV and DVD player. The cottage comes with its own deck complete with a hammock for those lazy afternoons.

Lana'i City Bar & Grille, Hotel Lana'i's in-house restaurant offers local favorites in a relaxed atmosphere. Whether enjoying dinner with friends or celebrating a special event, Lana'i City Bar & Grille is the perfect gathering place.

Attractions on Lanai

You'd be forgiven for thinking that Lanai's only activities are hiking, snorkeling, and golf.

Those, after, all, are the most popular activities and the best way to explore the outdoors, but there are also a number of traditional attractions that are scattered across the island.

In the cool uplands of Lanai City, where old plantation homes with wooden front porches are shaded by Cook Island pines, you'll find the Lanai Culture and Heritage Center across the street from Dole Park. Here in this small but informative center, visitors can learn the history of Lanai from settlement up through today, and peruse traditional Hawaiian artifacts and the collection of black and white photos.

In addition to being one of Lanai's best attractions, the staff can point you in the right direction for what to see on your trip, whether it's searching for shells on Shipwreck Beach or visiting the Luahiwa Petroglyphs. Or, for one of the best attractions on Lanai, experience a sunset at Keahiakawelo also known as "Garden of the Gods" where the deep red hues of the rocky landscape make it seem like the surface of Mars.

To visit a village site frozen in time, one of the best places to see on Lanai is ancient Kaunolu Village, where Hawaiian chiefs would spend their summers on the island's southwestern coast. When strolling the dry and rock-strewn shoreline, you'll see the imposing Halulu heiau that was constructed out on the point, and the notch in the cliff where King Kahekili would courageously leap towards the sea. The canoe house, or hale, still sits on the shore, and while reaching the site requires a couple miles of off road hiking, it's one of the best Lanai attractions for Hawaiian history and culture.

On the completely opposite side of the island, or the east coast facing Maui, historic Ka Lanakila church has a hauntingly beautiful way of portraying the modern day Keomoku ghost town. Here on a coast that's rung by palm groves and fronted by long stretches of sand, there was once a thriving, prosperous village and even a sugar plantation. All of that changed after 1900, when the plantation folded and pineapple was planted in the central Palawai Basin which led to construction of Lanai City and Keomoku's demise. Today, by hiring a rugged 4×4 Jeep, you can visit the historic Hawaiian church on a drive of the southeastern coast, continuing the journey to other Lanai attractions like Naha or Lopa Beach.

Finally, for one of the island's most photo-worthy sights and a great way to end the trip, take the short hike to Pu'u Pehe Overlook Lanai's most popular attraction. This 80-foot sea stack sits just off the point from the busy Manele Small Boat Harbor, and is a site that's steeped in Hawaiian legend of princesses, tragedy, and love. From the white sands of Hulopo'e Bay, enjoy the short, five-minute walk on a narrow and rocky trail, which then emerges at a hidden cove and a sweeping view of the rock. Of the dozens of different attractions on Lanai there's none more scenic or popular, and it's a spot as storied in tourist brochures as it is in ancient lore.

Lanai Beaches

If you're longing for a true tropical escape, you'll find seclusion, romance and beauty on the beaches of Lanai. The island has 18 miles of coastline dotted with remote beaches where you can sink your toes into soft white sand and gaze out at rolling blue waves. Here are a few popular Lanai beaches you can visit.

South Lanai

Hulopoe Beach Park is a sweeping crescent-shaped beach located on the southern coast in Hulopoe Bay, fronting the Four Seasons Resort Lanai. With fantastic snorkeling in the crystalline water, large tide pools to explore and Puu Pehe (Sweetheart Rock) just a short hike away, this is the Lanai's most popular and accessible beach. Restroom and picnic facilities are available.

North Lanai

Polihua Beach is harder to reach but worth the journey. Take a 4-wheel drive adventure about an hour northwest of Lanai City to find two miles of pristine and (more often than not) blissfully empty coast perfect for sunbathing or beachcombing. Note that strong winds and currents make the ocean too dangerous for swimming, and no restroom facilities are available.

Polihua Beach

Where: North Lanai

Activities: Sunbathing, beachcombing

While Polihua Beach may be harder to reach, it's worth the journey if you're looking for a secluded beach for sunbathing and beachcombing. Weather conditions permitting, take a 4-wheel drive adventure about an hour northwest of Lanai City. Or, hire a tour guide to take you to this beautiful two miles of pristine and (more often than not) blissfully empty coast. Note that strong winds and currents make the ocean too dangerous for swimming, and no restroom facilities are available.

Lanai Land Activities

Adventurous souls journey to Lanai from near and far to traverse 400 miles of dirt roads, hike trails peppered with breathtaking views and bask in the sun at 18 miles of secluded beaches. Take the rocky road to Kaiolohia (Shipwreck Beach) for dazzling views of Molokai and Maui, go horseback riding amid lush valleys and ironwood forests near Lanai City, amble the Munro Trail through the lush rainforest to Lanai's highest point at 3,370 feet the opportunities for adventure on Lanai are endless.

Hiking on Lanai

For a quick, 15-20 minute hike with a beautiful pay-off, head southeast from Hulopoe Bay to the cliffs overlooking Puu Pehe, or Sweetheart

Rock. For a much more challenging hike, set off on the Munro Trail. Winding its way from the Four Seasons Resort Lanai, The Lodge at Koele through mountain grasslands and rainforests filled with Cook pine trees, eucalyptus and native ohia lehua, you'll eventually reach the 3,370-foot peak of Lanaihale. Lanai's remote beaches like Polihua and Kaiolohia also give you plenty of real estate to stretch your legs. Please check with your hotel concierge for directions before setting off on your hiking adventure.

Puu Pehe (Sweetheart Rock)
What: An iconic Lanai landmark between Manele and Hulopoe Bay
Where: A short hike from the Four Seasons Resort Lanai

One hundred and fifty feet off the southern coastline between Manele and Hulopoe Bays, the iconic Puu Pehe, or Sweetheart Rock, rises majestically 80 feet out of the water. Besides being a picturesque natural landmark, Puu Pehe is also steeped in Hawaiian folklore.

Legend tells of two lovers, a Hawaiian maiden named Pehe from Lahaina and a young warrior from Lanai named Makakehau. He was so taken with her beauty that whenever he laid eyes upon her they would mist up in tears. Hence his name: Maka (eyes) Kehau (mist). He took her back to Lanai and hid her in a sea cave at the base of Manele's cliffs.

One day while gathering supplies he noticed a storm brewing and started back, only to find Pehe drowned by the surge of the storm waves. Stricken with grief, Makakehau gathered his beloved in his arms. He wailed out to the gods and his ancestors to help him climb the steep rock island where he eventually buried her. He then jumped from this 80-foot summit into the pounding surf below.

To get to Puu Pehe you can take a short hike from the Four Seasons Resort Lanai southeast past Hulopoe Beach and the rocky tide pools. Hike up the path along the rocky cliffs for about 15-20 minutes and you'll soon overlook this Lanai landmark. Sunsets here can be especially romantic with dramatic views of Hulopoe Bay. You may even spot the spinner dolphins that frequent these waters perched atop this scenic lookout.

Lanai Golf

Find your sweet spot in Lanai without even taking a swing. On this modest island, you'll find two golf courses of remarkable prestige. Along the southern coast, Jack Nicklaus created one of his most famous masterpieces, Manele Golf Course. With three holes built on the seaside cliffs above Hulopoe Bay, this target-style course roams across several hundred acres of natural lava outcroppings, using plunging ravines, native kiawe and towering trees as natural hazards. Each hole has five tee locations allowing golfers at all levels to enjoy one of Jack Nicklaus' crowning achievements in golf design. Manele Golf Course ranks among the best resort courses in Hawaii and the world by leading publications and travel guides.

Manele Golf Course

Award-winning Jack Nicklaus signature design golf course. Spectacular panoramic ocean views from every hole along with dramatic cliff side ocean golf holes. Facilities include VIEWS Clubhouse restaurant, logo golf shop, and driving range/practice facility

1 Manele Road. Lanai City, HI 96763

Local Phone: (808) 565-2222

US Toll Free: (800) 321-4666

Island: Lanai

High above the crashing surf of Hulopoe Bay, Manele Golf Course is an outstanding course that more than lives up to its name. Built on lava outcroppings, the course features three holes on cliffs which use the Pacific Ocean as a water hazard. The five-tee concept challenges the best golfers - tee shots over natural gorges and ravines must be precise. This dramatic, unspoiled natural terrain is a stunning backdrop, and every hole offers majestic ocean views. During the winter, you may even catch spectacular sightings of whales right from the fairways.

Lanai Gardens, Plantations & Parks

With tall, stately Cook pine trees and cooler weather due to elevation, Lanai is unlike any other island in Hawaii. Sitting just to the west of Maui, which gets most of the rain, the island is drier than other islands giving Central Lanai a more rustic feel.

Palawai Basin, once home to the world's largest pineapple plantations, is now a scenic, open plain. At the 590-acre Kanepuu Preserve on the north side of Lanai, visitors can learn about 48 species of endemic plants. Just north, experience a lunar-like rock garden at Keahiakawelo, the Garden of the Gods.

Keahiakawelo
What: Otherworldly rock garden
Where: A 45-minute drive from Lanai City. Get clear directions from your concierge.
More Info: A four-wheel drive vehicle or mountain bike is required

Keahiakawelo, also known as The Fires of Kawelo, is an otherworldly rock garden at the end of rocky Polihua Road. Located roughly 45 minutes from Lanai City on the northwest side of the island, its mysterious lunar topography is populated with boulders and rock towers.

According to Hawaiian lore, this windswept landscape is the result of a contest between two *kahuna*(priests) from Lanai and Molokai. Each was challenged to keep a fire burning on their respective island longer than the other, and the winner's island would be rewarded with great abundance. The Lanai kahuna, Kawelo, used every piece of vegetation in Keahiakawelo to keep his fire burning, which is why this area is so barren today.

The rock towers, spires, and formations formed by centuries of erosion are at their most enchanting at dusk. The setting sun casts a warm orange glow on the rocks illuminating them in brilliant reds and purples. And on a clear day, visitors can see the islands of Molokai and Oahu from these high elevations. Visitors should be aware that Polihua Road is unpaved and is only accessible via four-wheel drive vehicle or mountain bike. The removal or stacking of rocks is *kapu* (forbidden).

Horseback Riding on Lanai
Discover the timeless landscapes of Lanai on horseback with the Lanai Adventure Center. Ride into the hills surrounding Koele once the center of ranching operations on the island or explore the lush woodlands, home to axis deer, Mouflon sheep and turkey. Talk story with your wrangler as you pass through Ironwood forests to breathtaking vistas of neighbor islands. An assortment of trails meander through the wooded peaks and valleys of this extraordinary upland terrain, so riders of all ages and skill levels can saddle up.

Customized private excursions, children's and carriage rides and individual lessons are also available.

Lanai Water Activities

Water adventures begin in Hulopoe Bay in South Lanai, one of the island's most picturesque places to swim and snorkel. Thanks to its protected bay, it is perfect for sunbathing, snorkeling and exploring the many tide pools carved out of volcanic rock. You could even see spinner dolphins and the marine life playing just off shore. For scuba diving enthusiasts, the famous lava caverns of the Lanai Cathedrals off of the south coast are a must dive. And every winter to early spring, migrating humpback whales can often be seen offshore enjoying Lanai's warm waters.

Boating on Lanai
Take a sunrise or sunset sail from Maui to Manele Harbor on the southern coast of Lanai with Trilogy Excursions. Spinning Dolphin Charters of Lanai offers private fishing and boating tours. Or book a boat dive to the Lanai Cathedrals through Lanai Ocean Sports.

You can also take day trips to and from Manele Harbor and Lahaina Harbor in Maui through the Expeditions Ferry service. There are multiple round-trips daily, and during the winter months (December through May), you could even spot a humpback whale during your crossing. Ferry trips take roughly an hour.

Lana'i Ocean Sports

Lana'i Ocean Sports is committed to excellence by creating lifelong memories through personalized service delivered with Aloha. As stewards and sailors, we perpetuate our Hawaiian culture and protect our environment. As an 'Ohana, we value each other and inspire integrity, innovation, and community.

MANELE SMALL BOAT HARBOR. Lanai City, HI 96763

Local Phone: (808) 866-8256

Email: info@lanaioceansports.com

Island: Lanai

Lana'i Ocean Sports is a company committed to excellence by creating lifelong memories through personalized service delivered with Aloha. As stewards and sailors, we perpetuate our Hawaiian culture and protect our environment. As an 'Ohana, we value each other and inspire integrity, innovation, and community.

Expeditions: Maui - Lanai Ferry

Expeditions, the Lahaina-Lanai Ferry, provides affordable service between Maui and Lanai, five times a day, every day! Packages are available for a day of championship golf, luxury accommodations, Jeep rental, 4X4 Trekker Tours, Archery, Sporting Clays.

658 Front St Ste 127. Lahaina, HI 96761

Local Phone: (808) 661-3756

US Toll Free: (800) 695-2624

Email: reservations@go-lanai.com

Island: Lanai

Expeditions, the Lahaina-Lanai Ferry, provides affordable service between Maui and Lanai, five times a day, every day! Packages are available for a day of championship golf, luxury accommodations, Jeep rental, 4X4 Trekker Tours, Archery, Sporting Clays.

Snorkeling and Scuba on Lanai

For beginning snorkelers, Hulopoe Bay is the best spot on the island to get started. The calm waters of this protected marine preserve hosts a variety of colorful fish close to shore. Note that most other beaches in North Lanai like Polihua Beach and Kaiolohia (Shipwreck Beach) have strong currents so swimming is discouraged.

For seasoned scuba divers, the Lanai Cathedrals are Lanai's most popular dive spots. First Cathedral and Second Cathedral were formed from massive underwater lava tubes. When light shines through the holes in the lava, it looks like sunlight shining through the stained glass windows of an underwater church. It's a diving experience unlike any you've ever seen. Trilogy Ocean Sports Lanai is the only full service dive operation on Lanai or you can book a dive tour from neighboring Maui.

Expeditions: Maui - Lanai Ferry

Expeditions, the Lahaina-Lanai Ferry, provides affordable service between Maui and Lanai, five times a day, every day! Packages are available for a day of championship golf, luxury accommodations, Jeep rental, 4X4 Trekker Tours, Archery, Sporting Clays.

658 Front St Ste 127. Lahaina, HI 96761

Local Phone: (808) 661-3756

US Toll Free: (800) 695-2624

Email: reservations@go-lanai.com

Island: Lanai

Expeditions, the Lahaina-Lanai Ferry, provides affordable service between Maui and Lanai, five times a day, every day! Packages are available for a day of championship golf, luxury accommodations, Jeep rental, 4X4 Trekker Tours, Archery, Sporting Clays.

Lana'i Ocean Sports

Lana'i Ocean Sports is committed to excellence by creating lifelong memories through personalized service delivered with Aloha. As stewards and sailors, we perpetuate our Hawaiian culture and protect our environment. As an 'Ohana, we value each other and inspire integrity, innovation, and community.

MANELE SMALL BOAT HARBOR. Lanai City, HI 96763

Local Phone: (808) 866-8256

Email: info@lanaioceansports.com

Island: Lanai

Lana'i Ocean Sports is a company committed to excellence by creating lifelong memories through personalized service delivered with Aloha. As stewards and sailors, we perpetuate our Hawaiian culture and protect our environment. As an 'Ohana, we value each other and inspire integrity, innovation, and community.

Tours depart from Manele Small Boat Harbor and our current offerings include:

-Lana'i Snorkel Experience/One-Tank/SUP

-Whale Watch Expedition (Dec 15th-April 15th)

-Sunset Sail Expedition

-PADI Beginner and Advanced 3-day Certification Courses

-Private hourly tours aboard Lana'i and Kalulu

-Two Tank Cert Dive

Whether you are a guest at the Four Seasons Lana'i or just spending the day on Lana'i, come experience the Lana'i coastline in luxury aboard one of our three vessels. Bookings through the Four Seasons Activity desk.

Lanai Wedding

Imagine your own secluded island. Envision saying your vows as gentle trade winds blow off of Hulopoe Bay. Picture an intimate ceremony under the stars in the cool uplands of Central Lanai, shared with the ones you love. Through the luxury and impeccable service of its world-class resorts, Lanai provides an idyllic setting to take your first steps into a richer world.

It's no wonder why Bill Gates, one of the world's richest men, shared his vows here at the Four Seasons Resort Lanai on a dramatic bluff overlooking Hulopoe Bay. Whether it's with the deep blue of the Pacific as your backdrop or in the shade of majestic Cook pine trees, Lanai provides a more personal alternative to other destination wedding venues, making the day you've always dreamed of even more special.

Lanai Honeymoons

Lanai's isolation and tranquility make it the perfect honeymoon destination. With little or no crowds, personalized service and acres of unspoiled beauty, Lanai can make you feel like this intimate island was made for the both of you.

Start by choosing your lodging, from the plantation style inn of the historic Hotel Lanai to the opulent luxury of the Four Seasons Resort Lanai or the rustic grace of the Four Seasons Resort Lanai, The Lodge at Koele. Then choose your adventure. Snorkel, sunbathe and watch the dolphins off of romantic Hulopoe Bay. Hike up to Puu Pehe, also known as Sweetheart Rock. Or take 4-wheel drive to the remote sands Polihua Beach. The island is yours to explore together.

These are just some of the romantic experiences Lanai has to offer. Take advantage of our honeymoon resources and start planning the vacation of your dreams.

Relaxation and Romance
Ideas for Couples

Misty waterfalls, sun-kissed beaches, thrilling opportunities for adventure our six Hawaiian Islands invite you to slow down and savor the company of the one you love. One of the world's top honeymoon destinations, Hawaii's alluring landscapes provide an idyllic setting for intimate and relaxing escapes.

Here's a look at the couples' experiences on each island:

Kauai

Take hand-in-hand hikes into Waimea Canyon and Kokee State Park. Soak up unparalleled natural beauty at several botanical gardens and sail along the towering Napali Coast. Savor intimate dinners at romantic restaurants in Kauai's finest resorts, and rejuvenate your mind, body and spirit at the island's spas.

Oahu

Take a couples' surfing lesson on Waikiki Beach, and drive up the Pali Highway to Nuuanu Pali Lookout for spectacular vistas of the Windward Coast. Experience the serenity of a Buddhist sanctuary in the Valley of the Temples or browse the acclaimed collections at the Honolulu Museum of Art.

Lanai

Spot rainbow-colored fishes and protected tide pools at Hulopoe Bay's marine sanctuary. Embark on a short hike along the cliffs to Puu Pehe, also known as Sweetheart Rock. Feel the trade winds as you watch a quiet sunset from Kaumalapau Harbor.

Maui

Watch the sunrise wrapped in a blanket at the top of Haleakala Crater, or admire the sunset as you cruise along the golden Kihei coastline. Hike to one of East Maui's spectacular waterfalls, then enjoy a couples' massage at a resort in Wailea. Browse the charming shops of Lahaina and peruse the Maui Arts and Cultural Center.

Molokai

Sleep in at a cozy bed and breakfast on the island's West End and shop in the charming towns of Kaunakakai and Maunaloa. Catch unobstructed sunsets at Papohaku Beach, Kapukahehu Beach (Dixie Maru Beach) or Kapuaiwa Coconut Grove also amazing places for stargazing.

Island of Hawaii

Spend the day window shopping and sightseeing together in Historic Kailua Village (Kailua-Kona), the coffee and art town of Holualoa or beautiful Hawi. Take a road trip along the Hamakua Heritage Corridor, then wander the historic streets of Downtown Hilo. Set up a tee time at a spectacular golf course on the Kohala Coast, and hit the spa at one of the island's luxurious resorts.

Maui

Maui locals are often asked if they ever get "island fever." After all living full time on a tropical island must eventually get boring, right?

As it turns out, there are so many things to do in Maui it isn't really a problem. From the moment the sun rises above Haleakala Crater, to when it sets off Ka'anapali Beach, the island is rich in outdoor adventure and opportunities to explore.

Just take a look at the ocean activities found all across the island. Many of the best things to do on Maui are either out or under the waves, and between surfing, snorkeling, diving, canoeing, bodysurfing, kitesurfing, or fishing, there's always an activity to match the wind and wave conditions for that day.

On shore, waterfall hunters and swimming hole seekers can travel the Road to Hana one of the top 10 things to do on Maui for visitors and locals alike. Take a dip beneath Twin Falls or explore Waiʻanapanapa Caves, and a sunrise soak at the Pools of Oheʻo is the ultimate Hana escape.

Or, while it might seem like a lost art in an increasingly fast-pace world, one of the best things to do on Maui is to simply go out for a drive. If it gets too hot by the beach in summer, grab a jacket and head Upcountry for a drive through rolling green pastures. Stop at Grandma's Coffee House and relax on the covered front porch, before heading out to Ulupalakua for elk burgers and Maui-made wine. Or, take a drive around Mauna Kahalawai to the village of Kahakuloa, stopping en route at Nakalele Blowhole and hiking the trails on the coast.And, while many claim the cost of visiting or living in Maui is expensive, there are dozens of free things to do in Maui to help keep expenses at bay. Besides hiking, strolling down the beach, bodysurfing, or watching the sunset, there are festivals, markets, shows, and events that are completely free of charge. Once a month, on the Baldwin House lawn along Lahaina's famous Front Street, a free Hawaiian Music concert is held at 6pm. There are free hula shows at the

Cannery Mall, opportunities to volunteer, and free music on Wednesday nights in the courtyard of Shops at Wailea.

Finally, for some visitors (and even locals), one of the top things to do in Maui is simply spend a day shopping, in which case Pai'a, Makawao, and Lahaina are the island's best spots for gifts.

Myths, Legends and Geography

The demi-god Maui is a household name from Tonga to the Society Islands, to the Marquesas to Hawaii. Something of a trickster, Maui had a place in his heart for mortals and is celebrated throughout the Pacific for such feats as giving fire to humans (after stealing it from its supernatural guardians) and fishing the islands of the Pacific from out of their watery depths.

Over the millennia Maui's geography has changed drastically. Formed by six different volcanoes, the islands of Maui, Moloka'i, Lana'i and Kaho'olawe were once a single landmass known as *Maui Nui* ("Great Maui"). Rising sea levels eventually separated the islands, though they are still legally linked today all are part of Maui County.

What's More…

- ✓ Haleakala, whose name translates as "house of the sun," is the largest dormant volcano in the world. Not yet extinct, it is expected to erupt sometime in the next 200 years (it last erupted in 1790).

- ✓ The underwater valleys that once connected Maui, Moloka'i, Lana'i and Kaho'olawe are shallower than the surrounding ocean, providing shelter for an abundance of marine life including the humpback whales that migrate to Hawaiian waters during winter months to give birth to their calves.
- ✓ Temperatures on Maui range from 70 to 80 degrees Fahrenheit year-round, although the slopes of Haleakala Crater often see lows of 40 degrees. The lowest recorded temperature on Haleakala was 14 degrees Fahrenheit.
- ✓ Maui's official flower is the loke lani (pink cottage rose)
- ✓ Maui's official color is pink

Regions of Maui

Central Maui

Most visitors to the island will begin their vacations in Central Maui, arriving at Kahului Airport (OGG). Home to much of the island's population, this area offers plenty of interesting attractions and off-the-beaten-path treasures to uncover.

The top attraction in Central Maui is peaceful Iao Valley State Park, with fog-shrouded forests, lush valleys and burbling streams. Take an easy hike on a paved trail to view one of Maui's most iconic landmarks, the 1,200-foot Iao Needle.

At the gateway to Iao Valley State Park, you can browse local shops, restaurants and historic sites in the charming town of Wailuku.

The neighboring town of Kahului is a bustling shopping district with Maui's largest mall, and if you want to stock up for an epic trip, everything you need can be found here. The Hana Highway leads past town follow it toward Paia Town where the legenday Road to Hana begins.

Wailuku
What: County seat of Maui county and home to unique local businesses
Where: 10 minutes west of Kahului Airport

Just 10 minutes west from the Kahului Airport is Wailuku, a commercial center and the county seat of Maui's government. Visit Wailuku and explore the charming wooden storefronts around Market Street, showcasing dozens of family businesses, many of which have been in continuous operation for generations. These off-the-beaten-path "Mom and Pops" are home to local favorite shops, restaurants and bakeries.

Amid these cherished establishments, a new Wailuku is also emerging, featuring contemporary boutiques, stylish cafes and laid-back coffee shops. Check out both the classic and chic during Wailuku First Friday a fun monthly event celebrating local arts and culture. Packed with music, magicians, food, art, jewelry and fashion, this free community street party is held from 6-9 p.m., with Market Street closed to vehicular traffic from 5:30 p.m.

To find out more about this quaint town, take the "Rediscover Wailuku" walking tour developed by the Wailuku Main Street Association. The tour highlights more than 23 of the town's fascinating historical and cultural attractions, including Kaahumanu Church, the Bailey House, Pihana Kalani Heiau and the Iao Theater, built in 1927.

Nestled at the foot of the dramatic West Maui Mountains, Wailuku is also the gateway to lush Iao Valley, once a sacred burial ground for Hawaiian chiefs and home to the iconic Iao Needle.

Iao Valley State Park Maui
What: Historic state park home to iconic Iao Needle
Where: Central Maui, just west of Wailuku

Towering emerald peaks guard the lush valley floor of Iao Valley State Park. Located in Central Maui just west of Wailuku, this peaceful 4,000-acre, 10-mile long park is home to one of Maui's most recognizable landmarks, the 1,200-foot Iao Needle. This iconic green-mantled rock outcropping overlooks Iao stream and is an ideal attraction for easy hiking and sightseeing.

Aside from its natural tropical beauty, sacred Iao Valley has great historical significance. It was here in 1790 at the Battle of Kepaniwai that King Kamehameha I clashed with Maui's army in his quest to unite the islands. Even with Iao Needle serving as a lookout point, Kamehameha defeated Maui's forces in a ferocious battle that ultimately changed the course of Hawaiian history.

There is a well-marked, paved pedestrian path leading from the parking lot to view Iao Needle and the ridge-top lookout provides incredible views of the valley. The needle is sometimes covered in clouds, so an early start is your best bet for a good view. Families can also take a rainforest walk or explore interactive exhibits at the Hawaii Nature Center, which is also located within Iao Valley. Restroom facilities are available.

East Maui

When your mind imagines Maui, it probably looks a lot like the island's epic east side: cascading waterfall pools hidden in lush rainforests, roadside pineapple stands, hairpin turns around plunging sea cliffs. It's all here, along the legendary Road to Hana one big reason why East Maui is a must-see on any traveler's list.

The Hana Highway (HI-360) begins in the town of Kahului in Central Maui and snakes along the island's northern coast for 52 miles. The drive to Hana can take as few as 3 hours or last an entire day, depending on how many pictures you stop to take and food stands you sample.

After you've navigated the more than 600 white-knuckle turns and 50 bridges, you'll enter Hana a charming small town where time seems an abstract concept and aloha is a way of life. Just beyond Hana is the Kipahulu section of Haleakala National Park and the stunning Pools of Oheo (also called the Seven Sacred Pools), where a refreshing swim is the perfect reward after a long drive.

Hana Maui
What: A quiet and scenic town in East Maui
Where: The Eastern shore of Maui

Along Maui's rugged eastern coastline is the peaceful town of Hana, considered one of the last unspoiled Hawaiian frontiers. The legendary road to Hana is only 52 miles from Kahului, however the drive can take anywhere from two to four hours to complete since it's fraught with narrow one-lane bridges, hairpin turns and incredible island views.

The Hana Highway (HI-360) has 620 curves and 59 bridges. The road leads you through flourishing rainforests, flowing waterfalls, plunging pools and dramatic seascapes. There are plenty of opportunities to stop and enjoy the lovely views, so get an early start and take your time on your drive.

Historic St. Sophia's Church marks your arrival into Hana, where the pastures roll right up to the main street. The historic Travaasa Hana is a luxurious retreat in this village rooted in Hawaiian tradition. Browse the Hasegawa General Store and Hana Ranch Store for unique souvenirs. Swim and sunbathe at Hana Beach Park or Hamoa Beach, cited by author James Michener as the most beautiful beach in the Pacific. Snorkel at Waianapanapa State Park, a beautiful black sand beach. Or visit Hale Piilani, the state's largest heiau (Hawaiian temple), in Kanahu Gardens, one of five National Tropical Botanical Gardens in Hawaii.

Beyond Hana, venture 10 miles south to the outskirts of Haleakala National Park in Kipahulu. There you'll find the popular Pools of Oheo, where waterfalls spill into tiered pools leading to the sea. View these tranquil natural pools or hike up the Pipiwai Trail to the 400-foot Waimoku Falls.

Pools of Oheo

What: Tiered, swimmable pools located in the Oheo Gulch area of Haleakala National Park

Where: 10 miles south of Hana at mile marker 42

How much: $15 for a three-day park pass or $25 for an annual park pass. There's a $10 fee per car to enter the park

Just 15 minutes south of Hana on Highway 31 on the lower slopes of Haleakala are the famous Pools of Oheo in Oheo Gulch. Here you'll discover beautifully tiered pools fed by waterfalls. Weather permitting, you can take a dip in the tranquil waters, fed by streams starting 2 miles inland. Since Oheo is part of Haleakala National Park, the fee you pay here also admits you to the Haleakala Summit so save your receipt!

The Kipahulu area of Haleakala National Park also boasts plenty of self-guided hiking trails that weave through forests of bamboo, past roaring cascades to the green heart of the island. Consider the Pipiwai Trail, one of the island's best trails, which leads to the 400-foot Waimoku Falls. Make sure to consult park rangers at the Kipahulu Visitor Center before you embark on this three- to five-hour hike. Expect to get muddy, and don't forget your hiking shoes.

Arrive at Haleakala National Park early well before noon to avoid the crowds. If you plan to watch the sunrise from the summit of Haleakala, you'll need to plan ahead because the park requires reservations for watching the sunrise (to prevent overcrowding during dark hours).

South Maui

You'll find the sunniest, driest area of Maui on the peaceful southwestern coast. Blessed with miles of sandy beaches and clear views of the islands of Lanai, Molokini and Kahoolawe, South Maui is a place for lazy days and romantic nights. Explore the immersive underwater aquarium at the Maui Ocean Center in the whale-friendly Maalaea Bay. Golf at world-class courses in Wailea. Shop and dine in some of Maui's finest restaurants and resorts. Discover Maui's warm hospitality on its spectacular southern coast.

Kihei

What: Sunny coastal area with 6 miles of beautiful beaches
Where: Southwest Maui, about 25 minutes from Kahului Airport

Kihei is beach-combing territory on Maui's southwest shore, the sunniest, driest end of the island. Once a regular destination for sojourning Hawaiian royalty, Kihei features 6 miles of beaches offering clear views of Kahoolawe, Molokini, Lanai and West Maui. Along with swimming and surfing, you can also find great snorkeling and kayaking and you may even spot a giant humpback whale spouting or breaching the ocean's surface.

Kihei's Kalama Beach Park's 36 oceanfront acres are dotted with shady lawns and palm trees. The park is home to "the Cove" surf spot, beach volleyball courts, a roller-skating rink, a skate park, basketball and tennis courts, two baseball fields, picnic pavilions and a playground designed for younger kids.

A blink away are Kalpolepo, Waipuilani and the three beaches of Kamaole. Birdwatchers and nature lovers will find what they're looking for at Kealia Pond on the north end of Kihei. This National Wildlife Conservation District features endangered Hawaiian stilts and coots.

Also north of Kihei is Maalaea Bay, where pleasure boats launch to take visitors on whale watching expeditions, charter fishing excursions and snorkel trips to Molokini. Maalaea is also home to the family friendly Maui Ocean Center.

The town has a collection of affordable accommodations, with condominiums, small hotels and cottages to choose from along Kihei's beach road. You can also browse small shopping malls, a bustling farmers market and a spate of restaurants, all of which cater to residents and visitors alike. Nightlife here includes karaoke spots, dance clubs and sports bars ensuring your Kihei nights are just as fun as your days.

Makena Beach State Park (Big Beach)

Where: South Beach, Maui

Activities: Fishing, snorkeling, swimming

Amenities: Parking, lifeguard, picnic tables, restrooms, food concessions

Makena Beach State Park is one of Maui's signature beaches. With white sands extending nearly 2/3 of a mile long, it is one of the largest, undeveloped beaches in Maui. Enjoy relaxing on the beach with only nature in sight. Nestled between two black-lava outcroppings, Makena offers protection from the trade winds and provides great views of the islands of Molokini and Kahoolawe.

The area is divided into two beaches known as Big Beach and Little Beach. Big Beach is located south of Wailea near the Makena Beach and Golf Resort and provides a secluded alternative to more crowded beaches in Kaanapali and Lahaina. Little Beach is a small cove without amenities and no lifeguard. Although state park regulations prohibit nudity, Little Beach is frequently used as a nude beach.

Molokini

What: Tiny island for snorkeling and diving enthusiasts

Where: Located 3 miles off of Maui's southwestern coast

Molokini is a small, crescent moon-shaped island located just 3 miles from Maui's southwestern coast, The island stretches over 18 acres and rises 160 feet above reef-filled waters, offering visitors snorkeling and diving among a kaleidoscope of coral and more than 250 species of tropical fish.

When the United States entered World War II, the military used Molokini Crater for bombing practice. Years of protests and lobbying led the US government to deem Molokini Crater and the surrounding 77 acres a Marine Life Conservation District and Bird Sanctuary. The reef has restored its health and the fish have returned. Now the island is used primarily as a tourist destination for snorkeling and scuba diving.

Tours are available from nearby Maalaea Harbor and Lahaina. Early morning is the best time to explore this pristine reserve, and whale watching is a bonus during the winter months. If you're a scuba or snorkeling enthusiast, a visit to Molokini is a Maui must.

Wailea
What: 1,500 acres of luxurious beaches, resorts and attractions
Where: South Maui, about 35 minutes from Kahului Airport

Known for its five beautiful, crescent-shaped beaches and stellar golf courses, Wailea is a luxurious resort community in South Maui that spans 1,500 acres of land with staggering ocean views. The area exudes a sense of privacy, serenity and freedom spread across an area three times the size of Waikiki.

There are five hotels tucked into the town, including opulent resorts like the Grand Wailea Resort Hotel & Spa and the Four Seasons Resort Maui at Wailea. This resort community also includes distinctive condominiums and stately private homes.

The area's signature beaches include Wailea Beach, named "America's Best Beach" in 1999, Polo Beach, with excellent swimming and snorkeling, and Ulua Beach Park, where early morning and sunset walkers and joggers abound. The Wailea Blue, Wailea Gold and Wailea Emerald courses make up the 54 holes of championship golf that have made Wailea so famous.

Drive south about 6 miles down the coast and you'll reach Ahihi-Kinau Natural Area Reserve, which boasts a renowned snorkeling area and coastal lava field. Or continue for a couple more miles and you'll come to La Perouse Bay, where lava from Maui's last eruption flowed into the sea. The site has some nice hiking trails, including the Hoapili Trail, which winds its way along the coast through some shade and then strikes inland over the lava fields to Kanaio Beach 2 to 2.5 miles away.

Back in town, The Shops at Wailea is a destination in itself, featuring world-class restaurants and shops, along with regular entertainment programs. Wailea is also home to events such as the Maui Film Festival, February's Whale Week, as well as award-winning restaurants serving the best of Hawaii Regional Cuisine. Wailea's world-renowned spas round out an unforgettable Maui getaway.

West Maui

The sunny northwest coast of Maui was once a retreat for Hawaiian royalty and the capitol of the Hawaiian Kingdom. Today, West Maui is home to spectacular resorts, shopping, restaurants, a wealth of activities and some of the most amazing sunsets in the world.

The Honoapiilani Highway takes you from one sun-kissed resort to the next, each with its own personality. Traveling north from Maalaea and the Maui Ocean Center, your first stop is the historic whaling town of Lahaina. Rustic buildings recall its days as Hawaii's busiest port, while bustling shops on Front Street and winter whale watching make it a favorite port of call for cruise ship passengers.

A few minutes more on the Highway and you'll find yourself drawn into the vibrant Kaanapali Resort. Whether you're staying in the area or just passing through, a stroll on the Kaanapali Beachwalk is always in order. Families play on the beach, shoppers buzz in and out, and diners sit back and simply soak in the view.

On this side of the island, resorts melt into one another, and it doesn't take long to lead you to Kapalua, known for championship golf and private getaways. Here, the tone is a bit quieter, with understated elegance.

Despite their proximity to each other, and the other hotels nestled in between, there is one thing these resorts disagree on: which resort has the best sunset and the best view. The islands of Lanai and Molokai are just across the channel, and as the West Maui sun sets, its rays wrap around the islands washing the coastline in a magical glow. Which sunset is the best? You'll have to find out for yourself.

Honolua Bay Maui
What: Place to watch big wave surfers during the winter
Where: Roughly a 20 minute drive north of Lahaina

Honolua Bay on Maui's northwest shore is a favorite spot for experienced surfers. During the winter high surf season, Honolua has been known to have a hollow, powerful wave that offers incredibly long rides. The bluffs above the bay offer a great vantage point for visitors to watch the pros from a safe distance.

During the calmer summer months, Honolua Bay is a popular destination for snorkeling and scuba diving. As part of the Mokuleia Marine Life Conservation District, the bay has an abundance of fish and coral formations to explore. There is only a small rocky shoreline here, so sunbathing isn't ideal.

Surfing lessons are available, but note that during the winter, wave conditions at Honolua Bay can be extremely dangerous, so for your safety please heed all posted signs and use caution.

Lahaina, Maui
What: Historic whaling village and Maui hotspot
Where: On the west side of Maui, 45 minutes from Kahului Airport

Once known as Lele, which means "relentless sun" in Hawaiian, Lahaina is a historic town that has been transformed into a Maui hotspot with dozens of art galleries and a variety of unique shops and restaurants.

Once the capital of the Hawaiian Kingdom in the early nineteenth century, Lahaina was also a historic whaling village during the whaling boom of the mid-1800s. Up to 1,500 sailors from as many as 400 ships took leave in Lahaina, including Herman Melville, who immortalized the era in his classic novel *Moby Dick*.

Today, Lahaina is on the National Register of Historic Places. You can still get a feel for old Lahaina as you stroll down lively Front Street, ranked one of the "Top Ten Greatest Streets" by the American Planning Association. Visit historic stops like the U.S. Seamen's Hospital, Hale Paaho (Lahaina Prison), the Pioneer Inn, Maui's oldest living banyan tree and other sites on the Lahaina Historic Trail. Approximately 55 acres of old Lahaina have been set aside as historic districts.

Immerse yourself in Maui and the Hawaiian culture by learning about the ancient mode of seafaring by canoe, take a hiking tour with local guides at Hike Maui or fall asleep to the sound of breaking waves as you camp on the beach with Camp Maui-X.

Lahaina's sunny climate and oceanfront setting also provides the perfect backdrop for a variety of activities and entertainment. Get a fresh taste of Hawaii Regional Cuisine in Lahaina's fine restaurants. Get your tickets to some of Maui's best seaside luau where you can eat, drink and watch the traditional dances of Polynesia. The award-winning show Ulalena at the Maui Theatre offers a Broadway-caliber production showcasing the culture of Hawaii.

And during the winter months, don't forget to set sail from Lahaina Harbor on an unforgettable whale watching tour. The channel off the coast of Lahaina is one of the best places in the world to spot humpback whales. Even these magnificent creatures can't get enough of Lahaina.

Kapalua Maui

What: One of Maui's premier resort areas

Where: Northwest Maui, about one hour from Kahului Airport

Kapalua, loosely translated to "arms embracing the sea," is one of Maui's premier resort areas located at the foot of the verdant Kahalawai, or West Maui mountains. Kapalua's lovely shoreline is lined with five bays and three white-sand beaches, one of which was named "The Best Beach in America" by the University of Maryland's Laboratory of Coastal Research.

In the 1800's Kapalua was known as the Honolua Ranch and then the Honolua Plantation. Today the 23,000-acre, master-planned Kapalua Resort is home to the Ritz-Carlton Kapalua, award-winning restaurants, more than 20 boutique shops, historic sites and two renowned golf courses, including the Plantation Course, home to the prestigious PGA TOUR's Tournament of Champions (January) and the Bay Course, home to the 2009 Kapalua LPGA Classic.

Host of the renowned Kapalua Wine & Food Festival (June), this spectacular area, nestled amongst Cook pines and surrounded by acres of pineapple, is the perfect getaway to indulge in the luxurious side of Maui.

Kaanapali Beach

Where: West Shore, Maui, about 50 minutes from Kahului Airport
Activities: Swimming, cliff diving
Amenities: Parking $2/30 minutes, restrooms, lifeguard, shopping nearby

With three miles of white sand and crystal clear water, it's no wonder why Kaanapali Beach was once named America's Best Beach. Fronting Kaanapali's hotels and resorts, this former retreat for the royalty of Maui is now a popular getaway for the world.

Kaanapali was Hawaii's first planned resort and has become a model for resorts around the globe. Five hotels and six condominium villages face this renowned beach. Also fronting Kaanapali is the open air Whalers Village, a world-class shopping complex that features a variety of exceptional shops and restaurants, a renowned whaling museum and free Hawaiian entertainment. Kaanapali also has two championship golf courses, the Royal Kaanapali and the Kaanapali Kai, where you may even see a breaching whale as you try to line up a shot.

One of Kaanapali Beach's most famous attractions is the daily cliff diving ceremony off the beach's northernmost cliffs known as Puu Kekaa, or Black Rock. Held every evening at sunset, a cliff diver lights the torches along the cliff, diving off Black Rock in a reenactment of a feat by Maui's revered King Kahekili. To soar above Kaanapali's breathtaking coastline yourself, try a zipline tour by Kaanapali Skyline Eco Adventures and enjoy a royally good view of one of Maui's signature beaches.

Upcountry Maui

Golden beaches give way to rolling hills and misty mountains as you ascend into Upcountry Maui, which is located on the higher elevations surrounding Haleakala the island's highest peak. Since early times, Hawaiians have farmed the volcanic soil of Upcountry fields, growing taro and sweet potato. Today, you can take farm tours, visit a goat dairy or even sip Maui-made wines and spirits in the rustic outposts of Kula and Makawao.

Upcountry is also the stomping ground of the *paniolo*, or Hawaiian cowboys a culture that arose in the 19th century when King Kamehameha III invited vaqueros from California to teach islanders to wrangle cattle. Further east, the 10,023-foot Haleakala presides over the "Valley Isle," with epic sunrises and otherworldly landscapes that feel more like the moon than Maui. It's a dramatic departure from the coconut palms of Kaanapali and Kapalua, but a day trip to the Upcountry will bring you closer to Maui's heartland.

Paia, Maui

What: Historic Maui town featuring Hookipa Beach, the windsurfing capital of the world

Where: About four miles east of Kahului

Just four miles into your drive to Hana from Kahului, you'll discover the historic town of Paia on Maui's north coast. Divided into Lower Paia and Paia, this hospitable community was once a booming plantation town during the heyday of Maui's sugar cane industry. Today Paia is a town of colorful, rustic storefronts filled with local art galleries, one-of-a-kind shopping boutiques and restaurants.

Grab a fish burger at the popular Paia Fishmarket, then head to Hookipa Beach, the "windsurfing capital of the world." During the winter, the big north shore waves make Hookipa Beach a magnet for pro windsurfers and kite surfers. Watch the pros compete or swim and sunbathe in the calmer summer months. Another popular Paia beach is H.A. Baldwin Beach Park, which features a baby beach with a lagoon.

Note that during the winter, wave conditions can be extremely dangerous so please heed all posted signs for your safety.

Haleakala National Park Maui

What: A scenic national park known as the "house of the sun"

Where: Upcountry Maui to the southeastern coast

Towering over the island of Maui and visible from just about any point, Haleakala Crater is a force of nature in every sense. At 10,023 feet above sea level, this dormant volcano is the stage for a breathtaking range of landscapes and skyscapes. Haleakala means "house of the sun" in Hawaiian, and legend goes that the demigod Maui lassoed the sun from its journey across the sky as he stood on the volcano's summit, slowing its descent to make the day last longer.

Many visitors wake up early to drive to the Haleakala Visitor Center, the best spot to watch what may be the most spectacular sunrise on earth. As the sun peeks over the horizon, an ever-changing swirl of color and light dance across the vast sea of clouds a sight described by Mark Twain as "the most sublime spectacle I have ever witnessed." Perhaps just as impressive are Haleakala's sunsets and the bright, starry skies revealed at night. Remember, the NATIONAL PARK SERVICE NOW REQUIRES A RESERVATION FOR PERSONAL AND RENTAL VEHICLES TO VIEW THE SUNRISE FROM THE SUMMIT DISTRICT. Your RESERVATION is for parking at the summit and doesn't include the required national Park entry fee. Drive times from Kaanapali and Wailea to reach the summit average 2 hours.

Sunrises and sunsets are only two of the many reasons to pay Haleakala National Park a visit on your trip to Maui. Spanning more than 30,000 acres of public land, the stunning landscapes range from Mars-like red deserts and rock gardens near the summit to lush waterfalls and streams in the park's coastal Kipahulu section, near Hana.

There are numerous hiking trails that offer solitude and scenic vistas, while guided hikes and horseback rides provide an expert's insight in addition to the natural beauty. There are more endangered species here than any other park in the National Park Service, like blooming *ahinahina* (silversword) and *nene* (Hawaiian goose), the state bird. Visitors can also camp here, with separate campgrounds and cabins available.

Kula
What: Upcountry Maui town known for its farms and botanical gardens
Where: The higher elevations of Upcountry Maui

Found in the Upcountry region of Maui, Kula is a quaint, rustic area on the slopes of Haleakala. Located in the central part of the island, Kula is also at the center of its culinary resurgence, with much of the exotic produce served at Maui's best Hawaii Regional Cuisine restaurants grown right here in the rich, volcanic soil.

The fertile fields of Kula are an ideal place to stir up your appetite by taking a farm tour. Harvest your own veggies and let the chef cook them up into a truly fresh gourmet meal at Oo Farm or walk among the sugar canes and raise a glass to sustainable farming practices at Hawaii Sea Spirits Organic Farm and Distillery, producers of OCEAN Vodka. For a more floral affair, smell the sweet lavender and marvel at the stunning views at the Alii Kula Lavender Farm or see the protea at the Shim Coffee and Protea Farm Tour. The region is also home to the Kula Botanical Gardens, filled with blooming carnations, birds of paradise and orchids.

On the way to the gardens, visitors can also see Kula's most notable landmark, the brilliant white, octagonal Holy Ghost Church. A gift from the king and queen of Portugal to the island's Portuguese plantation workers in 1894, it has been recently restored. Kula also offers the best views in Upcountry Maui, with sweeping views of Maui and the Pacific Ocean.

Makawao, Maui
What: Paniolo (Hawaiian cowboy) town and a renowned art community

Where: Upcountry Maui

Located on the mid-slopes of Maui's Haleakala volcano, Makawao has one foot in its plantation past and another in its thriving arts community. This charming town was once named one of the top 25 arts destinations in the United States.

Makawao is the biggest little town in the region locally known as Upcountry Maui and is famous for its Hawaiian cowboys, or *paniolo*. Since the late 19th century, horseback-riding paniolo have wrangled cattle in Maui's wide-open upland fields. The Makawao Rodeo, held yearly on the Fourth of July, is Hawaii's largest paniolo competition and has been an Upcountry tradition for more than 50 years. The weekend events include a parade and traditional rodeo competitions such as barrel racing, calf roping and bareback bronco riding, all with a few Hawaiian twists.

For a snack, follow the locals to get a famous cream puff from T. Komoda Store. Established in 1916 by Takezo Komoda, a Japanese plantation worker, this little store and bakery does big business. Lines can be long in the morning when everything's fresh, so come early. The bakery is closed on Wednesdays and Sundays.

You can also spend the afternoon meandering through the eclectic shops, boutiques and art galleries. It's a town of working artists, where you can watch glassblowers, wood sculptors and painters as they fulfill your order. Makawao is also home to the Hui Noeau Visual Arts Center, where visitors can take classes and explore free gallery exhibits. The combination of its paniolo heritage and its lively artistic community make Makawao a unique stop on your visit to Maui.

Things to Do on Maui

Maui Restaurants & Dining

Pack a hearty appetite because Maui offers an exotic blend of savory dining. Indulge in the flavors of Hawaii Regional Cuisine, made from produce picked right from the farms of Kula and fish caught fresh from the sea. Try a traditional Hawaiian meal at a sunset luau or get off the beaten path to try some local favorites in small towns like Wailuku and Paia. On Maui you can feast on everything from haupia to hamburgers. Learn more about Maui restaurants in Kaanapali, Kahului, Kapalua, Kihei, Lahaina and Wailuku.

Japengo Maui

Serving up world-class steaks, seafood and sushi, Japengo at Hyatt Regency Maui provides Hawaii's freshest, locally-grown products and exotic Pacific Rim cuisine. Enjoy Japengo's indoor and outdoor seating overlooking Ka'anapali Beach, or watch as sushi is rolled to order in the chic Sushi Lounge.

200 Nohea Kai Drive. Lahaina, HI 96761

Local Phone: (808) 667-4727

Email: conciergeoggrm@hyatt.com

Island: Maui

Serving up world-class steaks, seafood, sushi and specialty cocktails, Japengo at Hyatt Regency Maui draws on Hawaii's freshest, locally-grown products coupled with exotic ingredients from the Pacific Rim. Take a culinary adventure showcasing modern Asian-inspired flavors with Hawaiian flair. Enjoy Japengo's indoor and outdoor patio seating overlooking the resort's waterfalls and famed Ka'anapali Beach, or watch as Maui's Best Sushi is rolled to order in the chic Sushi Lounge. Whether you are celebrating an intimate moment or entertaining a large group, Japengo provides the perfect ambiance for any occasion.

Ama Bar & Grill

Enjoy fresh garden salads, kiave grilled hamburgers, a variety of other sandwiches and assorted beverages at this poolside and oceanview restaurant which includes a swim-up bar.

4100 Wailea Alanui Drive. Wailea, HI 96753

Local Phone: (808) 875-4100

US Toll Free: (800) 659-4100

Email: info@kealani.com

Island: Maui

Kimo's

Historic landmark restaurant located on the water in Lahaina. Famous for fresh fish steaks and local fare. There's only one Kimo's!

845 Front Street. Lahaina, HI 96761

Local Phone: (808) 661-4811

Island: Maui

Historic landmark restaurant located on the water in Lahaina. Famous for fresh fish steaks and local fare. There's only one Kimo's!

Royal Ocean Terrace Restaurant

Full American breakfast buffet served daily, 6:30am-10am, with nightly Hawaiian and American dinner entrees served overlooking the Pacific. Enjoy afternoon and evening entertainment every night.

2780 Kekaa Dr. Lahaina, HI 96761

Local Phone: (808) 661-3611

US Toll Free: (800) 280-8155

Email: hhr@hawaiihotels.com

Island: Maui

Full American breakfast buffet served daily, 6:30am-10am, with nightly Hawaiian and American dinner entrees served overlooking the Pacific. Enjoy afternoon and evening entertainment every night.

Kai Cafe

Grab-and-go café located on the lobby level featuring homemade pastries, salads and wraps made with local, organic and seasonal ingredients.

1 Ritz Carlton Drive. Kapalua, HI 96761

Local Phone: (808) 669-6200

Island: Maui

Grab-and-go café located on the lobby level featuring homemade pastries, salads and wraps made with local, organic and seasonal ingredients.

Lahaina Grill

Lahaina Grill features cuisine using techniques and flavors from around the world with the freshest ingredients from Maui's local farms, dairies and surrounding waters. Voted Top 10 fine dining restaurants in U.S. for 2018 and Best Maui Restaurant for 26 years in a row. (1994-2019).

127 Lahainaluna Rd.Lahaina, HI 96761

Local Phone: (808) 667-5117

US Toll Free: (800) 360-2606

Email: reservations@lahainagrill.com

Island: Maui

Whether seeking a romantic dinner for two, a private group at The Chef's Table, or celebrating a family affair, Lahaina Grill will make your dining experience on Maui memorable. Among the signature favorites are the The Cake Walk - a sampler of Kona Lobster Crab Cake, Seared Ahi Cake, and Sweet Louisiana Rock Shrimp Cake. Entree selections encompass meat and seafood options. Try the Kona Coffee Roasted Rack of Lamb, Maui Onion Crusted Seared Ahi (considered by many to be the best Ahi preparation!), or the nightly fresh seafood design.

To finish the meal, delight in a slice of the famous Triple Berry Pie, or Road to Hana - a chocolate cake with a chewy macadamia nut caramel, and sour chocolate mousse, all enrobed in silky chocolate ganache. Don't miss a wine list that features over 350 selections. Open nightly from 5pm, 7 days a week. Reservations are recommended and the full menu is served at the bar. Recent awards include: top 10 fine dining restaurants in u.s. 2018 ; top 25 restaurants in u.s. 2014, 2015, 2016, 2017; restaurant of the year 2018 maui no ka oi magazine; best maui restaurant 26 years in a row 1994-2019 honolulu magazine; 100 best restaurants in america for 2016, 2017 open table; top 100 places to eat in u.s. 2016 yelp

Gannon's Restaurant

Voted one of the Top 100 Best Outdoor Dining Restaurants in America, Gannon's Restaurant in Wailea is a celebration of the classic dishes for which Chef Beverly Gannon is best known for her award-winning Maui restaurants.

Local Phone: (808) 875-8080

Email: thodge@bevgannonrestaurants.com

Island: Maui

Voted one of the Top 100 Best Outdoor Dining Restaurants in America, Gannon's Restaurant in Wailea is a celebration of the classic dishes for which Chef Beverly Gannon is best known for her award-winning Maui restaurants

Kahili Restaurant

The Kahili Restaurant welcomes you to enjoy our exciting location tucked away in the West Maui Mountains. A favorite meeting place where visitors and residents relax. The dining room and the lanai over look our amazing 18-hole golf course with spectacular views of the ocean and Haleakala Mountain.

2500 Honoapiilani Hwy. Wailuku, HI 96793

Local Phone: (808) 242-6000

Island: Maui

The Kahili Restaurant welcomes you to enjoy our exciting location tucked away in the West Maui Mountains. A favorite meeting place where visitors and residents relax. The dining room and the lanai over look our amazing 18-hole golf course with spectacular views of the ocean and Haleakala Mountain.

We are open for lunch every day with an extensive menu of salads, sandwiches, main dishes, and specials at affordable prices. Ample parking, wheel chair accessible, and Keiki menu make Kahili Restaurant very comfortable for families. A good reason to come to our scrumptious three famous buffets, All-You-Can-Eat Friday buffets and Sunday Brunch buffet are legendary. We are also available for private parties, weddings and receptions.

Royal Scoop

The Royal Scoop offers lighter fare with mouth-watering pastries and continental breakfast items, gourmet sandwiches and snacks, local Maui-made ice cream and frozen yogurt, and specialty coffees and smoothies. Outdoor seating is available, or for your convenience have your items wrapped to go.

2780 Kekaa Drive. Lahaina, HI 96761
Local Phone: (808) 661-3611
US Toll Free: (800) 280-8155
Island: Maui

The Royal Scoop offers lighter fare with mouth-watering pastries and continental breakfast items, gourmet sandwiches and snacks, local Maui-made ice cream and frozen yogurt, and specialty coffees and smoothies. Outdoor seating is available, or for your convenience have your items wrapped to go.

Maui Hotels & Accommodations

Adventure and enchantment await you on the welcoming island of Maui. Here you'll find a variety of places to stay. Gaze out at enchanting ocean views from your balcony at a luxurious resort in Kapalua or Kaanapali in the west, or relax in a spacious condo rental in sunny Kihei on the southern coast. Take the winding road to Hana in East Maui to discover your charming cabin hidden among palms and tropical flowers. Whether you seek a Five-Diamond hotel right next to the action or a peaceful seaside cottage all to yourself, you'll find what you're looking for in Maui.

Mana Kai Maui (CRH)

Oceanfront one- and two-bedroom condos located on the border of Kihei and Wailea. The luxurious Mana Kai Resort sits on Keawakapu Beach and enjoys amenities like an oceanfront pool, state-of-the-art fitness center, ground floor restaurant/bar, yoga studio, and so much more! Book exact condos!

362 Huku Lii Pl. Kihei, HI 96753

Local Phone: (808) 879-2778

US Toll Free: (800) 367-5242

Email: res@crhmaui.com

Island: Maui

Oceanfront one- and two-bedroom condos located on the border of Kihei and Wailea. The luxurious Mana Kai Resort sits on Keawakapu

Beach and enjoys amenities like an oceanfront pool, state-of-the-art fitness center, ground floor restaurant/bar, yoga studio, and so much more! This collection of condos are managed by Condominium Rentals Hawaii, which allow guests to reserve specific and individual condos that fit their tastes.

Paia Surf Vacation Home

Experience the ultimate vacation spot on one of the jewels of the Hawaiian island chain from the comfort of a newly-remodeled house on Maui's famed north shore.

15 Nalu Place. Paia, HI 96779

Local Phone: (808) 214-3171

Email: paiasurfvacationhome@gmail.com

Island: Maui

Experience the ultimate vacation spot on one of the jewels of the Hawaiian island chain from the comfort of a newly-remodeled house on Maui's famed north shore. You'll enjoy the finest land & water attractions, spectacular cuisine, and the best kind of R&R. Your Paia Surf vacation can be a memorable romantic getaway - or the ultimate family vacation, with plenty of shared experiences awaiting. The house is perfect for both.

WaileaEkahiVillage.com, Pauli Family Condos

Book the exact Wailea Ekahi Village condo you want from our luxury vacation rentals at one of Maui's most desirable beach front resorts. View our meticulous maintained & surprisingly affordable Studio, One & Two bedroom condos. Rates, photos, videos, virtual tours & reviews for each.

3300 Wailea Alanui Dr. Apt 11E. Wailea, HI 96753
Local Phone: (808) 868-4050
Email: matt@waileaekahivillage.com
Island: Maui

Book the exact Wailea Ekahi Village condto you want from our luxury vacation rentals at one of Maui's most desirable beach front resorts. View our meticulous maintained & surprisingly affordable Studio, One & Two bedroom condos. Rates, photos, videos, virtual tours and reviews for each. Group availability calendar. Site maps, floor plans.

Maui Kai

Our Maui oceanfront vacation rentals are perfect for family vacations & anyone seeking adventure. Each air-conditioned condos offer a panoramic view and immediate access to Maui beaches. We are close to the action in Lahaina, yet tucked away in a peaceful beachfront location offering fun & romance.

106 Kaanapali Shores Place. Lahaina, HI 96761
Local Phone: (808) 667-3500

US Toll Free: (800) 367-5635

Email: gm@mauikai.com

Island: Maui

Our Maui oceanfront vacation rentals are perfect for family vacations and anyone seeking adventure. Each of our air-conditioned condos offer a panoramic view and immediate access to Maui beaches. We are close to the action in Lahaina, yet tucked away in a peaceful beachfront location offering fun and romance. Wake up to the sound of the Sea!

Aston at The Whaler on Kaanapali Beach

Aston The Whaler on Ka'anapali Beach is at the heart of Maui's finest vacation destination. Just minutes from Lahaina, this resort offers spacious studio, one-, and two-bedroom oceanfront units complete with kitchens, private lanais and daily maid service.

2481 Kaanapali Pkwy. Lahaina, HI 96761

Local Phone: (808) 661-6000

US Toll Free: (866) 774-2924

Email: info@aqua-aston.com

Island: Maui

Aston at The Whaler on Kaanapali Beach is a luxurious, private beachfront condominium resort located on world-famous Kaanapali Beach, adjacent to Whalers Village Shopping Center. This resort offers spacious studio, one- and two-bedroom suites, each with its own large, private lanai. All units are furnished with fully-equipped kitchen facilities and central air conditioning. Amenities at the resort include a heated oceanfront swimming pool and jet spa, oceanfront barbeques and picnic areas, fitness facility and sauna, and tennis courts.

Sunsets in Paradise

One of West Maui's best kept secrets with breathtaking views of Molokai and Lanai, and a small secluded beach for snorkeling or just dipping your toes in the water. Great for watching the resident turtles return at sunset.

3975 Lower Honoapiilani Rd. Lahaina, HI 96761

Local Phone: (630) 377-8951

US Toll Free: (866) 530-9678

Email: info@sunsetsinparadise.com

Island: Maui

One of West Maui's best kept secrets with breathtaking views of Molokai and Lanai, and a small secluded beach for snorkeling or just dipping your toes in the water. Great for watching the resident turtles return at sunset.

Hotel Wailea Maui

The first and only Relais & Châteaux property in Hawaii. Set in Wailea, the ultra-private luxury hotel is designed uniquely for couples. From its perch, 300 feet above sea level, guests enjoy dramatic ocean views and 15 lush acres of pathways through tropical gardens, waterfalls and koi ponds.

555 Kaukahi St. Wailea, HI 96753

Local Phone: (808) 874-0500

US Toll Free: (800) 800-0720

Email: reservations@hotelwailea.com

Island: Maui

The first and only Relais & Châteaux property in Hawaii, Hotel Wailea offers travelers a European-inspired elegance infused with relaxed island luxury. Set in Wailea, the most exclusive resort community on Maui, the ultra-private luxury hotel is designed uniquely for couples. From its perch, 300 feet above sea level, guests enjoy dramatic ocean views and 15 lush acres of winding pathways through tropical gardens, waterfalls and koi ponds.

Hotel Wailea's 72 oversized suites each boast a chic beach house design with separate living room, private lanai and kitchenettes. Personalized guest programming is tailored to couples and centered on authentic island experiences that embody the spirit of Maui and laid back luxury. Hotel Wailea's locally-focused culinary program boasts a unique take on seasonal dining with Hawaiian staples and

Maui-grown ingredients, including from the hotel's own organic garden.

In the best of both worlds, guests of Hotel Wailea enjoy exclusive services at Wailea Beach by day, stunning panoramic views in the afternoon, poolside cocktails to a vivid sunset and award-winning dining at night.

Voted "#1 Best Hotel in Maui" Condé Nast Traveler Reader's Choice Awards 2014 & 2015; "#1 Hotel in Wailea"

Destination Residences Hawaii, Inc.

Destination Residences Hawaii offers an exclusive collection of premium vacation residences in beachfront and golf-front resorts in Wailea and Makena on the island of Maui. Come share our aloha, genuine Hawaiian hospitality and authentic Maui experiences.

34 Wailea Gateway Place. Wailea, HI 96753

Local Phone: (866) 384-4590

US Toll Free: (866) 384-4590

Email: drhinfo@destinationhotels.com

Island: Maui

Destination Residences Hawaii offers an exclusive collection of private vacation homes in seven beachfront and golf-front resorts in Wailea and Makena on the sunny south shore of Maui.

Select from studio, 1-, 2- or 3-bedroom residences with spacious living room with dining area, fully-equipped kitchen, bedroom(s) with private and semi-private baths, outdoor lanai and personal washer/dryer.

Indulge yourself in Maui's most exclusive beachfront villa resort and vacation in sophisticated and stylish luxury without crowds or cares at Wailea Beach Villas. Relax on secluded beaches at Polo Beach Club or Makena Surf. Play golf on the sun-drenched fairways of Grand Champions Villas or Wailea Ekolu Village, or enjoy spectacular snorkeling at Wailea Elua Village and Wailea Ekahi Village.

$155 in resort gift cards for Wailea restaurants and spas, parking, Wi-fi internet, local phone calls, a Maika'i grocery discount card and preferred rates at Wailea golf courses and the Wailea Tennis Center.

Polo Beach Club, A Destination Residence

With a prime beach front location on Polo Beach, relish the blissful view and lull of the ocean waves from every two-bedroom condo, featuring living room, dining area, kitchen and private lanai. Enjoy the pool, jetspa, BBQ grills or herb garden; with nearby entry to the scenic Wailea Coastal Walk.

4400 Makena Rd. Kihei, HI 96753

Local Phone: (866) 384-4590

US Toll Free: (866) 384-4590

Email: drhinfo@destinationhotels.com

Island: Maui

This hidden gem bordering the Wailea Resort is noted for its prime Maui beachfront location on Polo Beach. A breathtaking, idyllic beach, where guests have exclusive access to splash at the ocean's edge or venture further out to challenge the surf.

Resort amenities include a beachfront swimming pool with jet spa, barbecue grills and an herb garden.

Enjoy the sights and sounds of the ocean waves from each two-bedroom, two-bath suite. Enter through a marbled entryway that leads to a sunken living room with magnificent ocean views. Each suite offers a fully-equipped kitchen, separate living/dining area, bedrooms with private and semi-private baths, personal washer/dryer and ocean view lanai.

Self-parking, Wi-Fi internet, daily housekeeping, $155 in gift cards to Wailea restaurants and spas, and a Maika'i grocery discount card included.

Maui Activities

Fill your vacation itinerary with a variety of unique and entertaining attractions you can only experience in Maui. Whether you prefer living history or off-the-beaten-path adventures, these highlights will lead you in the right direction.

Land Activities
Biking on Maui
With all of the beaches, surfing, snorkeling, diving, kitesurfing, and paddling, Maui isn't a place that's generally known for land recreation.

The truth, however, is that biking on Maui is better than most people expect and a pleasant surprise for visiting cyclists who want to explore on two wheels.

The most famous ride on Maui, of course, is biking down Haleakalā, where visitors can ride over 6,000 feet down the slopes of the dormant volcano. Many of these tours are combined with watching the sunrise at Haleakalā Crater, and finish by biking all the way down to the beach at Pāʻia Bay. Along the 25-mile route, cyclists pass through pastoral scenes of farmland, ranches, and forests, and usually stop in the historic town of Makawao for breakfast.

There once was a time when tours would begin from the mountain's 10,000-foot summit, but due to liability concerns inside of the National Park, tours now start outside the park around 6,800 feet. That being said, it's still possible for independent cyclists to ride down all the way from the top as long as you provide your own transportation and bring along your own bike. It's only commercial operators who can no longer bike from the top. So, if you visit a local bike shop and rent one for 24 hours and then sweet talk one of your family members into giving you a ride to the top it's still possible to bike 10,000 feet down a dormant volcano on Maui.

Aside from biking down Haleakalā, other popular road cycling routes include circling the West Maui Mountains and riding along the 620 curves on the famous road to Hāna. On weekend mornings, groups of local cyclists gather to ride past Ulupalakua Ranch, starting from Kula and then biking back for coffee at Grandma's Coffee House.

For visitors interested in mountain biking on Maui, the team at Krank Cycles cut seven different trails in the trees of the Makawao Forest Reserve, which offer everything from technical single track to quad-burning climbs and a skills park. Surrounded by the scent of eucalyptus and pine, riders can get their heart rate up with a 30-minute climb up the mountain before dropping down over 1,300 feet on the fast and well-groomed trails.

If it's been raining too much in Makawao, there's an entire network of mountain biking trails in the Kula Forest Reserve, which range from hunting roads to steep single tracks and trails through towering redwoods. The air is cool here at 6,000 feet, and by riding all the way up the switchbacks of rutted Skyline Drive, it's even possible to mountain bike all the way to Haleakala's summit.

Family Activities on Maui

Remember that time you caught your first wave at the start of your Maui surf lesson? Or the silence, peace, and sense of calm from high in the seat of a parasail?

Maui is an island where memories are made the type that end up on Christmas cards and there's little wonder why families have named it the best island in the world.

With all the attractions, activities, and excursions that are offered around the island, one of Maui's best family activities is simply a day at the beach. Bodysurfing, after all, doesn't cost a dime, nor does building a massive sandcastle or scouring the tide pools for fish. For a few extra bucks you can rent some snorkels and maybe a couple of boogie boards just don't forget the reef-safe sunscreen since nobody wants to get burned. For family-friendly beaches in Maui, Kapalua Bay has easy access, showers, restrooms, and snorkeling, and Ka'anapali Beach is an island classic for snorkeling and jumping off "Black Rock." If the family is staying in South Maui, there's plenty of parking at Keawakapu Beach and a park at Kamaole III, or choose to hop from beach to beach while strolling Wailea's boardwalk.

To see all the action that's happening underwater without even getting your hair wet, head to the Maui Ocean Center Maui's best spot for families. Watch in wonder as rays and sharks go swimming above your head, and learn about turtles, coral reefs, and ways that Ancient

Hawaiians survived by living in tune with the sea. To up the adrenaline and soar through the trees, strap on a helmet, clip in a harness, and watch the family jump off a cliff while attached to a thin metal zipline. Every operator is a little bit different, and which company you choose to go with depends on the age of your children. Some companies, like Flyin' Hawaiian, have a minimum age of 10, whereas others like Maui Zipline Company take children as young as 5 years old as long as they're with an adult. For the chance to zipline side-by-side, Kapalua Ziplines has tandem lines where siblings can zip together, and Pi'iholo Ziplines often runs offers where children can zipline for free. To spend the day on another island as well as go sailing and snorkeling book an all-day tour to Lāna'i aboard Trilogy Excursions, a family-run company that's been making memories on Maui for 45 years. Snorkel the reef at Hulopo'e Bay, or even upgrade to Snuba, and the cruise between islands doubles as a whale watch when visiting Maui in winter. Or, for a budget friendly cruise to Lāna'i where the snorkeling is done off the boat, Pacific Whale Foundation often has deals where children snorkel for free.

Golfing on Maui
The game of golf came to Maui relatively late, when the Maui Country Club opened in 1925 in Spreckelsville. The island has done its best to make up for its slow start, now hosting fantastic courses, award-winning designs and championship tournaments galore.

The PGA Tournament of Champions, Kapalua, Maui

Perhaps the most well known golf event on Maui is the annual Tournament of Champions held annually in world-class Kapalua. Every January, top PGA golfers head to the Valley Isle to tee it up on the greens of Kapalua Golf's Plantation Course.

Best Golf Courses on Maui

With so many stellar courses on Maui, it's difficult to pinpoint "the best." That being said, Kapalua Golf's Plantation Course continues to be rated among the best in all of Hawaii. Kapalua Golf's Bay Course is not a bad alternative. Other standout Maui golf courses include King Kamehameha Golf Club in Wailuku, Wailea Golf Club, particularly the Emerald course, and the Kaanapali Golf Courses. Expect green fees of over $200 for these premium courses.

Hiking on Maui

Maui is known for its palm trees, turquoise waves and large surf, but few people know that at 6,500 feet above sea level, it has redwood trees and trails that crisscross fields of cinder and feel like the surface of the moon.

Experience the island's variety of landscapes on hiking adventures that range from treks through bamboo near Waimoku Falls, to strolling past world-class, white sand beaches on the Kapalua Coastal Trail.

The exceptional diversity makes hiking on Maui so unique that you could hike every day for 10 days and never encounter the same scenery.

Take, for example, the town of Waiheʻe, near the island's central valley, where three different hikes in a 10-minute radius offer wildly different experiences. At the Waiheʻe Coastal Dunes and Wetlands Refuge, a 2-mile trail runs right along a beach that's covered in white sand and driftwood. Just 4 miles away, the Waiheʻe Ridge Trail climbs 2,500 feet up the mountain on a fern-lined trail in the mists. And a mile up the road, a narrow trail in Makamakaʻole Valley leads down to a hidden waterfall, where hikers scramble down the roots of a banyan tree for a refreshing dip in the swimming hole.

If that last move sounds a little bit dangerous, it's important to remember that hiking in Maui can have it's fair share of consequences. Visitors should always assess their abilities, find detailed information on the trails and be sure to keep an eye on the weather since flash flooding can occur on parts of the island.

One place where flooding is rarely an issue is along the Hoapili Trail, a historic 5-mile round-trip hike that crosses the island's last lava flow in Keoneʻōiʻo, past Makena. This trail was commissioned in 1830 by Governor Hoapili and passes numerous cultural sites and ancient Hawaiian villages. It's as if time was frozen in stone as you hike on the desolate trail. Since there's virtually no shade on this section of coast, be sure to start early, bring lots of water and wear hiking boots for the lava rock.

Swap out the sunscreen you'd use on the Hoapili Trail for sweatshirts while hiking in Kula. Trails in the Kula Forest Reserve — or as locals know it, Poli Poli — range in elevation from 5,500 feet to the 10,000-foot summit of Haleakalā. Here you'll find stands of towering redwoods, plum, eucalyptus and pine trees and a well-marked network of hiking trails with the feel of the Pacific Northwest. Much of this land is open for hunting, so be sure to wear bright colors and watch for wild goats and pigs that often dart down the trail. If you're feeling ambitious and up to the challenge, you can give your lungs a high-altitude workout and hike "Skyline Drive" — a road that zig zags all the way up to the top of Haleakalā Crater.

If you packed a tent and sleeping bag — and don't mind being a little cold — Haleakalā Crater has some of Hawai'i's best backcountry hiking. There are three campgrounds in Haleakalā Crater that require quite a bit of walking — 8 miles to the closest Holua campground and 20 miles to the furthest Palikū campground.

But if hiking with a tent in 40-degree temperatures doesn't sound like a tropical vacation, stick to the shorter trails that hug the West Maui coastline. The Kapalua Coastal Trail connects Kapalua Bay with D.T. Fleming Beach Park — both of which have been previously named "America's Best Beach" by Dr. Beach. Take in all different shades of green while hiking through Honolua Valley to the shoreline of Honolua Bay, where vines dangle from a canopy of ferns and moss covers the tree trunks.

For a chance to spot whales during the winter months, hike the 2-mile Ohai Trail just past the Nakalele Blowhole or the rugged Lāhainā Pali Trail on the road between Lahaina and Ma'alaea. Both offer sweeping views of the coastline and are rarely ever crowded, which allows you just sit back and enjoy the scenery. That's what hiking in Maui is all about.

Nightlife on Maui
While nightlife on Maui isn't as hopping as Vegas or Waikiki, there's still a decent party scene for visitors who want to get dressed up and spend a night on the town. That said, only a handful of bars or nightclubs stay open past 10 p.m., and even fewer have designated dance floors you're legally allowed to dance on.

Because Maui is such an active location full of beaches, hiking and snorkeling, oftentimes people are simply too tired to party late into the night. It's a surprising reality for an island as popular and heavily visited as Maui, but there are all sorts of options for those just looking for dinner, drinks and a show.

The Triangle in Kihei

The highest concentration of nightlife on Maui is found at "The Triangle" in Kīhei, where so many bars are jammed into one courtyard, you can get lost in the "Bar-muda Triangle." Here you'll find everything from swanky martini bars and classic, no-nonsense dives to DJs spinning top-40 tunes until 2 a.m.

Best Ladies Night on the Island, Makawao

Another option is Casanova Italian Restaurant, located in Makawao, which hosts visiting bands and DJs on weekends and offers the island's best "Ladies Night" on Wednesdays until 2 a.m.

Lahaina Nightlife Scene

Lahaina, on the other hand, was once the island's party town with multiple late-night clubs, but only a couple of places are allowed to offer dancing. Longhi's is one of those spots and occasionally hosts DJs above their iconic restaurant on Front Street. Paradise Bar and Grill in Kāʻanapali is another popular late-night watering hole, and Black Rock Lounge at the Sheraton Maui Resort and Spa turns into a nightclub on weekends.

Bars on Maui

For what it lacks in nightclubs, however, Lahaina makes up for in bars and restaurants. Many of these establishments offer live music, and a couple of dives, like The Sly Mongoose, stay open until 2 a.m. The Dirty Monkey is the newest addition to Lahaina's late night scene and features a selection of hard-to-find whiskeys with music and DJs on weekends. Many of the bars around Lahaina Harbor, like Cool Cat Café and Down the Hatch, are good places to find the town's fishermen and boat crew as they festively drink through their tips. Kimo's is where to find slack key guitar by the flickering light of a tiki torch, and the Maui Brewing Company pub in Kahana is the original location of one of Hawai'i's largest and most popular craft breweries.

Maui's Best Date Night, Napili Kai

For a full evening of slack key guitar, the Slack Key Show at Nāpili Kai takes place Wednesday nights, and when paired with dinner at the Sea House Restaurant, is arguably Maui's best date night. Here you'll find Grammy award-winning guitar players in an intimate oceanfront setting who perform in a kanikapila style where they "talk story" with the crowd.

Live Music in Wailea

Another one of Maui's best shows is at Mulligan's on the Blue in Wailea, where local artist, Willie K, amazes the crowd with his range of styles from Hawaiian to opera and rock. Or, if you just want a casual cocktail while watching the sun go down, the lobby bars inside Wailea resorts offer live music and hula dancing most evenings around sunset.

Check out a Luau on Maui

Lū'au, of course, are also a big part of nightlife on Maui for visitors, and the favorite, hands down, is Old Lahaina Lū'au, located on Front

Street. Here you experience an authentic Hawaiian evening of entertainment that means no fire dancing since it's an art form that originates from Samoa. The Feast at Lele, on the other hand, offers a lū'au show with fire dancing and Polynesian cuisine, as does Wailele Polynesian Lū'au at The Westin Maui Resort and Spa and The Grand Lū'au at Honua'ula in Wailea. For a riveting performance on Hawaiian history without the feast catch a showing of 'Ulalena at Maui Theater in Lahaina.

A Night of Laughs on Maui

While it might not be the most intuitive way to spend an evening on Maui, Warren and Annabelle's Magic Dinner Show is a sidesplitting evening of comedy, dinner and magic on Front Street in Lahaina. The show takes place in a hidden parlor that's "haunted" by Annabelle, the ghost. Be warned, however, that if you sit in the front row, you'll end up as part of the show!

Catamaran/Nightclub

Finally, to combine a classic island activity with drinks, music and dancing, Club Ali'i Nui is just like a nightclub only it's on a catamaran. Trips depart from Mā'alaea Harbor on Wednesday and Friday nights and the party goes from 9:30-11:30 p.m., with hotel pickup included.

Ziplines on Maui

Though some countries   most notably Costa Rica   had ziplines well before Maui, the very first zipline in the United States was on the Valley Isle.

In 2002, when Skyline Eco-Adventures opened in Kula, they kicked off a trend that would rapidly become one of the island's most popular activities. Today the number of ziplines on Maui is eight. But that number is climbing, as it's not just the rush of adrenaline that makes it a popular visitor outing, but the views you get while standing atop the platforms.

Sweeping Views

At Skyline Eco-Adventures' Kāʻanapali location, guests are treated to sweeping views of the entire West Maui shoreline. These adventures take place on a mountainside slope that's closed to the general public. Same goes for Kapalua Ziplines on the island's northwestern coast, where the view not only looks out towards Molokaʻi and the white-capped Pailolo Channel, but the lines also span across forested valleys set high in the West Maui rainforest.

Family-Friendly to Adventure-Driven

The great thing about the different ziplines on Maui is that visitors now have the freedom to choose the adventure that offers the best fit. For travelers visiting the island with young children, Maui Zipline Company offers ziplining for children as young as five years old. Other operators, like Flyin' Hawaiian, cater to more adventurous travelers and has Maui's longest zipline that spans 3,600 feet. This 8-line course covers so much ground, you actually finish in a different town from where the tour begins.

Parallel Ziplines

Since ziplining on Maui is such a social activity for groups of friends and families, another important consideration is choosing a company with parallel lines so you can fly through the air together. Pi'iholo Zipline outside of Makawao offers parallel lines on their tours and the final zip of the 5-line course lets you fly more than 600 feet above the valley floor.

Hana and Haleakala Ziplines

Jungle Zipline on the Road to Hana is a way to break up the winding drive by soaring through a tropical rainforest. Or, bundle a trip to Haleakalā with ziplining on the original Skyline Eco-Adventures course and coast through groves of Eucalyptus.

Maui Zipline Guidelines and Tips

Finally, while ziplining on Maui is open to most travelers, every company has different requirements for who can zip on their course. All companies have weight requirements, which usually range from a 60-pound minimum to a 250-pound maximum. Every company is different, however, so be sure to inquire ahead of time. You'll also want to wear closed toe shoes and clothes you don't mind getting dirty. Also, bring a light jacket since the air is cooler in the mountains.

Attractions on Maui

Hawaiian vacations are meant to be relaxing, but there are so many different attractions in Maui that visiting can seem overwhelming. After all, how are you supposed to snorkel Molokini, drive the Road to Hana, watch sunrise at Haleakalā and still lie out by the pool?

This is one of the reasons that visitors return to Maui time and again; to experience the different Maui attractions they didn't see the first time around. Since trying to cram them all into one trip can easily sap the enjoyment, consider choosing a few Maui attractions and simply focusing on those.

For example, if outdoor adventure is the top priority, some of the best places to visit in Maui are snorkeling spots like Honolua Bay or scuba diving Molokini Crater. Start the day ziplining in Kapalua before driving to Nakalele Blowhole, and spend a day hiking and swimming beneath waterfalls while driving the Road to Hana.

Beaches, of course, are some of the most popular Maui attractions, and with dozens of sandy stretches of shoreline, Maui is a place where you could spend every day of vacation at a different beach. In fact, four of Maui's most popular beaches Ka'anapali, Wailea, D.T. Fleming, and Kapalua have been awarded the title of "Best Beach in America" in the rankings by Dr. Beach. Other beaches, like Hamoa Beach in Hana, consistently make the top 10, or you could always find a hidden beach that's well off the beaten path.For shopping, dining, and entertainment, nowhere has a higher concentration of shops than famous Front Street in Lahaina. Watch the sunset while eating mahimahi on the oceanfront deck at Kimo's, or shop for paintings, carvings, and crafts at the weekend Banyan Tree market. In the past few years, Pa'ia has started to rival Lahaina for artwork and fashionable boutiques, as has the Upcountry town of Makawao for jewelry and women's fashion.

Finally, Haleakalā Crater is undoubtedly one of Maui's top attractions, but there are other ways to visit the crater than waking up early for sunrise. Make the drive during the middle of the day and enjoy some afternoon hiking, or finish the perfect Maui day with a Haleakalā sunset. Just because sunrise is one of the most popular Maui tourist attractions, doesn't mean it's the only time to find magic up on the mountain.

Water Activities

Boating & Sailing on Maui

What's more exhilarating than being on a boat, wind in your hair, sunshine radiating from the skies, and the promise of wonder waiting to be discovered under clear blue waters? May it be to witness a majestic whale breaching, swim along a green sea turtle, or be off the grid for a few hours to reconvene with nature, any reason to climb on board and sail the great Pacific makes for an extraordinary day.

To explore Maui by water, boat tours depart from Lahaina harbor and Kaanapali Beach on the west side, the more centrally located Maalaea harbor by the Pali coastline, or Wailea Beach on the south shore. For adventures on smaller motorized rafts, the meeting spots would be Kihei boat ramp on the south side and Mala Wharf in Lahaina. Quick morning trips usually two to four hours, all-day boat tours, or a romantic sunset sail will take you to the most ideal sites for the day. Most boat tours include food and beverages plus a snorkel site or two.

Whale season brings two-hour whale watch trips in addition to the usual charters. Most of these trips include commentary from a naturalist on board and some hydrophone action to hear the mighty humpbacks sing.

On West Maui, the breath-taking Honolua Bay, Olowalu reef and Coral Garden are among the most popular destinations. If weather doesn't permit ideal visibility at these areas, there is always Mala Wharf, where a thriving reef grew from a collapsed fishing pier. It's an interesting reef with much to see, although it would've been free and fairly easy to swim to from the shore.

The southern coast's tours usually head to the Molokini crater, Makena Landing, or La Perouse Bay. Some boats will travel all the way to the jagged Kanaio Coast in the right conditions. One can also island hop to neighboring Lanai and frolic between the Hulopoe Marina Preserve and Manele Bay. A quick stroll to see Puu Pehe or the

Sweetheart Rock offers playtime at a tidepool and sea caves at an often-secluded part of the beach. Costs for the boat tours on Maui vary, but note that the more affordable boats are bigger and can load more people. During peak season, be prepared to share the day with more than 100 other passengers. If budget isn't an issue, a $30 to $50 difference per person could mean significant levels up in the quality of the boat, food and drinks, and personal service (not to mention ample space to leisurely move around or manspread to your heart's content). Most tour companies offer discounted rates for children and teens.

Dolphin Encounters on Maui
Unlike the leaping Humpback whales that visit Maui each winter, dolphins are full time Maui residents that can be spotted at any time of year.

What's more, the most commonly sighted dolphins on Maui Hawaiian Spinner dolphins can put a Humpback whale to shame when it comes to aerial antics, as the spinners can do up to seven full rotations when they jump up out of the water.

The Three Main Dolphin Pods on Maui
The most common dolphin encounters on Maui occur when out on a boat, particularly those between Lāhainā and Lāna'i where there's a large population of spinners. There's also a group of spinner dolphins that patrols the West Maui coastline and is sometimes found off

Kā'anapali Beach or up near Honolua Bay. The third distinct group of dolphins on Maui is found near La Perouse Bay, which is located at the end of the road in South Maui but best accessed by boat.

What to Do When You Encounter a Dolphin Pod

When you do encounter a pod of dolphins while boating or sailing off Maui, you'll often see the cluster of whitecaps and splashes before you'll notice the dolphins. Like a galloping cavalry of underwater horses, spinner dolphins will gather in pods that can number over 100 and create a white cluster of motion that moves like a large swarm of bees.

This is one massive swarm, however, where you hope to end up in the middle, to watch as spouting, leaping dolphins surround each side of the boat. In order for that to happen, however, it's up to the dolphins themselves. Boats in Hawai'i aren't allowed to intentionally drive through a pod of dolphins and must keep a distance of at least 50 yards between the dolphins and the boat. Try telling that to the dolphins, however, who often love to ride the wake in the front and the back of the boat. It's common for dolphins to approach a vessel and swim just feet from the hull, though it's illegal to jump out and swim with the dolphins since they're federally protected.

What Else You Need to Know About Dolphins on Maui

Aside from the feisty, acrobatic spinners, other dolphins that live around Maui are the larger, more solitary Bottlenose dolphin and Pantropical Spotted dolphins that live in deeper waters.

If you're simply snorkeling or swimming from shore, you're likely to hear any nearby dolphins but probably not get to see one. Their high-pitched squeaks and guttural chatter can be heard for hundreds of yards, but only in extremely rare instances will dolphins decide to mingle with snorkelers. In some ways it adds to their intrigue and mystery, in a beguiling, natural sense, that they seem to be curious, friendly and social but often just want to be left alone as they rest for their late night hunt.

Fishing on Maui
That's the phrase you hope to be screaming whenever you're fishing on Maui. It's Hawaiian slang for "hook up" or "fish on." Hanapaʻa can be screamed from shore or while trolling behind a boat as long as your reel is suddenly whistling and screaming right along with you.

Most of the fishing you'll find on Maui is deep sea fishing offshore, where anglers troll for *mahimahi, ono, ahi* and marlin. While the fishing on Maui is spectacular year round, there are still some notable differences in seasons in terms of what will bite.

The Best "Seasons" for Fishing on Maui

Summer, in general, is the best time of year for trophy fish like yellowfin tuna and blue marlin. The largest yellowfin tuna, or *ahi*, can weigh well over 100 lbs., and blue marlin can tip the scales at over 1,000 lbs. Spring is the best time for *mahimahi*, as well as wahoo, or *ono* and striped marlin become more common as springtime morphs into summer.

Bottom fishing is better in fall and winter. And while the overall quantity of fish might be higher, the fish on average tend to be smaller but still big enough for dinner. That said, Maui doesn't really have "seasons" in a strictly traditional sense, since trophy marlin and yellowfin tuna have been caught every month of the year.

The Best Fishing Spots on Maui

In terms of where to fish on Maui, all commercial fishing charters depart from either Lahaina Harbor, or in South Maui at Māʻalaea Harbor. In theory, you can cast your lines the moment you leave the harbor breakwall behind. But because the waters between Maui and Lānaʻi are only 200 feet deep, fishing charters with the best chances of success are those that leave in the early morning around 2:30 or 3 a.m.

The best fishing in Maui County is where the shelf drops thousands of feet off the western side of Lānaʻi, and where buoys, or FADs, have been placed to attract pelagic fish. The north shore of Molokaʻi is another spot where the bite is usually running. But since both places are two hours away, if you want to be at the buoys by dawn, then you better set an early alarm. Even if you leave a bit later, around 5:30 or 6 a.m., you can still make it out to the deep-water buoys by booking an 8-hour charter.

Fishing with the Family

If you aren't shooting for a trophy fish, or are planning to fish with your kids, spending a few hours bottom fishing might be more exciting. You don't need to motor nearly as far, and it's much more fun to catch a dozen fish than holding out hope for the big one.

Learn to Spearfish

Or, if you want to try something different and adventurous, there are also a couple of Maui companies that will teach you the sport of spearfishing. Learn how to equalize, or pop your ears, and how to increase your breath holds, all while hunting invasive fish that damage the island's reefs. Participants need to know how to swim, and should be comfortable breathing through a snorkel while keeping a calm, patient eye for that flit of color in the reef.

Scuba Diving on Maui

Have you ever engaged in a staring contest with a resting Hawaiian green sea turtle or felt the song of a Hawaiian humpback whale reverberate in your chest?

Those are just two experiences you'll find scuba diving on Maui, where Hawaiian green sea turtles are abundant any time of year and Hawaiian humpback whales peak, January through March.

Though Hawaiian humpback whales are seasonal visitors, one of the great things about scuba diving on Maui is there's never an "off-season." The water temperature can be 74 F in the "coldest" months of winter and warms up to 80 F by August and September. Turtles, dolphins, parrotfish and eels are year-round residents, as are colorful nudibranchs, sponges, corals, reef fish and urchins.

Scuba Diving from Shore

In terms of where to go scuba diving on Maui, the leeward coast near Wailea or Kāʻanapali are the most frequented locales. For beach dives, where you set out from shore, Ulua Beach is the most popular spot in the Kīhei/Wailea area, and Kahekili Beach Park and Puʻu Kekaʻa ("Black Rock") are the best in Kāʻanapali. Dives from shore rarely exceed 35 feet and are great for newly certified, novice divers.

Advanced Dive Spots on Maui

Veteran divers, on the other hand, will want to book a two-tank cruise to offshore reefs. Molokini Crater has a 100-foot visibility almost every day, and the "Back Wall" is arguably one of the best dives in the world. Because it can have strong currents, however, and the wall drops 300 feet, only advanced divers with a professional instructor should attempt any descent here. Dive depths on the inside of the crater, on the other hand, average about 75 feet and are much better suited for intermediate divers who book through a local dive shop. Here you'll find colonies of garden eels that slink into the sand and schools of jacks so large they'll often blot out the sun. Because Molokini is a marine reserve, only certified scuba divers are allowed at the crater.

Scuba Diving at Cathedrals, Maui

All dive boats in West Maui depart from Māla Ramp, with the exception of large-scale Lahaina Divers, who depart from Lahaina Harbor. Lānaʻi is the destination of choice for morning Lahaina dive charters. The boats cross to "Cathedrals," located off the Pineapple Isle's southern coast on a trip that usually takes about 45 minutes one-way. The underwater architecture at "Cathedrals" is world-famous, where subterranean caves and arches create the appearance of sunlight streaming through a cathedral's stained glass windows. You can also sometimes spot Hawaiian spinner dolphins as they cruise above the reef. "Second Cathedral," further down the coast, has a sprig of black coral that dangles from the ceiling like a feathery chandelier.

Dive Tours for Families

If you just want to explore the Maui coastline and not head over to Lanaʻi, Lahaina Divers has afternoon dives that search for turtles at Māla Ramp or Olowalu reef. If you're traveling with family or a large group where not everyone is a diver, Hula Girl is a sailing catamaran that departs from Kāʻanapali Beach and heads to Honolua Bay. Your travel companions can snorkel or lounge while you head out for a dive, and the entire family can meet back on deck for an outdoor lunch in the sun.

Something a Little Bit Crazy
Finally, if you're looking to do something a little bit crazy while scuba diving on Maui, Lahaina Divers has a once-a-week charter to Moku Hoʻoniki rock. Located off the tip of Molokaʻi, this rock was once a bombing target in the years following World War II. Today it is a deep-water gathering site of scalloped hammerhead sharks. Moorings aren't available at the rock, so you're drift diving, and depths can top out at 120 feet while searching for sharks in the blue. Because it's such an advanced level dive, everyone in the water needs dive computers, as well as a safety sausage. But for seasoned divers with the proper gear and knowledge of deep-water dives it's an unforgettable experience in one of Hawaiʻi's most isolated spots.

Snorkeling on Maui
Snorkelers in Maui, if nothing else, are blissfully spoiled for choice.

With 120 miles of coastline, Maui has dozens of snorkeling spots that are rung by coral reefs, and hundreds of colorful species of fish that call the shoreline home. Take a look out over the sand, out towards the open blue, and you may spot eagle rays flying on by, or turtles surfacing for air, and it's always fun when a camouflaged *he'e* (octopus) darts out from its home in the rocks. Snorkeling on Maui means the possibility of new experiences each day, and in winter it all takes place to the soundtrack of whales singing in the distance.

One of the most popular places to a go snorkeling in Maui is Kā'anapali Beach, at Pu'u Keka'a, also known as "Black Rock," in front of the Sheraton resort. Here at this volcanic promontory that juts out into the waves, Hawaiian sea turtles nibble on *limu* (seaweed), and silvery schools of *akule* and chubs patrol the fringe of the reef. Kahekili Beach, just one mile north is another popular spot, since the large reef helps thin the crowds and fish are found in abundance.

Further north, Napili Bay and Kapalua Bay are neighboring snorkeling hot spots, and Honolua Bay in the summer months has arguably the best snorkeling on Maui. In South Maui, Mokapu Beach and Ulua Beach are separated by a small, volcanic headland that teems with fish and sea turtles, and down in Makena, Kanahena Cove also known as "Dumps" is spectacularly rugged and remote. Or, for an easy snorkel in shallow water, check out the north end of Keawakapu Beach in front of the Mana Kai resort.

Despite the wealth of options, however, that run along Maui's coastline, none compare to the aquatic bonanza that's found at Molokini Crater. Just three miles off the coast of South Maui, this volcanic caldera is home to over 200 species of fish many of which are endemic to Hawai'i, only found here in the islands. Granted, because the spot is so popular, finding these different species of fish entails avoiding the crowds, so book a boat that gets there early before the onslaught begins. Even on days when the crater is crowded, the water clarity is reason enough to grab a mask and snorkel, and as is the case with snorkeling on Maui and Molokini in particular you never know what might swim by to put on an underwater show.

Water Sports on Maui
The next time you're driving down the highway on Maui, take a look at all the toys stacked in the back of trucks: quivers of surfboards and paddleboards tightly strapped down on racks, sails, booms, harnesses, and paddles for windsurfing, kitesurfing or canoeing. Then, of course, there's snorkeling gear and maybe a couple of scuba tanks to go along with a "three prong" for spearfishing or poles for casting from shore.

The ocean surrounding Maui is truly a playground and the number of different watersports can often be overwhelming. On a 10-day vacation to the Valley Isle, it's possible to do a different watersport every day and still go home having only scratched the surface.

The most popular watersports on Maui include snorkeling at places like Molokini Crater, or riding waves as part of a surf lesson in Kīhei, Kā'anapali or Lahaina. Even these standard offerings, however, have different sub-offerings to choose from like Snuba diving at Molokini

Crater rather than snorkeling, or surfing in an outrigger canoe instead of on a regular board.

Windsurfing and kitesurfing aren't quite as casual since they involve a fair amount of practice. But Maui is full of kitesurfing schools that offer weeklong lesson packages for visitors who really want to learn. If you just want to see some windsurfers in action, head to Hoʻokipa outside of Pāʻia and watch sails flip through the air or Kanaha Beach Park, near the airport, to see windsurfers, kitesurfers and hydrofoilers.

The sport of standup paddleboarding (SUP) is arguably the most popular watersport on Maui for visitors and locals alike. Morning hours are best for beginners since the ocean is usually calm, whereas afternoons are better for experienced paddlers who want thrilling "downwinders."

Scuba diving is another popular watersport on Maui where you can explore everything from scuttled whaling ships to caves off the coast of Lānaʻi even a sunken World War II bomber.

You can spend the morning paddling a kayak in search of Hawaiian green sea turtles or learn how to spearfish and help clear the reef of invasive species. There are even watersports on Maui like bodysurfing, where no equipment or money are required to splash around and have some fun in the sun.

That said, the caveat when it comes to watersports on Maui, is to know what's going on with the weather ahead of time. Wind, waves and runoff can affect your ocean experience.

Famous Honolua Bay, for example, is the perfect venue for snorkeling and diving from May through the end of September. Honolua Bay in winter, however, is a place where snorkels are swapped for surfboards since waves can reach 20 feet. Rain, too, can affect conditions, as runoff from a deluge on the mountain can cloud visibility.

Molokini Crater is another place that's greatly affected by conditions. The crater is perfect for snorkeling or diving during southern or easterly winds. When the wind direction turns north, however, the water becomes too rough and snorkeling tours are forced to look for more protected places.

North winds, on the other hand, are good for Kīhei "downwinders," which brings us back to why you'll see trucks stacked with so many toys. In a place like Maui, where there are so many options for having fun in the water, it's best to be prepared for whichever way the wind blows.

Whale Watching on Maui
If you're visiting Maui any time in winter, there's a decent chance you could spot a whale before even reaching the island.

Because the channels surrounding Maui house so many Humpback whales, it isn't uncommon to spot a whale from out your airplane window. If you don't end up seeing a misty spout before even touching down, rest assured that the whale watching in Maui is arguably the best in Hawaii, and the question isn't if you'll see whales but how many different times?

The peak season for whale watching on Maui is January, February, and March, though whale season in Maui officially runs from December 15-May 15. Early in the season, the first sightings are usually of males who have made the swim from Alaska, awaiting the females who usually show up between Thanksgiving and Christmas. For the next few months, the sea is alive with thunderous splashes, spouts, pec slaps, and breaches, as the 50-ton mammals will mate, give birth, and frolic here in these waters.

To spot whales from shore, head to Papawai Overlook on the twisting road to Lahaina, where the view stretches out from Ma'alaea Bay to the Au'au Channel towards Lāna'i. Honolua Bay is another good spot to look for breaches and spouts, which are best seen from the bumpy dirt road that runs atop the bluff.

To truly go whale watching on Maui, however, and experience the wintertime magic, you need to book a whale watching tour to see the Humpbacks up close. Boats, by law, cannot approach a Humpback whale any closer than 100 yards, but oftentimes the curious whales will swim up and "mug" the boat. Watch as they rhythmically slap their fluke, or erupt in a sudden breach using their massive peduncle muscle to thrust their body in the air. When it happens without warning, time literally seems to stop and no one can utter a word, as such an epic display of force can turn an entire crowd silent.

To book a whale watching tour in Maui, look for boats that leave from Lahaina, Ma'alaea, or Kā'anapali Beach. The catamarans in Kā'anapali are convenient if you're staying in the resort, but because they load directly from the sand require agility and mobility. Larger, more stable, diesel boats depart from Lahaina Harbor, and morning hours are usually best before the tradewinds pick up. In Ma'alaea, oftentimes the wind is howling by early afternoon, which is when most of the whale watching tours depart from Ma'alaea Harbor.

A little insider secret, however, is that any morning snorkeling charter will also stop to watch whales, so travelers pressed for time on the island can book a charter to Molokini and still get a morning whale watch. Granted, the amount of time you'll spend with the whales will be less than on a whale watch, since whale watching tours are custom geared towards following and learning about whales.

Finally, since whale watching in Maui is based around nature, no two whale watching trips or excursions will ever be the same. If you have a whale watch that's just mediocre, and don't experience much action, the best thing to do is just try again tomorrow's a brand new day.

Maui Beaches

There are plenty of beautiful beaches on Maui, each possessing its own set of unique qualities.

The question isn't whether or not to head for a beach, but how to pick the one that matches your mood and energy level. What makes one beach great for surfers and water-sport enthusiasts does not necessarily make for a great destination for families or vacationers looking to relax on the shore. Some beaches are more suitable for certain activities for instance, Launiupoko Beach, Breakwall in Lahaina and Cove Park in Kihei are great for beginning surfers; while wind and kite surfers flock to Kanaha Beach.

Maui has 120 miles of coastline and more than 75 beaches. Although hotels or vacation rentals front many popular shorelines; it is not difficult to find a secluded stretch of sand to get your dose of vitamin sea.

Top 5 Beaches on Maui

As an island chain, Hawaii is home to hundreds of beaches, each possessing its own set of unique qualities. What makes one beach great for surfers and water-sport enthusiasts does not necessarily make for a great destination for families or vacationers looking to relax on the shore.

To help narrow down the search for the your own personal perfect beach destination, the following list is a compilation of what are widely agreed to be the top five beaches on Maui.

Ka'anapali Beach

Similar to Waikiki Beach, Ka'anapali Beach is a hotbed of activity due to its location among Ka'anapali Resort and the many other hotels that sit along the shore. The 1.5-mile-long Ka'anapali Beach, however, is far less crowded than its Oahu counterpart, only feeling the strain of the masses during busy seasons such as Christmas. Located in West Maui, Ka'anapali Beach was once a retreat for Hawaiian royalty and today is often called one of the best beaches on Maui, thanks to its wide array of beach activities, including seasonal parasailing, surfing, volleyball and sailing. On the north end of the beach is Black Rock, a renowned snorkeling destination and home to a cliff diving ceremony that happens every day at sunset.

Keawakapu Beach

Hidden between Wailea and Kihei sits the lovely Keawakapu Beach. This secret south Maui paradise is an ideal getaway from the crowds of the islands' larger, more populated beaches. Don't let its small size fool you; Keawakapu has consistently good swimming conditions year-round, and its abundance of soft, white sand lends equally well to sunbathers and children wishing to build a sandcastle empire. An underwater reef just off the right side of the beach also offers a great snorkeling opportunity.

Kapalua Beach

With its beautiful sand and protected bay lined by palm trees and lava rock, Kapalua Beach is one of the most popular beaches in the state. In fact, this northwestern beach, located mere minutes from the historic whaling port of Lahaina, has consistently ranked among the top beaches in the nation by numerous travel publications. And it's little wonder why Kapalua remains a favorite beach for many families with young children. The calm waters offer great swimming, and natural tide pools give children the opportunity to see sea creatures up close. During the winter months, it is common to see whales migrating in the deeper waters. The nearby Shopping Village and hotels also offer ample shopping, dining and entertainment options.

Kahekili Beach

An extension of Kaanapali Beach, Kahekili Beach is actually separated from the busier and bigger Kaanapali by 250 yards of lava rock and a hotel. Named after the last king of Maui, Kahekili Beach is an ideal spot for snorkeling and scuba diving. Hidden rocks and strong currents, however, make this a dangerous spot for swimmers. The expansive, well-groomed sand beach also makes this a nice picnicking area.

Napili Bay

A charming beach with great swimming conditions, Napili Bay is well known for its golden sand, great snorkeling and picture-perfect sunsets. Located in Lahaina next to the Napili Kai Resort, the beach's large expanse of sand and gentle surf provide a great excuse for families looking to spend an entire day at the beach.

The End

www.ingramcontent.com/pod-product-compliance
Lightning Source LLC
Chambersburg PA
CBHW031055080526
44587CB00011B/687